NO
FEAR

ERNIE IRVAN: THE NASCAR DRIVER'S
STORY OF TRAGEDY AND TRIUMPH

by ernie irvan and peter golenbock
with debra hart nelson

HYPERION
New York

Library of Congress Cataloging-in-Publication Data

ISBN 0-7868-8940-3

FIRST PAPERBACK EDITION

Designed by Liane F. Fuji

10 9 8 7 6 5 4 3 2 1

To Kim,
my wife and guardian angel

CONTENTS

ACKNOWLEDGMENTS

Writing the acknowledgments for a book that covers a substantial portion of your life can be a daunting task. In writing a biographical piece of work like this one, you are reminded how many people have touched your life. In one way or another, the connections I have made have shaped my path. Therefore, thanks should be given to those of you whose presence in my life has helped contribute a great deal to the contents of this book and also to my days.

Clearly, I am indebted to NASCAR fans, and more specifically, to the fans that have followed my career, sharing my catastrophes and my victories. The fact that I have a driving career to write about is made all the more rewarding by those who come and participate as spectators. You have provided me with incredible encouragement and support so great that, at times, it has brought tears to my eyes.

The NASCAR officials work hard to put on a good show for everybody year after year, and I am very appreciative of their diligent efforts. Because of them, our sport has come a long way in a relatively short period of time and I'm thankful to be a part of it. They were also important when it came time for my comeback, a significant subject of this book.

To my fellow competitors, many of whom are my good friends and have provided some of the fun stories for this book, I would like to give a resounding thanks. The crews, too, have not only contributed to the stories in this book, but in various ways, to the success of my career. I am grateful for the times the team owners, the drivers, and the crews generously shared their insight, friendship, encouragement, and sometimes the car parts from their garage!

A special thanks to Pete Vargas, whose friendship I treasure and whose recollections helped to add to these pages.

Peter Golenbock deserves high praise for his enthusiasm and his willingness to work with everyone who helped shape this book. I know he spent many hours talking with family, friends, and medical personnel to provide the fodder for this work. After compiling all that information, he gave structure to this book.

I would also like to extend a sincere thanks to Debra Hart Nelson, who labored over the rewrites and editing. Her respect for our sport and appreciation for the kind of life the drivers and their families lead made her an obvious candidate for our writing team. I also appreciate that she has a great love for the written word. It is translated into her editing efforts in this book.

William Means deserves thanks for his contribution to the medical chapters (primarily Chapters 1–3). I am very appreciative of his interest in making sure these chapters were correct medical interpretations. I am grateful for his expert advice and even writing style.

Without my business manager, Brett Nelson, this project may never have come to fruition. Brett's unfailing loyalty is manifested not only in his attention to detail in financial matters, but in the many other tasks he undertakes on my behalf. This book is one of them and I know that he and Gretchen Young at Hyperion worked very hard to make sure the editing was done to everyone's satisfaction.

Thanks to Gretchen and her wonderful staff, my experience with Hyperion has been a remarkably positive one. At every twist and turn in our journey with this book, Gretchen was extraordinarily supportive, as well as the epitome of professionalism. This book-writing business was a new one to me, and her expertise and patient guidance laid to rest any reservations Kim, Brett, and I might have had.

To the medical staff who saved my life, it goes without saying that I owe you a huge debt of gratitude. I am also very appreciative of your willingness to talk about my medical difficulties as a result of the Michigan crash. I know a lot of the medical information was gleaned from conversations with Dr. John Maino, Theresa Canning, Kathleen O'Leary, and Dr. Eddie Erlandson. Thank you for that time.

As for my family, I know it wasn't always easy looking back and providing some of the material for this book. My mom and dad, Jo and Vic Irvan, have always helped to provide for me in one way or another, though, and words can never express the love and gratitude I have for everything they did to help me with this book, not to mention my life! As we prepared the chapters of this book, many of the details of their life was news to me. It served to remind me how many tough experiences they have been through and how proud I am that they managed to survive them in such a resourceful and productive way.

Not to be left out of the act, my sister Tracy provided some details that I had long forgotten, particularly about my childhood friend, Timmy Williamson. Thanks, Tracy, for being so willing to share your good memory! I think those details helped illuminate what racing can be like.

My wife, Kim, also spent countless hours going over relevant details about the racing industry and my crash at Michigan so that we could put together an accurate depiction. As my dedicated spouse, she insisted that my story was one of courage and triumph over formidable odds and that it needed to be told, and told well. Her love and commitment to me and our children has always been unwavering. I think that comes through in this book. There just are not adequate words to express the love that I have for her and the gratitude I feel for all that she does for our family. She is our number-one fan, and we are hers.

1

AGAINST THE WALL

Most of us don't dwell on dying. I didn't—not even the second before I hit the wall at 190 miles an hour. Like most race car drivers, I have friends on and off the track who have died, but I don't think about death. Driving fast and living as well as I can is more important. I don't care much for hospitals, and I try to avoid funerals. When a fan or a reporter asks me about the dangers I face, I deny the sport is dangerous. To me, being a racer is no more risky than being a teacher, a pilot, or a construction worker walking a beam seventy stories high. Yeah, accidents happen, but not to me. They happen only to the other guy. I was wrong.

When you're a race car driver, it doesn't make sense to be thinking about what can go wrong. What's the point? When you're out on that track, anything can happen, and more often than not, there's not a damn thing you can do about it. You learn when you're in my business that in order to win races, an awful lot has to go right. You must focus on the good because if you start dwelling on the bad, you might as well get out of the business.

No one—racer, banker, librarian, or accountant—

expects to get hurt or die. Every day you open your local paper and find a home owner who gets up in the morning and drives out of his driveway to his job, only to be T-boned by another driver who runs a red light. The paper lists the details of his funeral, but that guy never knew what hit him. That happens every day on highways across America. There are bumps and crashes on the racetrack, but not deaths. Even though I'm traveling at speeds approaching 200 miles an hour, it's still safer for me out on that track than it is for drivers making their daily commute to work. Everyone on that track is a trained professional. On the street all I know is that the driver is at least sixteen years old and can reach the gas pedal.

I have driven on racetracks since I was nine years old. The worst injury I had suffered was as a teenager driving a go-cart. I flipped the go-cart and ruptured my spleen. Another time I wrecked in a Busch Grand National race and broke my collarbone. Both times, I recovered quickly. I have driven thousands of miles in hundreds of races, and except for those two incidents, I barely had a scratch. Then, in the summer of 1994, my luck almost ran out. The timing couldn't have been worse. At the time of my crash, I was heading for the best season of my Winston Cup career. I was feeling very confident that I would be the NASCAR champion. I was driving the fastest car for a great race team. On August 20, 1994, I was headed for glory.

When I got up that day, dying was the furthest thing from my mind. I was thirty-five years old, the winner of fifteen Winston Cup races, and in my prime as a racer in the best run racing circuit in the United States. I was driving for

Robert Yates's racing team in the top Ford on NASCAR's Winston Cup circuit. I had replaced Davey Allison, who had been killed in July 1993 in a freak helicopter accident. I stepped into his shoes and won two races that first year. Then, in 1994, our team really began to click. I was battling Dale Earnhardt for the driving title—my goal had been to win that championship ever since entering Winston Cup racing in 1988—and I was sure I was going to win it. Beginning with the Michigan race in mid-August, there were eleven races to go, including four short-track races, my specialty. The Earnhardt team felt so strongly that we had them beat for the championship, they were building a new car for the short tracks. One of their crew members told Larry McReynolds, our crew chief, "This car will be our last chance to beat your 28 bunch at a short track."

For the first time in my career I was knocking on the door. In '94 I was leading in top-five finishes, in most laps finished, and in total money winnings. I had led in the points most of the season, and then in a race at Watkins Glen in mid-August Dale Earnhardt passed me for first place in the standings by only 27 points. I wasn't concerned because I knew deep down his lead was only going to be temporary. From my perspective, our engines were better, our chassis better, and we had more consistency than Earnhardt. My belief at that time was that as far as our race team—Robert Yates, Larry McReynolds and his crew, myself included—was concerned, no one could beat us. This was a race team that worked harder than anybody. Even after we won a race, no one slackened in his approach. Larry would tell the crew, "We gotta keep doing each week what we've done the previous sixteen or seventeen weeks that got us in this position." Larry was smart. He knew how fast things can go wrong. If you do your job, lead races and win races, you'll earn the points to win. I was anticipating that I would be sitting as guest of honor at the head of the table come Christmas at the NASCAR banquet at the Waldolf-Astoria in New York City.

The two-mile oval in Brooklyn, Michigan, is a fast track, and I was looking forward to running there. Our first day of practice was Friday, August 19, 1994. We were running okay, but we were struggling to qualify well. Michigan is a tricky place to qualify. There is a tendency to want to overdrive in the corners, and if I have a fault it's that I try to stand on the gas as long as I can. Sometimes when I'm driving at Michigan I will drive too deep into the corner, which causes the car to get loose, and my qualifying time will suffer.

I was always very serious about wanting to qualify well, and that weekend I qualified 18th, probably the worst I had qualified all season long. I was beating myself up pretty bad as the garage closed that day.

Our motor home was parked in the infield next to Robert Yates's. Robert was staying at the hotel with the team. His son Doug and his wife Carolyn, were spending the night in the motor home. That evening Larry McReynolds came over, and the three of us drank a beer, played Monopoly, and talked about our day. Larry was particularly upset with the way the car had handled. I told him, "Larry, don't worry about it. We're going to be just fine on Sunday. We'll figure out this Michigan track. We'll figure it out together." I gave him a reassuring pat on the back.

Practice began very early Saturday morning. We had been much too loose qualifying, and the team knew we would have to tighten the car up to run well in the race. The question was how much. Larry said to me, "As loose as it was yesterday, let's go ahead and leave it like it is, open a little front end, drop the pressures a little bit on the tires, and let's just go out and run a few laps. After you get acclimated to the racetrack, we'll work from there." We had about an hour and a half to practice.

We started around eight in the morning. It's always pretty smoky and hazy in the morning from the campfires and cookouts of the infield campers. You can't see much of the two-mile racetrack, except the front stretch. With high expectations I drove onto the track.

Larry and I decided we would run ten laps. We didn't say much that morning. Larry would give me lap times, and that was about it. I was practicing with Mark Martin in the number 6 Valvoline car and with two or three others. Mark Martin was beating me pretty badly in the center of the corners, which told me our car was running too tight. I'd run back up on him in the straightaway, and he'd pull back away from us in the corners.

I ran about ten laps, and as I completed that tenth lap, Larry came on the radio and said, "Ernie, that's ten," and he gave me my lap time. He said, "Why don't you come in here, and we'll go to working on the car?" I didn't say anything. I was concentrating on driving the race car. A lot of times I'd run an extra lap just to get that one last feel of the car. I should have listened to Larry that morning.

Larry and Raymond Fox, Larry's right-hand man, were standing on the truck watching me practice. They would lose sight of me going into turns one and two due to the smog, and after I crossed the start/finish line that tenth time, he ordered me to come in, but then I disappeared from their view.

Exactly what happened next, no one can say with certainty. It appears that at turn two I cut a right front tire, causing the car to veer suddenly in the direction of the concrete wall. I certainly do not remember hitting that wall head-on at 190 miles an hour. It's a wonder I'm still here to tell you about it. No, it's a miracle.

After I crashed, one of our crew began waving his hands to signal a caution. Larry called to him, "Who is it?" He pointed to himself and screamed, "It's us! It's us!"

Larry yelled into the radio, "Ernie, are you okay?" He got no response, and suddenly Larry had a sickening feeling in his stomach. He continued to call for me to answer, hoping that when I hit, my earplugs holding the transmitter had become unhitched. It's common in a crash, and then after a few seconds the driver will come back on the radio and say, "My radio became unplugged." But I was not responding to Larry's pleas of, "Ernie, are you okay? Ernie, are you okay? Ernie, answer me!"

Larry looked at Robert Yates, who was scanning the radios of the other race teams to find out my condition. What he heard from the other drivers who passed the wreck wasn't good. The talk was of how hard I had hit the concrete wall. Previously Robert and Larry had suffered through the tragedy of Davey Allison's helicopter accident and his death a day later, and the emotions they were feeling were all too familiar.

Robert and Larry climbed down off the trailer, and they ran into Buster Auton, who drives the pace car at Michigan. Whenever there's a bad wreck, NASCAR sends the pace car and some officials out to the scene. Auton came out of the NASCAR trailer in a panic. They asked Buster to drive them to the site. "Yeah," said Buster, who had a terrible look on his face. "Come on. Get in."

The pace car pulled within fifty yards of the wreck site. Larry looked at the car and remembered thinking that it didn't look all that bad. It was wishful thinking. The front had been demolished. A rescue worker ran up to Robert and Larry and told them, "You don't want to go over there." Larry said, "Oh God, what in the world?" The worker said, "I'm telling you, it's bad. You don't want to go over there."

Larry walked over to the wall at turn two, leaned over it, and threw up. Larry thought to himself, This can't be. My best friend is sitting in that race car dead. It can't be.

Steve Peterson, a NASCAR official, walked over to Larry and started talking to him. Larry only picked up bits and pieces of what Steve was saying. "They're going to cut him out of the car." "These are some of the best doctors in the world attending to him." "They're going to airlift him out of here." "He's alive."

Larry was now standing about a hundred feet away, and he saw what looked like a tremendous amount of blood. When you get hit as hard as I got hit, blood comes out of your ears and your nose. With blood, moreover, a little looks like a lot. To Larry it looked like someone had poured a bucket of blood on the track. His thoughts went to my wife, Kim. He began to wonder, Kim, poor Kim, where's Kim?

My wife, Kim, and our baby daughter, Jordan, were in our motor home parked in the infield. At eight-thirty there was a knock on the door. Jordan was still sleeping and Kim was watching TV. Carolyn Yates rushed in. Carolyn said, "Ernie's had an accident on the track." Kim asked if I was okay. Carolyn said, "I don't know. It's pretty bad. Hurry and get dressed. They're coming for you." Kim said, "Is he alive?" Carolyn weakly said, "Yeah." But there was hesitation in her voice.

There was nothing Robert or Larry could do while I waited for medical attention, so they got into one of the safety trucks and went back to the garage to meet with our race team. Larry and Robert told them what little they knew. Robert told them, "Sit tight and don't do anything. We'll call you and keep you posted. Don't unload the backup car. Go in the lounge of the truck and say your prayers, and we'll be back in touch with you."

What was so heartening was the sympathy and offers of help. Many of the race teams, especially members from the number 3 car of Dale Earnhardt, expressed sympathy and offered to help get the car ready to race. But Robert and Larry weren't concerned with the race, only with me.

They headed from the garage to my motor home. Max Helton, the preacher for Motor Racing Outreach, had already arrived, as had my dad. He looked pitiful. Larry put his arm around him and said, "Vic, don't worry. He's strong. He's going to be fine." My dad had tears in his eyes, and he shook his head.

As Kim stood outside our motor home, Mark Martin came by. Mark, who is one of my closest friends in racing, told her, "He's really bad, but he's alive."

2

DESPERATE MEASURES

I'm alive only because of the immediate response of the emergency care medical staff at the Michigan track and the quick thinking of Dr. John Maino, the physician in charge. Dr. Maino had worked at the track since 1985, and he says my accident was the worst he ever saw.

Dr. Maino and the other members of the response team raced to the accident site in a Suburban van converted to an ambulance from their station in the infield. When they arrived at the turn, they saw that my car was up against the wall, its front end compressed and demolished. I lay unconscious in the driver's seat, bleeding profusely from my nose and mouth. Dr. Maino ordered a wrecking crew to cut away part of the top of my car so they could get me out quicker. I was pulled up and out of the car and then laid on a board placed on the ground. I was strapped to it to prevent further spinal damage while the doctors worked on me.

Normally I would have been taken to the infield care center, but Dr. Maino was so concerned about my condition that he ordered the helicopter pilot to start up, lift off, fly to the crash site just beyond the apron of the track, and keep the engines going while the medical team treated me. This usually isn't done because the whirring rotors present a danger to everyone around. Dr. Maino wanted the helicopter to be able to take off for a trip to the hospital as soon as possible. He felt my condition was so critical that he wanted to save the valuable few minutes that would have been needed to cool down and then restart the helicopter's engine. The helicopter medical crew, Dr. John Holmes, the flight physician, and his assistant Kathleen O'Leary, had seen the crash on the TV monitors while stationed inside the infield hospital, and they and the pilot had run for the helicopter immediately.

Dr. Maino had only minutes to save my life. As a first step, he ordered one of the attending paramedics to put a plastic tube down my throat to clear my airway and help me breathe. But I was bleeding so badly in the back of my mouth that such a procedure was impossible. My larynx had been crushed, my lungs had collapsed from the impact of the blow, and I was drowning in my own blood.

The helicopter medical staff brought over a pulse oxymeter, which registers how much oxygen is in the blood that goes to the brain and vital organs. If your oxygen level is under 90 percent, the lack of oxygen to the brain, heart, and kidneys puts you in grave danger. When the doctor read the machine my oxygen level was 15 percent. Dr. Maino saw my chest wasn't moving and informed the others, "He's not breathing on his own." If I didn't get oxygen quickly, he knew, I would probably die, and if somehow I managed to live, I would be a vegetable. My brain cells were dying second by second.

Dr. Maino asked Dr. Holmes, "John, when was the last

time you did an emergency trach?" A tracheostomy under these circumstances is risky and is done only as a last resort. The doctor takes a knife and cuts a hole below the Adam's apple or larynx and inserts a tube into the airway. A machine then forces oxygen into the tube, allowing the patient to breathe. If it is not done right—if the incision is made in the wrong spot—the patient will die from asphyxiation or hemorrhage.

To Dr. Maino's question whether he had ever performed the operation, Dr. Holmes, an anesthesiology resident at the University of Michigan, said one word, "Well," and that was enough of a hesitation to let Dr. Maino know that he had better perform the surgery himself.

First he inserted a needle to make sure he had the right location, and then he requested a scalpel. Dr. Maino was informed that the handle which was supposed to come in the kit with the blade couldn't be found. Losing no time he said, "Give me the blade then." Dr. Maino located my Adam's apple and started to cut the area just below it. Holding the blade tightly in his fingers, he cut into my airway. As soon as he heard air coming through the trachea, he inserted a hemostat into the first ring of the trachea, spread it open, and while he held open the lower portion of my trachea, Dr. Holmes inserted a tube into the opening. Dr. Maino removed the hemostat, pushed in the tube, pumped 100 percent oxygen into my lungs. When he checked my oxygen level, it read 90 percent. My life was saved at that moment.

While Dr. Maino taped the tube to my neck and secured it in place, the rest of the team immobilized my body so there would be no further injury to my neck, and they inserted two large IVs into my arms in order to replace the blood I had lost. They then placed me inside the helicopter and flew me to St. Joseph Mercy Hospital in Ann Arbor. The reason I went to St. Joe's was that in addition to the severe head injury I had suffered, the doctors also were concerned that as a result of the severe deceleration caused by my hitting the wall at high speed, I had badly bruised or even torn my heart and lungs. Dr. Maino knew that St. Joe's had a cath lab to study my heart, and if I needed a cardiac bypass, St. Joe's was the place to do it. Many months after the accident, I heard individuals had asked if my seat belts were on. Had they not been on, I would have died. I can assure you I had my seat belts on securely. Although I never hit the steering wheel, internal injuries still occur when the heart and lungs smash into the chest wall.

Time seemed to stand still for the people in the stands watching the medical staff work on me. When the helicopter lifted off, it had only been twenty-three minutes from the time I hit the wall. It took them eight minutes to get me out of the car, and fifteen minutes to work their magic. Those doctors clearly saved my life, and I will always be grateful to them.

After the helicopter left, Dr. Maino was talking with Gene Haskett, the general manager and vice president of the Michigan Speedway. Haskett wanted to know what my chances were.

"Eighty to 90 percent he's not going to make it," Dr. Maino told him, "but if he makes it through the next twenty-four hours, then all bets are off."

Everybody watched in silence as the helicopter took

off. A member of the Dale Earnhardt race team came over to our motor home and asked if there was anything he could do to help. He had a car. He drove Larry, Robert, my dad, Kim, and Brian Vandercook, Texaco's PR man, to the hospital in Ann Arbor. If you've ever been to Michigan, you know that to go from the track to town takes an hour. That was the longest ride of everyone's life. Nobody talked all the way there. The trip seemed to take forever.

Larry periodically would reach in front of him and pat Kim on the shoulder. She had left our daughter, Jordan, back at our motor home with Carolyn Yates, and she rode in silence staring out the window. In the backseat Larry was reliving the horror of Davey Allison's crash, rushing to the hospital, and waiting in a room the next day to hear the tragic news that he had died. In addition Larry had been the crew chief for a driver by the name of Butch Lindley. They were racing at a track in Bradenton, Florida, in 1985 when Lindley hit the wall hard, was knocked unconscious, and lay in a coma for six years before he died. Recalling what Lindley's wife and family went through, Larry began to pray: "Dear Lord, it's not fair for God to take somebody's life, but if your plan is for Ernie to be less than 100 percent husband and father, go and take him to heaven with you." Kim's prayer was less complicated. "Dear Lord," she prayed, "just let him live."

After they drove up to St. Joseph Mercy Hospital in Ann Arbor, everyone got out and grimly went inside.

Once the helicopter took off, the flight medical team checked to make sure the IVs were secure, that I was getting the fluids into me that I needed, while they monitored the pulse oxymeter to make certain I was getting enough oxygen. My racing suit was cut open while I lay on the gurney, and two large EKG patches were placed on my chest to monitor my heart. They also took my blood pressure. I was later told the top number (systolic pressure) hovered at 90. I was still alive.

Kathleen O'Leary, Dr. Holmes's assistant and a nurse-anesthetist student at the University of Detroit, was struck by the severity of my head injuries. She saw I wasn't responsive at all. The trip didn't take a half hour, and when the helicopter landed on a pad right in front of the emergency room, my chances were not good.

Theresa Canning was one of the members of the medical staff when I was wheeled into the ER. The day before she and a friend had been part of the helicopter emergency crew at the track. She had waved over to me, "Hey Ernie," and I had waved back, and when she found out I was the one being worked on, she shuddered. Only the day before, I was walking and talking and alive; the next day I'm lying on a gurney, near dead, waiting for surgery. As I was rushed into the ER, Theresa heard another member of the medical staff say, "His brain is really swollen. His prognosis is poor."

Dr. Errol Erlandson, the staff surgeon responsible for trauma, was in charge of the medical team in the ER. There must have been twenty doctors and nurses, each one working feverishly, inserting a tube or giving medication or monitoring my vital signs. Few race teams could have moved with such skill and coordination as I lay unconscious, fighting for my life.

Robert Yates, Larry McReynolds, Brian Vandercook, my father, and Kim arrived at the hospital and quickly headed for the emergency room. Brian tried to lead Kim into the

ER where I lay, but the doctors stopped them from going in there because they were preparing me for surgery. Kim was very upset because no one would tell her anything. When she asked the NASCAR officials whether I was alive or dead, they wouldn't say. And now she was in the hospital where I lay only a few feet away, and they wouldn't let her in to see me. Kim was living a nightmare.

After an interminable wait, a nurse asked Kim to go in and identify me. Brian went with her. They walked through the doors into the emergency room where I was lying on a gurney at the back in a big room. Though in a state of shock, Kim could see there must have been twenty medical people in there working on me. They had cut my uniform totally off, and all Kim could see was blood everywhere on the floor. A hose was connected to my neck; a machine was breathing for me. Although still disbelieving, she said, "Yes, that's him."

Immediately they hauled me out for a CT scan. That was the last Kim saw of me for two hours. Kim can remember a lot of people coming in and administering to me, and during this time she kept going into the bathroom and crying hysterically. Rice Speed, Lake Speed's wife, was with her, trying her best to pull Kim back together.

Eventually they moved everyone upstairs to a private waiting room where Kim, my parents, and a group of others concerned for my life sat there waiting. And waiting. And waiting.

Robert and Larry, meanwhile, had to figure what the race team was going to do. I was hurt very badly, and the chances of my surviving were slim. Robert and Larry huddled in the corner of one of the waiting rooms. Robert said,

"We need to make a decision. We have to dry the tears from our eyes for a few minutes and decide what to do bcause we've got seven or eight crew members sitting at the race-track waiting to hear how Ernie's doing and what to do." They reviewed their options. They asked themselves, "What would Ernie want us to do?" They knew very well that I would have wanted them to go out there the next day and run. They hashed over the option of running the car with Hut Stricklin in it. Hut had not made the Michigan race in his own car, and he was available, but Robert said, "It doesn't make any sense going back to the track and safely preparing the car for another driver when all our thoughts are back in Ann Arbor with Ernie lying in that hospital bed, not knowing whether he's going to live or die." They didn't think it was fair to whoever they put in the car or to themselves. They also remembered that when Davey was killed, rather than going to the track, they stayed at the hospital by Davey's side. Like they did that day, Robert and Larry elected to stay with me and not run. They were in the championship hunt, but they realized that it didn't matter any more if I wasn't behind the wheel. They decided if I couldn't drive the car, they would load up and go home.

Finally, one of the nurses came back and told Kim what had happened to me and what to expect. Nevertheless, when Kim walked in the room, she felt quite a shock when she saw that I had fourteen tubes in me including two chest tubes and an intracranial pressure monitor (ICP), besides being hooked to a respirator. I didn't look like I was alive. I looked more like an experiment in a horror movie.

A nurse walked Kim back to the waiting room where Robert and Larry were sitting. Dr. Saeed (pronounced Sid)

Farhat, my neurosurgeon, came over to speak with my family and friends. Dr. Farhat, whose neurological skill was one of the prime reasons I was flown to St. Joseph Hospital, was asked about my chances for survival. "What percent?" he was asked. He wore a very concerned look, and with his head down, didn't look anyone in the eye. He said, "Right now at this hour Ernie has a 10 percent chance of making it through the night."

Larry thought, This just can't be. This just can't. Kim felt a renewed sense of panic. She thought to herself, He's not going to live.

Carolyn Yates drove our daughter to the hospital. Jordan had just celebrated her first birthday the week before. Kim wondered whether Jordan would see her father again. Kim considered sending Jordan home, but she decided she needed her there. For the next month Kim and Jordan would live in a room attached to the hospital. One of our crew members drove the motor home onto the hospital grounds, but it was filled with memories of me and a lot of good times we had together, and she just couldn't bring herself to go back in there and sleep in it.

The way Dr. Erlandson explained it that first night, I had serious injuries to three major systems, any one of which could be fatal. The trauma Dr. Erlandson worried about most was to my heart and lungs. I had a cardiac contusion, a bruised heart muscle. As he explained it, the heart moves inside the chest cavity, and when I hit the wall and decelerated from 190 miles an hour to zero in less than a second, the heart keeps moving and slams against the breastbone. I suffered bilateral pneumothoraces—collapsed lungs—and had to have air pumped into them, so tubes were inserted into my chest cavity. If I was going to survive until the morning, the functioning of my heart and lungs had to stabilize.

The other serious injuries were to my brain. I had severe brain contusions, which is a bruising of the brain, and I also had fractures at the base of my skull. It's what happens on impact at high speed, when the brain moves in the cranium and the cranial bones absorb the shock.

I was in a coma. Doctors worried how my head injuries would affect my perception, memory, and previous motor skills, including my ability to drive a race car. Even if I recovered fully in one area, they knew there was no guarantee the other functions would return. But it was too early even to think about recovery. The questions of that first day had much more to do with my survival. Dr. Erlandson didn't hold out much hope for my making it through the night.

The doctors gave me steroids to keep the swelling down in my brain. They attached a pressure monitor that goes right through the skull and around the brain, and they watched my pressure from minute to minute.

Despite the general gloom there were a few hopeful signs. The doctors showed Kim major spots on my brain scan to indicate that the damage wasn't going to be permanent. What they didn't know was whether I would survive.

Around midday Robert and Larry drove back to the racetrack to look after our crew. I had been slated to run in the Busch race that day, and my Busch crew was very concerned and needed direction. After Robert and Larry talked to them and told them to pack up and go home to Charlotte, they briefed the NASCAR officials about my condition as best they could. Robert and Larry then drove back to the hospital, and that evening they were joined by their wives and others, who flew in, and for a couple of hours they sat and waited, paced and waited, along with my family and several members of Dale Earnhardt's race team. Everyone was waiting for me to take a turn—one way or the other. Larry had sat in just such a waiting room in 1993 waiting for news about Davey Allison, after his helicopter crash. Every time the door opened and a doctor or nurse came through it, Larry would sit at the edge of his seat and hold his breath. It was like a recurrent nightmare. Finally, a grim-faced doctor from the trauma team came out and said I was still alive but my chances were slim.

That evening, exhausted, Robert went to a local hotel to get some needed rest. Larry and Linda McReynolds stayed until nearly three in the morning. Kim, my sister Tracy, Linda Siegars, an employee of Irvan Enterprises, and Brett Nelson, my financial manager, stayed all night and slept in the waiting room.

Dr. Erlandson and his staff watched me minute by minute throughout the night. When morning came, Dr. Erlandson felt gratified that I hadn't succumbed. By the morning he felt I had a good chance to get to the second stage of recovery. It would be a couple of more days before he would be able to tell.

When Robert and Larry returned to the hospital Sunday morning, they found that my condition had changed little. I wasn't getting worse, but I wasn't getting better. My family and friends continued to prepare for the worst. Marc Reno, whom I had known as a teenager from California when I

was racing on short tracks and who built my first Winston
Cup car, flew from Florida that Sunday to see me. Marc was
sitting with my mom and dad when Dr. Farhat came in. Dr.
Farhat told them, "If he makes it through the next forty-eight
hours, it'll be a big plus." When asked my chances, the doctor was a little more optimistic than he had been the day
before. He told them, "He still has only a 10 or 15 percent
chance of making it." Marc thought to himself, Wow, to me
50–50 is not real good odds. Ernie's 10 to 15?

When Marc saw me, he said I looked "scary." Marc was
impressed more than anything by the number of tubes running into me and the plastic shunt screwed right into the top
of my skull to relieve the pressure on my brain. When he got
home that afternoon, he told his wife, Teri, "If I'm ever like
that, don't ever let them do that to me. Just pull the plug."
(Now when people ask Marc about it, he tells them, "You
never know what you can come back from.")

Mark Martin also came up that Sunday to peek in on
me. Mark too didn't think I'd make it. He saw that prepara-
tions were under way in the likely event I didn't survive, and
he left feeling very upset.

That afternoon Robert and Larry met again to discuss the
future of the 28 car. They had obligations to sponsors that
didn't stop even after a calamity like this. Robert had made
the decision to continue my salary the rest of the season,
and to do that the team needed to race to earn money and
to give the sponsor the exposure it was expecting on the TV
broadcasts. Robert decided that he and Larry would return
to the shop in Charlotte and make plans to finish out the
season.

When they returned to their shop, they found a pile of messages from just about anyone who ever drove a race car seeking to replace me in the 28 car. Robert and Larry approached their selection of their new driver with the certainty that not only would I not die, but I would possibly return the next year. Using that as their operative theory, they decided to pick Kenny Wallace as their driver for the remainder of 1994. Kenny is a very upbeat, happy-go-lucky guy, and he had no illusions as far as his role was concerned. Kenny told Robert, "I'm not looking for a full-time ride. I run for Fil Martocci in Busch events, and we run a few Winston Cup races. If I can help you out—and obviously it will help me—I'll race whatever races you'd like me to race as long as you need me to do it." Robert and Larry liked Kenny's approach, and they hired him. Kenny did a fine job. He usually qualified well, and he gained his first top-five finish in Winston Cup in a race at Martinsville in late September.

After three days, prayers were answered. I started responding to the doctors' prodding and prying. I hadn't opened my eyes, but I knew people were in the room. Dr. Erlandson was talking to me. I made facial responses with my eyebrows, and Dr. Erlandson knew then that I could understand even if I couldn't speak. When he asked me to squeeze his hand, I would. Dr. Erlandson was hopeful—it was an emotion short of optimistic, but it was a start.

On the fourth day, I started waking up, which was another big step toward recovering. When you wake up after a coma or anesthesia or surgery, you become very agitated from the trauma. The pain is severe and you become delirious. To keep me calm, the doctors gave me sedatives. One time Marc Reno visited me when the doctors were trying to bring me out of my coma, but as I came to, I was so upset they put me right back under again. They gave me morphine and also a paralysis drug. I later had hallucinations that people were trying to kill me, and when I woke up that time I was almost violent. I didn't recognize anyone, and I was afraid of everybody. Dr. Erlandson sat with me and tried to calm me down and talk me through it.

Larry returned to Ann Arbor on Friday, five days after the accident. He had been talking with Kim twice a day on the phone. During that entire time Kim had never left my side, and she was also in constant contact with Robert, giving them updates on my recovery. By Friday my chances for survival had improved. The question now was whether I would be brain damaged. There were few clues, some indirect signs, but the doctors really had no way of knowing for sure.

Kim told Larry, "He's in a semicoma. His eyes are open, he can look at you, but it's like there isn't a whole lot going on in there." When Larry and his wife, Linda, rode the elevator to my floor on Friday, he felt afraid at what he might find. When they walked into my room, I was lying in bed holding one of Jordan's baby shoes in my hand. The doctors were putting familiar objects in my hand in the hopes of stimulating my brain to consciousness. Even though I was still in a coma, I knew they were there. I squeezed Larry's hand. But Larry realized that though I was looking at him, I was looking right through him. And yet, remembering what I looked like back just five days before, despite the tubes and the wires and the endotracheal tube in my airway, Larry said, "Ernie's looking better."

Two days later, Dale Earnhardt and Mark Martin came

to visit me. I was still in a state resembling unconsciousness but I could recognize their voices, was very excited that they had come, even tried to sit up and started waving my hand around, but I couldn't respond in a meaningful way. I had been communicating with Dr. Erlandson by squeezing his hand, and when Dale and Mark came, I started reaching for their hands. Mark, who had seen me the day after the accident, was encouraged, though like Kim and everyone else, he left that day very much afraid that I was going to end up brain damaged or something less than 100 percent. Dale and Mark left with a sick feeling in their gut.

Mark tried to put his best face on it when he talked about me to Ken Schrader, another of my close friends. He said I was doing really well. A few days later Schrader came to visit. After he left, Kenny was devastated. He told Mark, "I don't call that doing very good." I guess Ken had expected that I'd be sitting up in bed talking.

Less than a week after my accident, Linda Siegars and Brett Nelson came back to visit. They had arrived in Michigan through the generous efforts of D.K. Ulrich, who flew them up in his plane. This was but one example of the generosity shown to me. I am grateful to all the many people who donated time and resources on my behalf. You really find out who your friends are in the bad times. Nonetheless, when Linda and Brett came back to visit, they were shocked. They had not seen me the first time and had heard from my sister Tracy how good I looked. As soon as they walked into the room and saw me, they turned and quickly left. On the way back to North Carolina they agreed there was no way possible I could have a normal life again. I would prove them wrong.

It was ten days before I could speak. It was a lot longer before I could put words together. Kim's biggest fear was that I would be brain impaired. You can't be greedy, but at first all she asked was that I survive, and then as I began to respond, she kept asking for more and more. According to Kim, when I first started to talk with an endotracheal tube inserted in my throat, I made no sense. Later I could say words, but the words had no meaning. It was like somebody took a bunch of words, put them in a bucket and shook them up, and what you got was what I said. Kim would walk around the room crying because she thought I'd remain like that.

On other occasions she thought I was going to die. Thoughts of my dying rarely left her. The big reason she refused to leave my side was that she feared that if she didn't watch over me, I would die. She was my guardian angel.

Eventually two of the nurses convinced her that they would watch me as closely as she did. They promised her that if anything happened to me, they would call her, and so she felt confident enough to go to another room and sleep.

And one night my heart started fibrillating. My heart was so bruised, it was causing an erratic heartbeat. The cardiogram started making wavy lines. To Kim, it was like a fire alarm going off when she heard the heart monitor shriek.

A young intern was on duty that night, and he panicked. And when he did, so did Kim, who demanded they call the cardiologist. It was over the weekend. The intern said, "I don't know if I should." But Kim was insistent, and she got one to come, and he performed an EKG on me. After fourteen or so hours, it straightened itself out, but that whole time Kim kept thinking I was going to have a heart attack.

Another problem was that after being on the feeding tube for so long, my stomach wouldn't digest food. They kept waiting for me to eat but I couldn't get any food down. It took a while.

On other occasions I couldn't keep food down. One night I drank several Dr. Peppers, when suddenly I started throwing up everything. I was feeling terrible. I began feeling better when I received a visit from Jack Roush, who owns five Winston Cup race teams including Mark Martin's car. He talked to me for about four hours, about racing and airplanes and all sorts of things. That's the longest I ever spoke to Jack Roush, and it meant a lot to me that he came.

About three weeks after the accident in early September, Dale Earnhardt called me on the phone to see how I was doing. Earnhardt was headed to Richmond to go test. I had just had the trach taken out, and my throat hurt, but I was glad to be able to talk again, if you want to call what I was saying "talking."

It was painful for Kim to watch me try to get the words out. My mind was working, but my mouth wasn't. The nurses would show me pictures, and I had a terrible time trying to identify some of them. They would show me a picture of a camel, for instance. I'd say, "It's got two humps. I know that one." But I couldn't remember the word *camel*.

And yet, the fact I could talk meant so much to my friends. A few days later Kim called Larry on the phone. She said, "Larry, I have somebody who wants to talk to you." And she put me on the phone, and we talked. It wasn't much of a conversation, and my voice was very scratchy, but

Larry didn't care about what I was saying. He kept repeating, "Ernie, it's just so great to hear you!"

Just before the Dover race on September 18 Larry and Rusty Wallace flew up to Michigan to see me. Rusty was another friend who had come up regularly. By this time, the doctors were saying I had improved enough to fly back to Charlotte to continue my rehabilitation. I was out of intensive care, resting in a private room. I was still under a nurse's care, but I was out of the woods. I would survive.

When Larry and Rusty came to see me, they couldn't believe the progress I had made. Said Larry, "Anybody who saw what Ernie went through during this three-week period could not deny there's a God."

3

My recovery did not always progress smoothly. There were times if I made one step forward, I'd take three backward. I got pneumonia, but the doctors treated me and I recovered. Dr. Farhat permanently inserted a shunt valve, a little tube underneath the skin behind my right ear to relieve the pressure from cerebral spinal fluid, which is the fluid that bathes the brain. When it becomes blocked, excessive amounts of fluid build up and the normal drainage system can't manage it. The shunt drains that fluid directly back into my vascular system, going from the brain into a vein into my neck. What was tricky about having the shunt implanted was that when the fluid drained out too quickly and the pressure got too low, I would become nauseated. When they flew me by medical jet from Michigan to Charlotte the weekend of September 18, 1994, I felt sick the whole way.

When the plane landed in Charlotte, it taxied to the end of the runway to an isolated part of the airport, and an ambulance came to meet me and take me to the Charlotte Institute of Rehabilitation, connected to the Carolinas

Medical Center downtown. We did this because we felt it important that I not let the media see the condition I was in. If I was going to return to racing, I wanted them to see me healthy and robust, not weak and unfit.

When Larry returned from the Dover race that Sunday evening, he came over to see me. He lit up when he entered the room. He said, "Man, I can't believe you're back in Charlotte." For the first time since the accident Larry saw that I was going to be able to live a life, and he was relieved. As for my being able to drive a race car again, I don't think at this point deep down any of my friends thought I would ever drive again.

Neither did Dr. Jim McDeavitt, who was in charge of my rehabilitation program. I asked him, "Doc, how long do you think it will be before I'll be able to race again?" As far as I had come, he was looking at a patient who could barely walk, who lacked proper balance, who essentially had one good eye. He said, "Ernie, racing is shooting for too much. Let's shoot for something more reachable, that some day you will be able to drive your little girl to school." I became very emotional. I was about to cry, and I cry every time I recall it. I said, "Doc, you don't understand what you're saying. I'm a race car driver. It's who I am. It's what I do." He repeated, "It will be a miraculous day if you can drive your little girl to school."

He was looking at someone who had suffered a serious head injury. I was looking at it like, "What's the big deal? It's not like I can't walk." Dr. McDeavitt told me he had had thousands of patients with similar injuries to mine, and that I was very lucky to have survived. Still, I simply could not accept the limits Dr. McDeavitt was proposing for my future.

Dr. McDeavitt's recovery program included different kinds of therapy. I worked with physical therapists to improve my mobility, balance, endurance, and strength. I received treatment from occupational therapists who helped me relearn how to dress, bathe, and groom myself. I also worked with speech therapists. With diligent effort, I improved day after day. Though I was still weak, I was much more stable on my feet, and my head was beginning to clear. My biggest problem at this point was the nerve damage to my left eye. My eyes couldn't focus properly, and I had to wear an eye patch to prevent double vision.

Dr. McDeavitt and I disagreed about whether the eye patch would prevent me from returning to racing. He didn't think it possible. He asked, "How can you think of getting in a car if you only have one eye? You have no depth perception. You won't be able to tell how close or far the other cars are, much less judge the distance between you and the wall."

I said, "Doc, I know all the tracks. I know all the spots I have to hit when I'm going through the corners. You don't need depth perception." He disagreed. "How can you move in and out of traffic without having depth perception?" he asked.

I proved I could do it on a miniature scale in the rehab center. The husband of one of the nurses brought me a small remote control Texaco race car, and I found that despite wearing that eye patch, I could run that little car out my room and into the hall and back with great dexterity. I'd chase the nurses and little kids with it, and I could make it turn around and bring it back as I wished. Marc Reno came to visit, and when he saw how well I steered that miniature car, he was really impressed that I could steer the opposite way to get the car to return to me. He marveled that I still had my coordination. I had no doubt in my mind I would be able to do the same thing on the racetrack.

When I checked into the rehab clinic in Charlotte, Brian Vandercook made sure that security was tight. I checked in under a pseudonym, and the only way callers could get through to me was to ask for me under my fake name. Visitors were screened very carefully. Brian didn't want any unauthorized photos of me or any interviews before I was more fully recovered. Reporters had been calling, but Brian told them, "No, Ernie's not ready to meet the press."

About five days after I began my rehabilitation, one morning I was listening to the John Boy and Billy Big Show on the radio. Their show is syndicated throughout the South and has a large audience. John Boy and Billy are friends of mine, two very funny comedians who love country music and stock car racing. As I was listening, I decided it would be fun to call them on the phone and let them—and all my fans—know I was recovering and was going to be fine. I called John Boy and Billy, and we chatted for a while. I enjoyed talking with them.

Sometimes you forget the power of radio—everybody and his uncle apparently had heard me on the show—and it wasn't long before the phones started ringing off the hook in the hospital. Every reporter who wrote about motor sports racing now knew that I was capable of giving an interview, and so many requests poured in that we decided to hold a press conference that afternoon.

Dr. McDeavitt was wary. My endurance still was not what he felt it should have been, and he was concerned that by the end of the day I would become weak. He was afraid I might be asking too much of myself to conduct a press conference in front of dozens of reporters. ESPN was there and all the motor sports reporters. That evening the press conference was broadcast nationally. If I had stumbled and fallen in front of the national media, that sort of publicity would not have aided my comeback at all, but it turned out I did fine.

In early October I said, "Doc, I want to attend the Charlotte race." He said, "That's only in two weeks." I said, "Yes, it is, and I want to go to it." He said he didn't think I would be able to go. Two weeks later, I was happy to know he was incorrect.

I went to the Charlotte Motor Speedway, watched practice, and held another press conference. When I walked out onto the track, I heard the cheers, and I was moved to tears. It meant so much to me that the fans were behind me. Without their loyal support, I don't know if I'd have recovered quite as quickly. I don't think anyone really thought I would ever drive again, but in my mind there was no question about my returning. If I'm nothing else, I'm determined. When I want to do something, it's rare that I don't succeed.

For the most part, I enjoyed my day at the track. I was like a kid in a candy store. I enjoyed teasing Brian Vandercook, who was given the unenviable job of keeping an eye on me. Whenever I could, I would purposely give Brian the slip. I wasn't supposed to climb the ladder and go to the top of the Texaco/Haviland truck, but I did, and every time I climbed up or down that ladder, poor Brian would wring his hands. I was having the time of my life trying to lose him. I was excited being at the track that day, but it was a bitter pill to swallow when I watched all my colleagues out there on the track, knowing I wasn't in the lineup. And when I went to the garage area and saw Kenny Wallace sitting in my 28 car, I felt rage. My anger wasn't directed at Kenny, who did a fine job while he was in the car, as much as it was that I was not seated in that car. It only served to make me more determined to make a full recovery and get back out on the racetrack.

Less than two weeks after checking into the rehabilitation center, the doctors cleared me for outpatient care. I went home, and began a workout at a local health club to improve my stamina and strength. I worked hard, climbing the Stairmaster, running on a treadmill, and lifting weights. I'm in better shape now than I ever was before my accident.

The further along I went in my recovery, the more anxious I was to race again. By December 1994, I was going crazy. Robert Yates kept telling me, "When you're ready to come back, we'll run you in a car." Robert had announced that in 1995 I would be his driver, but he also said that until I was able to return Dale Jarrett would drive the 28 car. "When Ernie is ready to come back, we'll run a second car," he said.

Even though he said that, I didn't know whether he truly believed it would happen. By the NASCAR awards banquet at the Waldorf-Astoria in New York in December, my frustrations had grown to the point where I was driving Kim and everyone on the race team crazy.

During our New York stay, Kim and I met with the Ford racing executives in Dan Rivard's suite at the Waldorf. I was feeling physically fit and confident about my ability to race competitively. At the meeting I expressed my certainty that I would return to racing, somehow, somewhere, no matter what, in 1995. At the meeting were Robert Yates and Larry McReynolds, and Dan Rivard and Lee Morse from Ford. I told Robert, "I'm capable of driving right now, and I want to get it done. I'm going racing, with you or without you, so you better have a car for me at Daytona." Robert could tell I was serious.

It was only four months after the accident, and I was very impatient. I didn't want to sit out a year. I wanted my life back. I asked Robert, "Are you going to have a car for me at Daytona? If not, I'll go drive for someone else." Robert did what he could to put me off.

Dan Rivard, who is in charge of the Ford racing program, understood my impatience. Dan is a great guy. He is a very thoughtful person who thinks things through. Like everyone else, Dan was sure it was far too early for me to race, but he knew if he set up a plan that would lead to my return to Winston Cup racing, I would calm down and stop making everyone else so uncomfortable with my demands to drive again so early in my recovery.

Dan said, "Ernie, what we need to do is set goals. What you are looking for is a plan, and I'm going to outline the various steps that will lead to your racing again. Every goal you reach will take you one step closer to your getting back into a Winston Cup car to race." What Rivard was doing was wise. Ford didn't want to look irresponsible by allowing me to race too soon. Naturally they were concerned about criticism from the media and the fans. At the same time Dan was protecting me from myself. By setting up a plan, Ford could set aside their fears I would do too much too soon.

Dan wisely wanted to be sure I was ready before climbing into a race car again.

Dan said, "Ernie, if we don't stick to the plan, it will be disastrous for everyone, but mainly for you." I was perfectly agreeable because I had heard what I wanted to hear—that the race team had something concrete in mind for me. Understandably NASCAR was going to be very careful about letting me run. Even if Robert had said I could run at Daytona in February, NASCAR couldn't allow it. NASCAR needed to see an executed game plan too. In addition, the doctors had to give their blessing.

As the first step in my return to racing, Dan had arranged a series of tests about two weeks after the banquet on Ford's test track in Naples, Florida. Ford had built a new experimental Thunderbird, and it had a lot of computerized features that allowed the technicians to monitor the performance of the car and the driver. I suspect it's possible that they set up the test just for me to be able to go down there and drive some, but Ford brought along Dale Jarrett, and they made it seem like we were going down there not only to test our skills but to test what this new experimental car could measure. The car's computer was able to test a lot of things, including my reaction time. D.J. ran, Robert Yates ran, seven or eight of us took turns behind the wheel of that car. Though they had to have been nervous about it, they let me run as they said they would.

They worked with Dale first. He ran smoothly, and his reflexes were good. I got in behind the wheel. Dan Rivard got in beside me—a show of confidence in me on his part. It was a passenger car Thunderbird, but its suspension was strongly modified. It only had two seats because the rest of the car was filled with data acquisition equipment. It was a road course, and though the car was not a race car, I was able to get up to speeds of 80 miles an hour. To drive it, you had to be fully aware, competent, aggressive, and smooth. They were entrusting me with a million dollars' worth of experimental automobile and equipment. I was still wearing an eye patch over my left eye. That day I was assessing myself as much as everyone else was.

I drove several laps, and when I came in, Dan was smiling from ear to ear. He told Robert and Larry, "This cat hasn't lost anything. He's as smooth as they come." Their encouragement was certainly appreciated.

According to Ford's computers and timers, I was as fast as D.J. any time I was on the track. Though my brain may have been a little slow for certain functions away from the track, it didn't impair my driving skills at all. Robert told me my reaction times were as quick as they ever were. We did a lot of stopping and starting, and we tested the handling of the car, and everyone was surprised I hadn't lost my skills after all the damage to my body and brain. It was a relief to pass test number one with flying colors, I can tell you.

Larry marveled at my day-to-day improvement. He knew me as well as anyone, and could see I was getting better.

After driving the Naples test track, I was completely convinced I was going to race again. For me the next step was to get into a Winston Cup car. Others still weren't as confident and preferred that I take a few interim steps before racing at full speed. In January 1995, I went with the race team to Daytona where we were testing with Dale

Jarrett behind the wheel. Robert and Larry didn't want me racing at Daytona. They felt it was too soon. Dan Rivard didn't want me skipping any of his steps, and he had specified that he wanted me to run on a short track before I attempted to run at a superspeedway like Daytona or Talladega. But I was impatient and confident, and I kept pushing Robert and Larry to let me get in a run at Daytona. I kept saying, "Robert, I just want to make a couple of laps." Robert really didn't want me to do it, and it was clear I was putting him in a tough position. He said, "Oh man, I knew you'd ask me." I kept insisting, "Just let me sneak in a couple of laps." I begged him. Robert knew that if the press or NASCAR knew I was running down at Daytona there'd be hell to pay.

There were seven or eight other cars testing at the time. Toward the end of the third and final day of testing, I again approached Robert and Larry about letting me go out to run a few laps.

Larry asked Robert, "What do you want to do?" Robert said, "I'm going to go to pit road. You do what you think best." Larry said, "Oh, thanks Robert. I appreciate that." Robert added, "That way I don't have to lie to the press when they come around and ask about it." Neither Larry not Robert were in an enviable position, but I will always be grateful that they respected my desire to push ahead—fast, with no hesitation.

Larry told D.J., "You go out and test, and we'll give Ernie a uniform. After you finish, drive into the garage, and go into the van, and Ernie will wear one of your uniforms. He'll get in the van, and we'll shut the doors. Then Ernie will get in the car pretending to be you, and he'll go out and test."

And that's exactly what we did. When the two race cars were in the garage along with our passenger van, I put on one of Dale's uniforms and my helmet and climbed inside the van. After we pulled the garage doors down, D.J. went into the van. Then I left the van and got into the race car while he stayed in the van out of sight as I pretended to be him.

As anyone can imagine, Larry was very nervous about it. He kept saying, "Man, just be careful. Take it easy. Go slow." I said, "You know me, Larry." He said, "That's why I said that."

As I drove onto the track, Larry climbed on top of the hauler to watch. We decided not to talk on the radio to try to prevent anyone from discovering I was in the car. When our spotter said, "Clear," I remained silent. I took off down pit road, entered the Daytona track and ran wide open. I never lifted. I went all the way around, ran within hundredths of a second of what D.J. had run, real close to 190 miles an hour, and I could see that everything was fine. Better than that, everything *felt* fine.

I had forgotten how much I love the smell and sound of racing. I badly missed the adrenaline rush that comes when you roar out onto that track, flooring that gas pedal. To be back on a racetrack, getting up to speed, taking the perfect line to get around Daytona sent a thrill run through me that I hadn't experienced in too long a time. After being told by everyone that I would never have these experiences again, my joy at being back on that racetrack was unadulterated pleasure.

When I came in and swapped back again with D.J., everyone was on pins and needles, afraid someone would find out. Until now no one knew for sure that I had done this except for a few of us.

Larry was tickled by my performance. Larry told me the whole time I was running out there he was both scared and thrilled. He knew that if I had wrecked, NASCAR would have been furious. Every time I completed a lap, Larry shouted, "Yes." Only after I pulled back into the garage and swapped back with Dale did he relax. I will always be grateful for the risks Larry took with me, and remember our successes together as some of my best moments.

Members of other race teams had seen us pull the garage doors down, and they became suspicious and began putting two and two together. That night we returned to Charlotte for the All Pro banquet where the top drivers, crew chiefs, mechanics, and tire changers from the previous year are honored. Before we arrived word had beaten us back that I had been driving the car at Daytona.

Robert Yates denied he knew anything about it, which he could do because he didn't know for sure, and Larry was forced to double-talk the reporters. When they asked him, "Did Ernie drive the car today?" he said to them, "We were down there testing, and Ernie was down with us, but Dale did the testing for us today." He was tiptoeing lightly around the truth though.

Driving those few laps at Daytona that day was important to me. I realized that it's not that big a deal to drive a car fast at Daytona when you're out there by yourself, but if I had had any doubts about whether my abilities had been hampered by the crash, my running that day dispelled them. I saw I was able to hold a good line and keep the gas pedal to the floor with ease and comfort, and that day in Daytona I knew I could still race.

The first time I tested publicly was around the first of March at Darlington. Dan Rivard wanted me to test my Busch Grand National car before I drove a Winston Cup car. The Busch cars are a little slower, but Darlington is a tricky racetrack, and it was the first time I ran there since they repaved the track surface.

I had asked Mark Martin to come with me. He went out and made sure my Busch car was driving all right before I got in it. As Mark put it, "I was just watching out for my buddy." Some of the members of the Texaco/Havoline race team were upset that I hadn't asked D.J. to warm up the car for me. But in truth it really hadn't occurred to me. Mark and I went back a long ways, and I wanted Mark with me that day. Mark had prayed for me often, asking God to return me to my family so I could lead a normal life. He'll tell you today my recovery was a "miracle from God."

Mark went out onto the Darlington track and ran a 30-second flat lap. I got the uniform on and went out in the car. I took it easy for two or three laps, then ran about a 30.40 lap. I told Larry, "Feels good, but it's a little too tight." The next time I went out, I ran two-tenths faster than Mark. I came back in, went back out, and ran about six-tenths faster than Mark—two-tenths faster than the track record from the year before! Mark was impressed but also very relieved that it had gone well. I'm very lucky to have good friends like Mark Martin.

As I got faster and faster in my Busch car, I asked Robert, "How about letting me run in one of the Cup cars?"

Robert and Larry looked at each other as if they were both asking, "What do we do now? We can't very well tell him no." Dale Jarrett was standing nearby, and very generously offered, "Why don't you let him drive the car over there? That one is driving pretty good."

Dale had been running 29.70s with the Cup car. I got in, headed for the track, and by the fourth lap I ran a 29.72.

Larry was standing on the top of our truck watching me test. Darlington can be a complicated racetrack. Turns three and four are almost like a long straightaway. When a car is really running well there, the driver will get back on the gas in the middle of three and four. As he comes across four and cuts to the bottom of the corner, the left side wheels sometimes hit that apron, and the car will wiggle. You have to stay on the gas, though, and keep going. About the third lap, I drove through three and moved the car up high and got back on the gas. I cut down across four, leaving the left front wheel dipped down. The car wiggled, but I didn't lift a bit. I was flying. Larry noticed.

He told Robert, "Man, this guy could race tomorrow if he had to and he'd be better than 90 percent of the drivers out there." Robert just grinned along with Larry. Robert said, "You're right, but we still have to make sure we follow the game plan."

At the very end of the day I made a ten-lap run in my Busch car, and decided to run one more lap. I relaxed too much as I went into turn one, spun and hit the fence. As Kim said, two steps forward, one step back. The day was filled with success, even though I brushed the wall. I wasn't hurt, and I was still feeling very positive. Larry was afraid the incident would affect my confidence, but he had nothing to worry about. I hated that I had crashed, but I knew it was because I hadn't been in a car for a while, not because I had lost any real ability. In fact, from the moment I was able to think straight after my wreck in Michigan, I never once questioned my driving ability. I knew I would come back and be just fine. It was just a matter of time and opportunity.

One of the decisions I had to make in 1995 was what to do with my Busch team. In addition to taking me out of Winston Cup competition, my accident kept me from continuing as a driver in the Busch Grand National series events. While I was recovering, I continued to pay my employees. But if I couldn't drive the car, keeping it going didn't make a lot of sense. In the spring of 1995 I was approached by Mark Simo to go into partnership in the truck series.

At the time Mark made the offer he had no idea whether I would ever drive again. The way he put it, he wasn't hiring Ernie Irvan, the driver, but Ernie Irvan, an experienced, knowledgeable Winston Cup veteran. He wanted my overall expertise, and at the time of his offer he was providing me with the only way I could participate in racing. Mark's offer was very generous, and the timing could not have been better. I would furnish the shop and all the equipment, and the Simos would finance the team. It was an excellent opportunity for me, in large part because during the period when I wasn't racing, mostly I was sitting around grousing over not being able to race. I was making everyone's life unpleasant, and overseeing the Irvan-Simo truck team gave me the chance to use my talents for something constructive. And so I changed my Busch team into a truck series team. We hired Joe Ruttman to drive, and

Coca-Cola was our sponsor. We actually had a pretty good season, finishing second in the points standings.

The third of Dan Rivard's steps was to run on a track with some other cars. Since I now owned a truck team, we decided to do that in one of my trucks. We went to North Wilkesboro in April to test. Joe Ruttman drove one of my trucks and I drove another. Robert came up and watched. This wasn't any Sunday stroll. Ruttman and I drove hard against each other. We ran side by side at top speeds. We even rubbed sheet metal a couple of times. I needed to know whether I could compete going all out, and so did Robert.

He was impressed by how well I was doing. When he returned to the shop he told Larry McReynolds, "The guy is as good as he ever was. He wore Ruttman out. He let Ruttman get by him, and he would set him up and drive right past him."

Again, I can't say enough how supportive Robert was during this time. He could have concentrated on D.J. and ignored me, but he went out of his way to ease my return to racing, more than many other owners might have.

Joe and I next went to Martinsville for more testing. Robert stated what he had said before: "Larry, he hasn't forgotten a thing." He told NASCAR that too. I believe that Robert's credibility is such that NASCAR easily accepted his expert opinion.

Nonetheless, I was still concerned that NASCAR wouldn't let me race again. As it turned out, they did everything they could do for me while also ensuring they covered their bases. NASCAR selected a doctor to clear me. I feel sure NASCAR was well aware that these type of comebacks made good stories and would bring favorable coverage to the sport if it turned out well. Thankfully it did.

I was hoping to return in June 1995. We went to Road Atlanta and tested the road course car, where I was able to consistently run well and competitively with D.J. Actually, I felt pretty confident on the road course. Larry wanted me to drive conservatively, but by this time I knew I was as good as ever. For me there was only one way to drive—flat out. As far as I was concerned, I had recovered. There was no longer any reason to pussyfoot around the racetrack.

I kept telling Larry, "We need to put new tires on the car because it feels loose." He said, "If we put tires on it, you're going to go out and try to set the track record." I said, "I'm telling you, if you don't put tires on this thing, I'm going to end up in the gravel." Robert kept checking carburetors and running laps. Again I said to Larry, "I'm telling you, put new tires on this thing or I'm going to crash." He said, "Go out one more time without the new tires." I went out one more time and in turn one I spun and got stuck in the gravel pit.

I didn't hit anything, but Robert could have used that incident as an excuse to let me go if he had wanted to. It would have been very easy for Robert to say, "Man, I don't want to mess with this. I'm taking too much of a risk. Ernie could get hurt again." But Robert never did. I will always be grateful to Robert for giving me the chance to come all the way back.

4

ALL THE WAY BACK

In late April 1995 the doctors discovered I had an aneurysm. I had been tested and scanned at St. Joseph's in Michigan right after my accident, but there was so much blood and swelling and bruising that the CT scan wasn't able to see the area where the aneurysm was found. Dr. Farhat had arranged for the rehab institute to repeat the test. Dr. Jerry Petty, a neurosurgeon who has worked with NASCAR for many years, examined me. After he studied the imaging study of my brain, he determined that the three nerves which allowed me to move my left eye had been damaged. The only place where that can happen was in or around the carotid artery. He had an arteriogram performed showing where the artery had been damaged, and prescribed an operation to correct the weakness.

At first the doctors were nervous about the potential danger I was in. I was like a time bomb that could explode at any moment. I could die. Fortunately the aneurysm was inside an artery. If it did erupt, Dr. Petty said, I could go to the hospital, and they could repair the damaged area. I went through three surgeries to have it corrected.

It turned out the aneurysm was what caused my double vision. When it ballooned, it pinched off the nerves that went to my left eye. When I first went back to driving, I continued to wear an eye patch. A lot of people thought I was blind in my left eye, but the problem wasn't my vision. I've always been able to see. I had double vision because my left eye was pointing at the wrong angle. I later had eye muscle and eyelid surgery to correct the problem. My vision basically is back to normal now.

I owe Dr. Petty a huge debt of gratitude. If he had not diagnosed the problem at the beginning, it wouldn't have been treated properly, and perhaps I still would have a paralyzed eye.

After the initial surgery, my eye developed enough muscle to move left to right. However, it still didn't move up or down much. The surgeons had to go back and do surgery to align my eyes and get the muscles to work together. It took a full three years for everything to work right again.

The fourth nerve makes your eye move and makes your eyelid open and close. Before the surgery my left eye was drooping, and I could barely open it. It was difficult to see out of it very well. I had to open it up with my fingers. The surgeons got the eyelid to open. Now the only problem—the only lasting damage from the accident to speak of—is that my left eye doesn't shut well enough at night. If that muscle is all right, the eye will roll back in your head when you sleep. Because my eye doesn't close tightly enough, too much air goes to the cornea, and I have to use a thick cream at night to protect and moisten the eye.

The Friday before the Sears Point race in May, I was operated on in a hospital in San Francisco. Everything went well. Ten minutes before the Sunday race, I walked into our pits at the track in street clothes. Larry and the crew seemed very surprised. But at every stage of my career, I cannot imagine operating without an immense amount of determination. I was not to let my injuries keep me from racing again. I was determined to succeed. My determination, plus God's will and all the prayers and encouragement, helped to hasten my return.

My comeback was delayed from the spring to the fall when my doctors discovered that the aneurysm they had operated on in May still allowed blood to flow.

After the surgery in May, the doctors had asked me to wait until the middle of August to check my condition again. NASCAR made it clear that they wouldn't let me race until the aneurysm was repaired. NASCAR said, "In three months we'll recheck. If everything is fine, we'll sign off and let you race."

When they rechecked, they felt there was still a problem. They advised me to have one more operation in mid-August. The doctors attached more coils. When it was completed the doctors were totally confident it was 100 percent.

I had to wait another month for the doctors to check the aneurysm one last time. My goal had been to get in ten races in '95, so we could plan for '96, but the aneurysm sharply cut back on my plans. We were shooting for the September 9 race at Richmond, but the release didn't arrive until September 16, 1995, before the Martinsville race, when I was cleared to drive again. It was a little over a year after my accident when the doctors returned my life back to me.

■　■　■

I still had a couple of more hurdles before I could run the full Winston Cup series. As a precaution, NASCAR first wanted to see me race in my truck because it's a slower race. Then they wanted me to drive in a short-track Winston Cup race.

We went to North Wilkesboro two weeks before the actual race on October 1 and tested. Dale Jarrett and I both ran fast in practice. I won't apologize for the fact that I was very happy I ran very fast. The racing press also noticed my speed. Consequently there were plenty of questions to be answered. I went into the media center and did interviews. My eye patch brought many comments. I was told over and over, "You can't race with only one eye." They were wrong. I could, and for a while, I did.

I was scheduled to race my truck at Martinsville, but it rained. Because qualifying was rained out and I didn't have any points, I didn't get to compete. Despite my initial disappointment, I didn't stay upset long. I told Larry, "It can't rain for forty days and forty nights. It's got to clear up eventually."

The next week, we went to North Wilkesboro, where I was scheduled to run in the truck race first and then in the Winston Cup race. Before I started in the truck race, everyone wondered whether I'd be able to run in traffic wearing that eye patch, whether I'd be able to judge distances.

The truck race at North Wilkesboro was my first official race back after my accident. I knew I needed to show everyone that there was no reason to be afraid of me, that I had the same skill I had had before my crash. And I needed to do it quickly. My race team and I worked hard on getting that truck ready for qualifying. Late in the day I went out onto that track and I could hear the thousands of fans in the grandstands rising as one, the cheering was so loud that I could hear the excitement over the roar of the car engine. I was energized by their encouragement, and when I took the checkered flag and my time was posted, the crowd stood on its feet and continued to cheer when they saw I had qualified second, missing the pole by only a hundredth of a second! It was one of the most satisfying performances of my life. I was putting everyone on notice—the other drivers, NASCAR, the fans—that I was going to be as good as ever.

Early in the race I led, a tremendous thrill, and in fact I led much of the first half of the race. We just missed on the setup, and halfway through we got real loose and fell back to third or fourth. There was a five-minute break, and we decided to change the sway bar, but we couldn't get it done in time. It was our mistake. Then the truck had mechanical problems and we had to drop out. But when the truck was working, I ran well, and people seemed to be taking notice.

The next day I ran the Winston Cup car. Dale Jarrett, who had taken my ride in the 28 car, stayed where he was, and Robert Yates put me in the 88 car. Robert swore to me that both cars were identical. The only difference, he said, was that Dale's car had an orange number 28 on it and mine had a yellow number 88.

Larry was the crew chief for both cars. He had hired a few crew members for my race team. We didn't have enough equipment at the time for both cars, and so, to make Larry's life easier before the race, NASCAR was good enough to let our two cars park close together in the garage. One crew worked on D.J.'s car and another on my car. Larry ran back and forth between the two of them. That week he must have worked a hundred hours. Larry knew that if I didn't qualify I wouldn't get to run in the race because I hadn't raced that season and didn't have any points for a provisional starting spot.

Wilkesboro always has a large crowd to watch qualifying, and when I drove out onto the track, I thought those people were going to tear the grandstand down they made so much noise. It was a sound I welcomed. And when I came around and took the green flag, the entire place erupted with cheering that left me with tears in my eyes. The fans in our sport are very loyal to their favorite drivers, but it seemed that *everyone* there was cheering my return. Perhaps each had a sense of just how hard it had been for me to get to this point.

When I came around and took the checkered flag, I was third fastest. It was a thrill, but I was particularly happy for Larry and the crew. Larry told me later that when my time was announced, he felt as though the weight of the world had been lifted from his shoulders. Three cars later D.J. went out and ran two-hundredths of a second faster than I had run, and we started the race sixth and seventh, a credit to Larry's hard work. At the end of the day I slept like a baby.

Some members of the press told me that my run at Wilkesboro was followed more intensely throughout the United States than the Daytona 500. I think because I was still wearing that eye patch, a lot of people didn't expect me to be able to perform up to par.

In the race both cars ran decently. D.J. and I both led part of that Wilkesboro race. D.J. even had a shot at winning it. Robert was acting as my crew chief, and during the race, I radioed into him. "How am I running?" Robert said,

"You're fifth, and you're ten seconds behind the leader." I asked him, "Who's leading?" And Robert kind of hesitated, like he really didn't want to tell me. He finally said, "The 28 is leading."

Dale had the fastest car that day. Then with about a hundred laps to go he ran into one of the lapped cars, knocking the toe out. I finished sixth, and Dale ended up right behind me. At the end of the day Larry was exhausted but elated. I shared his enthusiasm when he told me, "It doesn't get any better than this."

After Wilkesboro, I saw a doctor who suggested I get glasses with a prism lens. I had vision in my left eye, but because it was not pointed the same way as my right eye, I was seeing double. By giving me prism lenses, I could see straight ahead and also have peripheral vision. It was 100 percent better, though not completely fixed. For instance, I still had real trouble playing Ping-Pong—I'd see four or five balls coming at me, but the glasses certainly helped me on the racetrack. Those prism glasses were a major step.

Charlotte was the next race after Wilkesboro, and NASCAR asked me not to run there, but to run in the next race at Rockingham, a shorter, slower track. NASCAR wanted me sticking to the steps they had set out. I can't tell you I wasn't disappointed, but I was committed to honoring our agreement.

After the Charlotte race Dale and I went to Rockingham and tested. Because Larry felt it was too much for him to be the crew chief for both cars, he and Robert hired Todd Parrott from the Roger Penske team to be my crew chief, and Larry worked as crew chief for the 28 car.

On Friday we went to Rockingham to qualify, but it

rained, leaving only one day to make the race. Unfortunately, on Saturday right before the practice session was to end, I collided with another car, spun, and hit the wall. We had to unload the backup car, I got no practice, and the car didn't run fast enough to make the field. It was Todd's first effort as a crew chief, and he was very disappointed, but it certainly wasn't his fault.

We went to Phoenix and qualified well. Then with ten minutes left during Happy Hour (the final hour of practice), I got loose between turns one and two, spun, and hit the wall. Once again we had to unload our backup car. Todd did an excellent job getting the car ready. He also had a great attitude. I was always confident that Todd would make the most of every opportunity to make sure I would run fast.

It pleased me that for a while I was able to give that Phoenix crowd quite a thrill, as I led most of the race. At one point I had almost a straightaway lead, before the engine gave out at the end.

We went to Atlanta and had a reasonable qualifying run. I ran in the top five all day long. With about ten laps to go, we had to pit for fuel, and I ended up finishing seventh. Atlanta is the third fastest track on the Winston Cup circuit, and this was the last and final step of my recovery before NASCAR would clear me to race. I had run competitively side by side all day, despite my patch. A lot of drivers were uncomfortable with my patch, but I think I was able to show everybody that it didn't impede by ability to run fast and safely. My performance should have been proof.

During the off-season Dr. Buckley performed muscle surgery on the left eye, making it unnecessary for me to wear glasses at all. If I wanted to play baseball or racquetball, I'd have a hard time. But when you drive a race car, you're strapped in and you look straight ahead, and everything is fine. I'm not hindered at all.

My comeback was now complete. Looking back on it, it seems only natural that I would come back and race again. But anyone who saw me that dark day of August in Michigan will tell you that my chances of survival—forget the likelihood of racing again—were grim. When they saw I was going to survive, they said I'd be lucky if I could drive my daughter to school again. But as I will describe in more detail later, in 1996 I won races at Loudon and Richmond, and in 1997 I returned to Michigan, where three years earlier I had crashed, and I rode the 28 car to victory.

It's definitely a miracle. God works in mysterious ways.

5

KIM'S NIGHTMARE

There is no question but that my accident created an immediate crisis for my wife, Kim, too. When I hit the wall, the shock and damage to my body was instantaneous. I would feel the emotional impact later. As I lay on the stretcher on the way to the hospital Kim was learning of my near-fatal accident. The news sent her emotional world spinning and crashing as surely as my accident sent my body reeling. Although I remained virtually unaware of the significance of everything for almost a month, Kim had to cope with the magnitude and the aftermath of the situation immediately. I was not surprised to learn later that, after she was told the devastating news, she faced our circumstances with the strong faith and solid character that I, and our daughter Jordan, and many others would need to rely on in the unpredictable days that lay ahead.

Kim Irvan: Before Ernie's crash at Michigan I lived in a comfortable state of denial. I put the possibility that something might ever happen to Ernie out of my mind. I am sure it is much the same feeling that a policeman's wife must have every time her hus-

band walks out the door to start his shift. Subconsciously, you appreciate that this may be the last time you see your husband alive. For the sake of your sanity, though, you cannot afford to dwell on it. It could drive you crazy. If you tried to stop your husband from doing what he loves most, it would drive him crazy. I know this is the only career to which Ernie has ever been seriously devoted. Every time Ernie goes on the track, he risks his life, and I risk my heart. I knew that was the way it was when I married him. Now, though, after the accident, my state of denial is not quite as comfortable, but I still can't afford to dwell on it. I also know that nothing can prepare you for the moment when your worst fears are realized.

The look on Carolyn Yates's face when she came to tell me about the accident left no doubt in my mind that something horrible had happened. We both knew what I meant when I asked her if everything was all right. Her answer was as discouraging as the look on her face. "I don't know. I think he's alive. I don't know. I think he's okay. I don't know."

My mind instantly registered a sense of great panic that I hope I will never have to know again. The subconscious fears I had tried to keep neatly tucked away from my everyday conscious mind had been realized and for a moment, I seemed paralyzed. I had to get to Ernie, that much was clear. I was anxious to get to him as quickly as I could, but I was overwhelmed by a complete sense of helplessness and by the horrible images that my mind could not seem to block out. I knew that once I reached him, it was not in my power to save Ernie, or protect our daughter from the possibility that she might have just celebrated the first and only birthday she could with her father. It was devastating to even remotely consider what my future might be like without the man I married.

On my way there I was remembering the words our friend Mark Martin told me as I was leaving the track. "Kim, he's alive. But he's very, very bad." Mark had been on the track and saw Ernie's lifeless body being loaded onto the ambulance. He was trying to prepare me for what I would encounter when I got to the hospital. On the way I started praying the simple prayer, "Lord, please just let him live. I don't care under what conditions, just please let him live. I will take care of him. Just let him live." The sense of helplessness would, at times, become so great that I would break down and cry. It was precious little relief.

My sense of frustration was only beginning, however. When I got to the hospital, no one would tell me how Ernie was doing. While he was undergoing emergency procedures I had to sit in my anguish and my growing anger because I was absolutely in the dark about exactly what injuries he had, how he was doing, what his chances were, or what they were doing to him. Try as I would to keep my emotions in check I would periodically run to the bathroom and cry until I could pull myself together. I really couldn't say why, but ever since I was a child it seemed important to stay composed in public. When my dad died of a heart attack when I was fourteen I remember trying to stay collected through the funeral. Understandably, I couldn't keep from crying, but I did escape to the bathroom to do my sobbing in private. Standing in that hospital rest room, it was unfathomable that I would, once again, lose the man in my life. The immediate support of friends and family helped immensely.

At some point between the waiting, crying, praying, and more waiting, I was asked to come into the emergency room that Ernie was in and identify Ernie. I thought, *Identify him?* I could not comprehend what I was being asked to do. It was hospital procedure that he be positively identified before he left the emergency room, and the staff was getting ready to whisk him away to radiology for a CT scan. As I walked through the doors and stood along the perimeter of the room in which my husband lay, I was amazed that I could stand, let alone utter the words, "That's him." Seeing his battered body with all the tubes and medical equipment around him was almost too much to bear. If the life was draining out of his body and was heading for another world, I thought surely some of my lifeblood might be leaving too. I managed to make it back to the waiting room with my heart filled with fear and my nerves all but shot. There was nothing to do but wait for what seemed like an eternity and pray to God that His will would answer my prayer—to let Ernie live. That first night the doctors were not at all sure that was going to be the case.

Once Ernie survived that first night, I couldn't help letting my hopes grow just a little bit. The doctors warned me that it was still touch-and-go and that it was still up to God and Ernie. Dr. Erlandson never held out false hope, yet I knew even when he would gently tell me the worst news that there was always room for some optimism.

Little by little, day by day, we would learn of one obstacle after another that Ernie had made it past. First and foremost, he survived. When God generously answered that prayer, I and many others tried to renegotiate with Him. I would humbly whisper my thanks and then ask, "God, please heal Ernie. Please don't let him be in a vegetative state for the remainder of his life."

When Ernie was trying to talk and I couldn't make any sense of it, I became so upset I ran out of the room. It was hard to see my husband, who just a short month earlier had been so vibrant and easily talkative, struggling so hard to reason and communicate now. I had to leave the room because I did not want Ernie to know that his trying to communicate was anything less than the miracle it was. I continued to pray. I had to ask God for more for Ernie. All the while Jordan and I would be near him everyday and often many nights. I hoped that with Jordan and me there, Ernie's motivation to live and get better would be greater.

Our friends and family too would come by to offer support and comfort. Those seeing Ernie for the first time since the accident would often walk away discouraged by the sight of all the tubes and machines around Ernie. As hard as it was to see their friend in such a bad way, I hope they all know how much their visits bolstered Ernie's spirit as well. It helped immeasurably to know that family, friends, and fans were sending their prayers and love Ernie's way, as cards and letters poured in.

As Ernie made his way through all the medical milestones that someone with his injuries comes to endure, we had many sources of support for which we were and always will be very grateful.

The part of his story that makes his miracle complete has been the inspiration Ernie has been able to provide to others as a result of his ordeal. When we went to Pocono this year, we were introduced to a man who had had an aneurysm (bleeding on the brain) that caused similar eye problems to those Ernie had. This man wore an eye patch like Ernie did. The man told us that he had his aneurysm on the day Ernie returned to drive in the truck race. He said he had watched everything Ernie had gone through, and when it happened to him, instead of giving up, he was determined to follow Ernie's example and work toward coming back 100 percent. Needless to say, our meeting with this individual was for us very emotional. Ernie and I both hope that there are more patients out there who will take a page from Ernie's book and keep fighting.

The bottom line for me is that as a result of Ernie's accident I still share Ernie's joy and elation when he wins, but winning has taken on a new meaning for me. It is all the more wonderful because it is a miracle he can drive again. Winning just doesn't have the same place of importance that it once had in my competitive spirit. It is far more important to know that, win or lose, our family is intact.

When Ernie first got back in the car to practice at Darlington and wrecked, I felt like that big emotional scar I carried around from the wreck in Michigan was being ripped open. I felt nothing short of cold terror. Again I had to remind myself that it was God's will that Ernie was saved back in 1994, and I am still very grateful for his second lease on life.

You always hear about people who have encountered tragic experiences saying that they no longer take life for granted. Well, it's true for me too, although occasionally I find myself slipping back into complacency. The emotional scars are there forever, though. They will always be in my heart to remind me of how precious life is and how quickly it can be snatched away. We really do appreciate every day and all the good people who helped us through that very difficult period. When we say we are blessed in so many ways, we really mean it.

6

CHILDHOOD ON WHEELS

It's a miracle, when you stop to think about it, that I was born at all. My mom and dad each were married to someone else before they married each other. I'm not saying divorce is necessarily a good thing, but in my case, it was helpful. After they married a doctor told them it would be impossible for them to conceive. Happily, that doctor was wrong.

My mother, Jo, grew up in Oklahoma during the Depression in the late '30s and early '40s. She was the oldest of seven kids. Her dad worked as a welder. After the war was over, things got really bad. There wasn't any work, so in 1946 my mom's parents decided to leave Oklahoma behind and move to sunny California. Mom was eleven. She tells me a popular song at the time talked about the oranges, peaches, and sunshine of California. They also had relatives living in Southern California. All in all, it sounded a lot better than where they were living—the dreary, overcast Dust Bowl. They got in Grandpa's '37 Packard and headed west, pulling a trailer behind them. Just like many other folks who were victims of the Depression, they took with them everything they owned. Grandpa stuffed a mattress in between the front and back seats, and they, my mom, five sisters, and one brother rode for five days, heading for Paradise. It was like a scene straight out of *The Grapes of Wrath*.

When they finally got there, they discovered very quickly that California wasn't all oranges and peaches. They settled in the town of Hanford, in the San Joaquin valley near Fresno. Grandpa worked as a laborer, forking the hay and doing manual labor in the heat, while my mom and her sisters worked in the fields picking peaches and apricots to make dried fruit. Mom said she never minded doing any of that work, even though that part of the country is the hottest place in the world. However, after three months Grandpa couldn't stand the heat anymore, and he moved the family farther north to live with other relatives in the coastal town of Monterey.

My grandparents went to work in the fish canneries. Mom, to help the family, picked tomatoes in the fields. She got ten cents for every crate of tomatoes she could fill. In the fall she worked in the cotton fields, which, she says, was no fun.

Halfway through tenth grade Mom dropped out of school so she could help support the family. As the oldest, she realized there were a lot of mouths to feed. She worked in the fish canneries packing sardines into cans, but she found the work nasty and became a waitress. She made three dollars a day flat salary, and three times that in tips.

My grandmother wanted a better life for her daughter, so she arranged dates in hopes that Mom would find a husband. The first person she arranged for Mom to date was my father. She was fifteen. He was twenty. My grandmother had set up their first date with Dad's mother. Mom says she fell in love the first day, but after dating for a short time they broke up. When her mother pushed her to marry another man, she married him instead. She was only sixteen. During this time Dad also married someone else.

After three months Mom knew she didn't want to be in that marriage. She hopped a bus back to her grandpa in Oklahoma City and got an annulment. When Mom came back to Monterey late in 1950, she learned that Dad's marriage had also broken up. It wasn't long before they took back up where they left off.

My dad was also born in Oklahoma, in 1929, near the town of Freedom in a cabin out in the middle of nowhere. When Dad was four, his family moved to northwestern Arkansas, and then returned to Oklahoma. When the Second World War started they moved southwest to Arkansas. It was at this time that they too became enamored by that popular song about California. Dad even remembers some of the words: "Hey, Okie, have you seen Arkie? Tell him Tex has got a job out in California picking prunes and squeezing oil out of olives." As my mother also remembered, Dad said the song mentions oranges and peaches. In the minds of my dad and his family, California seemed so much nicer than where they were living. Like a lot of poor folks living in dusty Oklahoma at the time, they too decided to see whether or not the state could live up to the song it inspired, where the streets supposedly were paved with gold. They weren't, of course, but at least they were paved.

My dad's father had an uncle in the service living in Monterey, who told him the canneries needed workers. So

Dad and his family took the train west to California to work in the canneries where they had high hopes of getting rich. Not surprisingly, it didn't happen. I've been told when Dad was a boy, he never did stay in any one place for very long. When he saw that the money just wasn't there, well, he didn't stay long.

Dad started the tenth grade in California, but didn't care much for school. He quit to pick tomatoes and cotton to help out the family. He was quick to see that there was no future in that. At seventeen, he went into the Air Force, where he was trained to work in a control tower. He was based in Las Vegas. Even though he had intended to stay in the service, he changed his mind when it came time to reenlist, and moved back to Arkansas where he worked in a sawmill with his cousin.

After six months of drudgery Dad decided to move again, this time back to California. That's where he met Mom and dated for the first time, broke up with her, and married someone else. Like Mom, his marriage lasted three months. In 1952 he started going with Mom again. After dating three months, they got married.

When my dad was in the service in Las Vegas, he started going to stock car races in San Diego. Then, when he came back to live in Salinas, he started going to stock car races in Monterey. Around this time Dad and his best friend, Bill White, started an auto dismantling business in Seaside, the Avenue Auto Wreckers. He would buy wrecked cars, take them apart, and then sell the parts. Because he had the engines and the car parts in stock, Dad decided it might be fun to race his '37 Ford at the track in nearby Salinas.

It took Dad a little while before he won a race. However, during his early years he did win a few. One weekend at Salinas he cleaned house: he had the fastest time, won the heat race, and won the main. He told me he brought home a grand total of $33!

Once Dad got the racing bug, he gave my mom, who had reservations, the ultimatum: "Either you let me race, or I'm leaving you." Mom decided that if he was going to race, she would too. She drove Dad's '37 Ford in a powder puff derby in Salinas. She won right out of the box! She says she can remember before the race being scared and shaking badly, but as soon as they waved the green flag, she didn't have any problems at all. She ran in powder puffs for years and won a lot of races.

By 1955 racing in California was dying out. Dad was racing in San Jose, sixty miles from home. The traffic was bad, and he decided to quit as a racer. In fact, he decided to quit California. As I said, Dad was never one to stay in one place very long. He sold his wrecking yard and auto parts business, got out of racing, and he and my mom moved back to Oklahoma.

Of course, my dad being the way he was, he wasn't in Oklahoma very long before he turned right around and came back to California. After Dad came back to California, he started a new wrecking yard. One of his employees was building a '46 Plymouth that he raced at a dirt track called Watsonville. Dad would go with him to watch him race, and he'd blow an engine, have all kinds of problems. Finally sometime in 1959, the year I was born, the man let Dad drive the car. This time he was hooked for good. Dad earned the nickname "Vic the Villain." He was called that because if you got in his way, he would move you. Dad had one style of racing, wide open all the way, move it or lose it. He drove at all the local tracks, Merced, Antioch, Watsonville—at least a half dozen within a hundred miles of Salinas. He drove at Watsonville for twenty years, and he holds the track record with sixty-three wins. The first year he ran up front a lot, and then all of a sudden he started winning races big time. All told he won well over a hundred races in his career.

After my parents were married they were told by the doctors that they wouldn't be able to have children. They adopted two baby girls, Susan and Sheryl. About the time they adopted Sheryl, they defied the doctor's prediction and had a baby themselves. I came along on January 13, 1959. Two years later my younger brother, David, was born. When David was two, there was a car accident in our driveway and David was thrown out of the car and killed. To this day, it's tough for Mom and Dad to talk about it. It was a terrible tragedy. My sister Tracy, their youngest child, was ten months old at the time.

My parents, who loved racing, always had it in their heads that I would become a stock car racer. When I was five, Mom would get out the tape recorder, and as I pretended to be holding the wheel, she would announce a stock car race as though I was driving one of the cars. Always she would have me cross the finish line first, which, she says, gave me a lot of pleasure. Meanwhile, Dad would tell people I was going to be the next Richard Petty. It is interesting that he even knew about Richard Petty. Living in California, we were three thousand miles from the Carolinas, and in those days there was very little NASCAR being shown on TV. In fact, the only NASCAR race I can remember watching as a young boy was the Daytona 500, which was aired on CBS. But Dad would talk about Grand National (Winston Cup) racing, and so I gained a modest awareness of Petty and the NASCAR circuit back East. I was lucky because a lot of other kids who grew up racing in California, for whatever reasons, never expanded their sights beyond a couple of hundred miles from where they lived.

I was eight when Dad bought me a quarter-midget racer. We took the quarter-midget to the track only to find out that I had to go to two weeks of driving school before I could compete in a race. Well, Dad, who has been known to be impatient, decided we didn't have the time to spend going to a course. He wanted me racing, right now. He junked the quarter-midget and went out and bought me a go-cart. As they say, I was off to the races. People ask me how you learn to race, and I really don't have an answer. I'm not really sure how you know how to do it, except that you just go out and do it. The more you practice, the better you get. There is no written book to read on how to do it. You have to figure it out for yourself. Just like life, pretty much.

For the most part Dad was too busy racing himself to teach me. He'd take me to the go-cart track and let me run laps. I can say that gaining experience was essential. Thanks to Dad, I always had good equipment. Being a driver himself, he knew how important that was. He bought me the best chassis, and if I asked for a top-of-the-line motor, I could usually talk him into getting it for me.

Dad also did a lot of the work on the go-cart during the

week when he wasn't racing. At the same time he taught me about engines and body work. A pretty tough taskmaster and one who wanted to make sure he wasn't doing all the work, Dad would say to me, "If you want me to tune the engine, first you need to finish the body work." Dad wanted to make sure I'd learn as much about my machine as I could. He knew that the drivers who won were usually the ones who knew how to make the needed adjustments to stay ahead of the competition. I will always be grateful to him for that. As a perfectionist, he felt it important that I be able to do my job right. He believed that if your job was to fix something or make a part, you had to make it perfectly. If you had to measure something, you had to measure it perfectly. For instance, when we were go-cart racing, one of the tools Dad used to measure the carburetor was his Bank of America Visa card. You know how they have a white line around the outside of the card? Well, he figured out that the width of that white line was exactly where the float level needed to be on the carburetor. That's what he used to tune the carburetor—perfectly.

Dad had a mindset about the way things should be done, even if they seemed unusual. If you didn't do it his way, you would be inviting trouble. But one thing is for certain—I learned early never to do a half-assed job.

I raced all around the Salinas area, at Kerman, a well-known go-cart track, and Laguna Seca. During the years I raced go-carts, I brought home a bushel of trophies. Class was set by height and weight, not so much age. After I was twelve I would race against adults. Under my parents' guidance I had an understanding at a young age of what I had to do to win.

They fostered my determination and sense of fearlessness. In a go-cart, you never know if you will end up on your head. Fortunately, it didn't happen too often to me. I did have a nasty incident in one race in Salinas at the airport. I flipped my cart, flew out of it, and landed hard on the pavement, rupturing my spleen. I was in the hospital a few days but recovered just fine. Crashing never bothered me. I learned early it was just part of the sport. I was young, and like all racers (like many who get behind the wheel of a street car as well), I never thought about the dangers of the sport. I still don't. None of the racers do. I won a few races, and when I didn't win, as often as not it was because my equipment would blow up. Those two-cycle engines could be awfully testy. It seemed like most of the times I didn't win it was because of engine failure.

There were others who played a part in my early racing career. I couldn't have been as successful as I was without the help of the Williamson family. When I was five, I became fast friends with Timmy Williamson, who was three years older. Our families knew each other through racing. My dad raced, and Timmy's dad, Chuck, loved racing. When they got older, both Timmy and his older brother Charles worked for my dad at the wrecking yard. We'd take apart cars, alternators, learn how the different parts worked. Timmy had raced go-carts a short while before I did. Timmy was a great go-cart driver, and Charles did a lot of work on his car.

When I started go-cart racing, my dad didn't know much about go-cart engines. He felt we needed somebody to help us prepare for racing. Dad enlisted Timmy's older brother, Charles, and his dad. They knew who to buy the right body from and exactly what kind of engine to get. Later, when Timmy turned sixteen and started driving stock cars, my dad helped him. Charles didn't race, but he was a very good mechanic and a great help to me. Charles took me under his wing.

Because Timmy was three years older than I was, he ran in the senior class while I ran junior class. Once I turned twelve and could run in the senior class, we would run against each other. Timmy was an outstanding racer. In 1973 Mom, my sisters Tracy and Sheryl, and I took a trip to Quincy, Illinois, to compete in the go-cart national championships. I drove hard, but flipped my cart the first or second day. That year Timmy won the national go-cart championship in his class. The next year I drove all over Northern California and won the California championship. It was a point accumulation. I just happened to have some good luck and won that thing.

I used to race against my friend, Pete Vargas, on the local roads. Pete would be the first to tell you he wasn't any good. He had this old '64 Impala. It was lowered in the back, a fine piece. One time when Pete was visiting me at home, we decided to go into town. I was fifteen and didn't have my driver's license yet. Pete, who was two years older and had his license, had left his car in town. Because my parents were away racing and it was the weekend, I had no choice but to drive him into town to get his car. I was left in the care of my two older sisters. Finding the keys to our El Camino, Pete and I were off without my sisters knowing. Just for the record, I didn't sneak off very often.

It's amusing that Pete, being older, was supposed to be

a "good influence" on me. My role model and I drove to his car and began racing up and down San Benancio Canyon, doing around 75 in a 30-mile-an-hour zone. As luck would have it Pete missed a turn, drove down the bottom of a ditch, and took out about a hundred feet of chain-link fence that surrounded the local tennis courts where I used to play.

Fortunately Pete wasn't hurt. We got back into my car and drove home to get my dad's wrecker so we could get his car out of the ditch. I had to wake my sister up to do that. When we returned for Pete's car, the highway patrol had arrived. Amazingly he didn't get a ticket, but we had a lot of explaining to do, both to the cops and to our parents.

By then, racing was in my blood. In addition to go-carts, I also raced dune buggies in autocross races. Dad and I joined a dune buggy club. We fabricated a dune buggy body and installed a Porsche motor in it. That baby really could go. I felt ready to go too.

I turned sixteen in January 1975. Immediately I got my California driver's license, a requirement for getting your NASCAR driver's license, unless you're Mark Martin, who raced on the local tracks of Arkansas before he was sixteen. The first time we raced against Mark, we were in Las Vegas. Everyone was talking about this young kid. He was all of about five feet tall, weighed about a hundred pounds, but could race with the best of them. He had had a tractor license, so NASCAR gave him a racer's license before he was sixteen.

Dad had bought a '66 Chevelle down at Riverside, drove it the entire '74 season, and then brought it home for us to work on. The plan was for me to drive that car at the

Watsonville Speedway, which was a local dirt track where
my dad was a star.

Dad and I spent the entire winter getting that Chevelle
ready to race there. When I got to the track in early April for
opening night, the inspectors ruled that the car was ineligible
to run. I'm sure even before I arrived everyone had heard that
Vic's son was coming to Watsonville with this fast new car,
one that was better than the cars most of the guys drove. It
was certainly safer than anything else out there. It was like I
was bringing a Winston Cup car to a local track. They told
me, "We've never seen this or that on a car. You can't race
that here." I was incredibly disappointed. I knew it was the
safest car out there. Structurally, the car was built a lot better
than what the other drivers were racing, which were '55
Chevys mostly, cars like that. Mine was new, and it was fast.
I guess the inspectors felt it would be unfair. At the time,
that's what I thought of their decision. I had been working on
the car since January, getting ready for this day. It was tough
news to accept when they said they wouldn't allow me to
race. But looking back, that was one of the most important
events in my life. I didn't know it at the time, but it may have
kept me from staying there instead of expanding my hori-
zons. It's possible that had they let me drive at Watsonville,
today I would be the all-time Watsonville dirt track champion rather than a Winston Cup competitor.

Dad wasn't as unhappy as I was. He could see further
down the road. All along he felt I had a bigger future than
just racing on dirt at local California tracks. He knew that
dirt had all but disappeared from Winston Cup racing. He
saw what I couldn't because of my frustration—that it
would be best if I started my racing career on asphalt.

We waited until July Fourth weekend, where I raced for the first time on asphalt at the Stockton 99 Speedway. The Chevelle had been hard for Dad to handle because it was tough to turn. But that car and I got along. I was excited when I qualified for the semimain event. I was thrilled when I won it. I went with my mom, my sister Tracy, and Pete Vargas, and we were elated, because we assumed I would then be able to move up to the main event. Once again I would face disappointment when we learned the track had a rule you had to have raced in several races before you could enter the main event.

Looking back, the couple who owned the Stockton Speedway, Whitey and Annie Rich, who were friends of my parents, ran a tight ship. Today I can say in all fairness, they really knew what they were doing. Their rules were designed to protect the drivers. The local fans really supported the track, and it was one of those places where you thoroughly enjoyed racing.

At the end of that first year, when I was sixteen, I ran a half a dozen races. Then in 1976 I started running regularly. For thirty weeks during the summer on Friday nights, Mom, Tracy, Pete, and I would drive two and a half hours to the town of Madera to race. Mom and Pete would be in the pits, and Tracy would keep the lap times from the stands.

After the race, we'd leave and drive through the central valley of California to Merced or Atwater, where we'd camp out near a river and relax or work on the car. The next day we'd drive to Stockton and race. Dad was still racing at Watsonville, so I did most of the work on the car myself—I learned a lot from my dad, and Pete helped out. Sometimes Mom would handle the tools if she had to.

Around this time Timmy started racing stock cars on the local dirt tracks, making a name for himself. His brother Charles was the chief mechanic on his car. In between races Timmy and I would come down and help in my dad's wrecking yard, making money on the side. We became the closest of friends, like brothers. In '74, Charles and his dad took me out to the national go-cart championship, where I finished second in the country in my class.

Timmy and I loved to race. I had good backing from my father, and Timmy was able to race because all of his relatives, parents, cousins, in-laws, everyone, pooled their money together to buy him his equipment. Their efforts were worthwhile. Simply put, Timmy was awesome. As a youngster, he won big races at Ontario and Riverside. As we got older we talked often about running against each other in Winston Cup racing.

As a matter of discipline and training, Timmy's father always made him start a go-cart race dead last. It didn't matter if he qualified first and was sitting on the pole. He'd run Timmy in every class he could enter. Timmy's dad would go to the races with five or six go-carts with different motors and weights. Timmy would run a race, grab another cart, get to the back of the line, and race again. Timmy's father's tough training really taught Timmy how to pass cars and win races. He was very efficient at cutting through traffic to get back up front.

His equipment always looked brand new. He would arrive at the track with his stuff painted and buffed. He had ten to twelve people working on his rig to make it look so great. My stuff, in contrast, tended to look a little junky. My working crew usually consisted of myself, and occasionally

Pete or my sister Tracy. I grew up learning to work on my equipment. I had to. You can bet I accepted whatever free help I could get. If there was no one to help me, I knew how to do it myself. The contrast between my racing gear and Timmy's helped me to know what I might attain. It raised my standards.

By the time I turned seventeen, I was faster than everyone else around. We were having trouble getting the Chevelle to handle as well as we wanted; so Dad decided to build me a brand-new Nova. We went to Modesto to the race shop of Jack McCoy, a West Coast racer. The man who actually built the car was Ivan Baldwin, a fierce, aggressive racer himself. Dad bought the engine from a motor builder by the name of Dennis Fisher. I can remember the excitement of driving to Modesto to sit in that car as they were building it. They fit me for the seat, making sure it was exactly the way I wanted it. I was just a kid, so I really didn't appreciate the advantage Dad was giving me. Few kids (or adults) had custom-made cars like this one. My dad, however, did have one. He bought his from Frank Denny. In that car Dad won one of the last races on dirt at Santa Maria in a Winston West race.

As for my new Nova, it "fit like a glove." That car and I seemed to really understand each other.

Dad and I raced a couple of times against each other. You would think it would be interesting watching competition between father and son. But in fact we were too similar in style to be competing against each other. One race I remember was in San Jose, a race Dad was promoting. We were in a trophy dash. Dad started on the pole. I was in the back. We got through the first turn, and we were going down the back straightaway. I blew by him with my ass end wiggling so badly Dad wondered if I was going to spin out. It was father and son togetherness at its most fun for me.

I had a major disappointment in high school, when, as a senior, the tennis coach at North Salinas High protested that I was ineligible because I was making money driving stock cars. I liked to play tennis. I was good at it. I didn't take a lot of lessons, but I had good reflexes and was a quick learner. I was an average student—my favorite classes were industrial classes, wood and metal shop, rather than math and English. I particularly enjoyed the camaraderie of playing sports, and I would sorely miss playing tennis and football my senior year. This was an era before pros could play in the Olympics, when any time you made any money at anything, you lost your amateur standing in everything. It was frustrating having a coach complain because I made money racing, but there wasn't much I could do about it. Today, I'd be allowed to play under those circumstances. Times have changed.

I had to choose, tennis or racing, and I didn't have any problem choosing racing, but I did think the whole issue was petty, and I was mad about it for a long time. I wasn't really making any money racing. Dad spent thousands and thousands of dollars on my car. The expenses were great, the purses minimal. The average winning purse was $400 or $500. That barely covered the gas and food for me and my crew. It was Dad's money I was racing on, not any winnings, which were spent as quickly as they came in. What my dad did for me was similar to what it would be like if a parent rented a skating rink so his kid could learn to ice skate. There would be no monetary gain, only the satisfaction that it was done for your child's benefit. Dad did this to get my career going and because it was a fun family sport. It worked out that Dad couldn't go with us much, unfortunately. Nevertheless, he was home every night in the garage working on my car.

To give you an idea how little money was in racing back then, one year I was sponsored by Frank Viglietti, my girlfriend Karen's dad. He owned a general store. I put the name of his market on my car. For doing that he gave us four cases of Dr. Pepper for the weekend. When we got older, he gave us beer.

We got to know the owner of a gas station called Viera Canyon Shell, in Gilroy, a town thirty miles north of Salinas. The station was on the way to Stockton. The owner became a sponsor in exchange for fifty gallons of gas every weekend. One year Dad was sponsored by Olympia's beer. We all found that funny because nobody liked Olympia's. We all drank Coors. When the sponsors came around, Dad would have Olympia's on top of the cooler, but Coors inside.

The night I graduated from North Salinas High, I was unable to attend. I was racing at Riverside, one of the tracks where I competed against Marc Reno, who would later be a big help to my career. Marc raced out of San Diego, a long way from us, but he would also travel north. We could always count on seeing him at Riverside. Marc Reno, Timmy and Charles Williamson, and I all became good friends.

Once I graduated, I decided that the best way for me to advance my racing career was to move out of the house to live near Ivan Baldwin's race shop. My mom and dad were having a rough time getting along, and the tension made everyone uncomfortable. It just seemed to make sense at that point to move to a town near Modesto, where Ivan was based. I left Salinas, my parents and my sisters, and my girlfriend Karen, and went to work for Ivan, who had quit Jack McCoy's race shop to go off on his own in Modesto, which is twenty miles south of Stockton and about a hundred miles east of San Francisco.

Ivan was about thirty-five when I went to work for him. He had come from San Bernardino, raced in the Winston West circuit, then started building cars. Ivan was an unbelievable innovator who just loved building things. He built the first coil-over cars that were ever run. (Coil-over cars are built with the spring outside the shock.) To this day most of the short-track cars, the All-Pro cars, are coil-overs. There was no question that Ivan's workmanship far and away surpassed everyone else's. Ivan was an incredibly talented guy. He built everything from the ground up and drove too. That's why he was so good. He knew what the cars were. He was also extremely aggressive. Nobody liked to race against Ivan.

In fact, Ivan was one of the best drivers in the country. Marc Reno puts him in the category of the top ten drivers of all time in the United States. Some people might not agree, but anyone who ever knew him and saw him drive would have to admit he was phenomenal.

Ivan quit driving because he said his eyes were bad. I'm not sure whether that was the case or whether he just lost interest. Anytime he wanted, he could get in anybody's car and run faster than the owner did. When Ivan was working for Bill Elliott, Marc Reno saw him get in and test Bill's Winston Cup car—this was after he said his eyes were bad and he hadn't driven in years. He ran faster than Bill in that car.

Ivan was wild—wide open all the time. From the minute he opened his eyes in the morning until he passed out at night, he was absolutely wide open. If you were going to run with him, you'd better keep up. When he moved from one end of the shop to another, he didn't walk. He ran. The guy gave new definition to the term *hyper*.

He didn't believe in second place. People give Ivan credit for teaching me all his bad habits. With Ivan you didn't finish second and come home happy. If you didn't win, you had better bring the car back to the shop to get it repaired (meaning you had crashed trying to win). That's the way Ivan drove. His motto was "the front bumper better be lying on the ground if you didn't win the race." He drove that way and preached that way. He pushed me hard to be like him, and I was happy to work hard to do that. I respected his all-out attitude.

It was Ivan's car in which I won that championship at Stockton. Ivan built two coil-over cars and gave me one of them. He told me, "If you touch anything, I'll kill you." He said, "If it's not working right, bring it back to the shop and I'll set it back up, but don't touch a jackbolt." Once again it was just my mom, my sister, and I working on the car, and I had no problem doing it Ivan's way.

From the start, I knew Ivan believed I had talent and potential. He wouldn't have bothered with me otherwise. My personality and Ivan's were similar in important ways. We weren't buddy-buddy guys. We were tough competitors focused on one goal—winning races. Sometimes that meant that competitors might get upset as we fought to get to the finish line first. Ivan and I bucked heads a lot, but we always respected each other. I always had a win-at-all-costs attitude, and Ivan did too.

Working for Ivan was a good deal for both of us. I didn't get paid a lot. But in exchange, Ivan worked on my car.

The year before I graduated and went to work with Ivan, I remember being encouraged by my success. I was dominating the Stockton 99 Speedway. That year I won twenty of the twenty-nine main events I entered. At Stockton, we ran twenty-lap races in '72 Novas with 302 horsepower motors. We had to race on eight-inch tires, a fairly small tire, but it really helped me to learn to race under less than desirable conditions. Like my friend Timmy, I could negotiate through traffic. Incidentally, that same year, the rule was that the fastest driver to qualify started last. In other words, you went out and qualified, and before the start of the race, they inverted the field. Twenty times I had to come from last to win. That often meant I didn't make a lot of friends along the way.

One time I was set down for rough driving. I was in the grandstand watching the races, and I got into a fight. A fan hit me. Back then, fighting was commonplace. It was nothing if someone made you mad and you just went over and "handled it." Nowadays, conflicts are handled on the track. Back then, two or three times a year we'd handle it after the race. In fact I have a few scars on my face—mementos from times when you weren't done racing until you were done fighting. My mom, who was a pretty aggressive woman, could hold her own when the occasion called for it.

The racing crowd was that way. It wasn't just Mom and

me. It was a rough-and-tumble place and time. Killer drivers came out of the Stockton 99 Speedway, and you had to be ready for them. These were very short races, and there wasn't any time for politeness. You started in the back, and the only way to get to the front was to move cars out of the way. It's fair to say I did my share of fender bending. I didn't necessarily total cars, but I'd rub them to move them. I'd say it's normal not to like somebody who bangs your car to pieces and then beats you in the race.

Stockton was an unusual racetrack. It had a high bank on one corner and was flat at the other. You really had to learn some driving to run it. It was hard to get it to work in both places, a tough track to figure out.

Most of the drivers I raced against were adults. Not many teenagers could afford to race. At times, I felt other drivers started to resent my success. It didn't help that I was a smartass kid. The older guys grew particularly resentful, and it showed. One time the other drivers banded together to raise $100 needed to protest my engine. Failing that, they began whispering behind my back that because my parents knew the Riches, who owned the Stockton track, I was getting all sorts of special treatment, and that's why I was winning races. That was nonsense, of course. I won because I had a great car, and because I was working hard at learning how to drive and make the car run fast and well.

In July I set the Stockton track record. I was on my way to the track championship when with six races left in the season, I totaled my car. It was a wreck that would take at least two weeks to fix. Timmy Williamson, who was also running a car at Stockton, generously loaned me his car. For the next two weeks I won races in Timmy's car.

With two races to go, I led Rick Meyers, a racer from Riverbank, California, by 25 points. In that second-to-last race, once again driving my own car, I was fastest to qualify, I won the heat, the trophy dash, and the twenty-lap main event.

Even after doing all that, with one last race to go, my lead over Rick Meyers was only 37 points. Under track rules, the points for the last race were doubled. I had nineteen wins and Meyers only had one. Amazingly, he could have ended up champion if I had gone out early. I never was sure how they added everything up, but it sure made for some intense and exciting moments to watch and report.

In my mind, there was no way Meyers was going to beat me that day, and he didn't. It was my twentieth win in a main event out of 29 races, including 9 in a row. That 1977 season I was the Stockton champion. That year I also finished third in California for the overall NASCAR driver's championship.

Timmy Williamson kept talking about driving Winston Cup, but my only goal was to be able to continue racing. I felt like I was as good as anyone I had raced against. Winston Cup seemed so farfetched—to race with Richard Petty? Yeah, right. When I won the Stockton championship in November 1977, I was sitting on top of the world. It was a high that would last exactly one month.

7

A CHRISTMAS SURPRISE

Life is funny. Sometimes when something happens, it might be the most important event in your life and you don't know it. That's what happened to me in the mid-1970s when the town of Seaside decided to condemn the whole area around where my dad had his wrecking yard in order to turn it into an urban renewal project. As part of that deal, the city bought my dad's land.

At that point Dad didn't know whether he wanted to open another wrecking yard or not. When you run the same business for a lot of years, it's hard to imagine yourself doing something different. Suddenly, Dad wasn't in that business anymore. This was a big change and adjustment for my dad. He kept looking around other parts of the city, trying to figure out if he could start his business somewhere else. As it happened, he didn't. He ended up surprising us all. In the wake of his decision, all of our lives were changed.

On Christmas Eve, 1977, I was still living near Ivan Baldwin in Modesto. When my mom, three sisters, and I came home to celebrate Christmas together, we found Dad gone. Him not being home wasn't anything unusual. The note he left that I found when I went upstairs to my room, however, was. In the note he essentially said he needed to leave for a while. He and my mom had been having some problems, and he believed that in order to try to make some sense of them, he needed some space to do that.

"Ernie," he wrote, "it would be really good if you could help Mom to make it work." I didn't know what he meant until I found out he had taken the $300,000 or $400,000 he and Mom had gotten from selling our wrecking yard as part of the urban renewal program. He said Mom could keep the house, which was paid for, and any of the car parts left behind. And the brand new pickup truck he had bought for my little sister Tracy, who had just turned sixteen. It wasn't like he didn't want anything to do with us kids. He just felt he had to leave, and he did.

I had no clue Dad was going to do this. I guess that's because I wasn't around him much. Most of the week our paths didn't cross. I was living on my own, and we always seemed to be racing at different tracks. In 1977 when I won the Stockton track championship and was learning how to build race cars, Dad was in a different part of California. If we got together at home, we'd meet Sunday night or Monday. I certainly never expected that he wouldn't be home on Christmas Eve, much less with no plans to return. It was really strange to find that Dad wanted to leave his old life and start over again. A troubled marriage can make a person act unpredictably.

We learned we had no cash. He had taken it all. In his letter Dad said he needed to be where he was going, but he didn't tell us where that was. He may have just gone twenty miles down the road or traveled cross country. We didn't know.

I can remember how mad and hurt we were that he had left. Even though I was only eighteen, I was and am the type of person who subscribes to the motto "when the going gets tough, the tough get going." Nobody had to tell me that things were tough. Our family got going. We had a shop with hundreds of car parts in it, and to make quick cash, we sold a lot of it. Mom's job, though, was to be the primary worrier. At eighteen, it was hard for me not to worry more about girls, my friends, and going to the racetrack. I know it wasn't fair, but I had a lot of confidence in my mom making sure everything would work out. She did, in fact, make things work out. Eventually she also discovered where Dad was and was able to patch things up with him.

Meanwhile, Dad's selling the salvage yard had been hard for me. My whole life had revolved around car parts and fixing cars. As a child I didn't take Disneyland trips. Racetracks were my Disneylands. Dad's disappearance was traumatic and emotional for all of us in part because it was so unexpected, so sudden. I saw my family breaking up before my eyes. My whole life had revolved around the salvage yard and my mom and dad. Not only was the salvage yard gone, but Dad had moved on as well. Even at eighteen, I didn't understand the reasons. I felt abandoned, angry, even thought for a little while that maybe somehow it had been *my* fault Dad had left.

Christmas, of course, was not very festive, and when I returned to Ivan Baldwin's shop to continue my racing career, it now was on a pay-as-you-go basis. I would no longer have Dad's money for new pieces. This time I was *really* on my own. If I had been a dirt track racer, that wouldn't have been such a big deal. But being an asphalt racer put me at a real disadvantage. Not having money for parts made me have to work that much harder.

At the dirt tracks, the drivers didn't have much money to spend on equipment. They were just happy to be out there and race. At the asphalt tracks, everyone was looking to move up the ladder. One thing I learned from Ivan and the rest of the asphalt racers: you never stand still in racing. He showed me that either you improve your car or everyone else passes you by. What they constantly sought was an edge over the competition. They wanted to discover that one little detail that might make you just that much better than the other guy. The asphalt tracks, like Winston Cup tracks, have rules to keep the costs down, but that never stopped the asphalt track competitors from working on the car just one hour longer in order to gain one extra horsepower on everyone else. This was one of the important lessons I learned from Ivan. Some people say I patterned myself after him, and in some respects perhaps that's true. He was aggressive and talented, and he worked hard, and I admired him. He had been instrumental in my early success because he had built the car. He had an interest that I do well at Stockton because if I did well, people would know who the car builder was and buy chassis from him. We made a hell of a team. Ivan passed away in 1996 from a heart attack, and I'll never forget him and his influence is imprinted on my driving style.

When I went to work for Ivan, I moved to the small

town of Ceres, close to Modesto, where I rented a small apartment that I shared with another mechanic. I had my race car, but with Dad gone and no more money to race it, times were hard. I stopped being a dominating racer, which was an experience unto itself. There were times on the track I'd lose my temper and say things I shouldn't have said. After what had happened at home, I wasn't in a very good frame of mind.

After my dad left, I got my first shot at the Winston West circuit. I drove for Jack McCoy, with Bob Martin as my crew chief. Jack had been a Winston West champion. I had always run against him the years I raced. In 1978 Jack asked if I would drive some races for him, and I agreed.

We didn't have a whole lot of success. I only ran four or five races. But Winston West racing was very expensive, and we were unable to get a sponsor. It was a bad time for me. I didn't have my head screwed on too tight. With my dad gone, I felt directionless and lost a lot of the time. I had gone from feeling like the king of the world, not having a whole lot of cares, to a sense of loneliness and failure. After my experience driving for Jack McCoy, I seriously considered leaving racing and doing something else to make a living.

Then in November 1978 I suffered one of the great tragedies in my life. As I mentioned, my best friend growing up was Timmy Williamson. Tim's older brother, Charles, for many years had worked for my dad at the salvage yard. His dad, Chuck, owned a dry cleaning business in Salinas, and as kids Timmy and I would work there to earn some extra money cleaning up the store.

Timmy and I had the same birthdate, though he was three years older. We grew up racing go-carts together, and we had plans to be stock car champions together.

After running dirt, for a couple of years Timmy concentrated on driving asphalt. He came to Stockton with me, and we ran around the West Coast entering a lot of open competition. They had an international driver's challenge, where drivers would go up to Canada and race for a week and a half. Timmy used to race there. He was as competitive as anyone in racing.

In 1977, when I was running for the championship at Stockton, I blew a motor and needed a replacement. Timmy wasn't running for the points, and as I said, he lent me his car for two weeks and I was able to win twice more to stay in the lead. It was a time when we were inseparable, just the best of friends.

While I was still running at Stockton, Timmy got a ride in the Winston West competition. He competed in the Grand American circuit, which was held on Saturdays, and did very well. He had a sponsor, and he won Rookie of the Year in the circuit and at the same time ran second for the points championship. Nobody had ever done that before.

Timmy's goal was to run the Winston Cup circuit, and it looked like he was going to fulfill his dreams in the fall of 1978 when he was hired by J.D. Stacy to come back east and drive for him. He entered his last race at Riverside, a fast and dangerous road course, before starting his Winston Cup career.

I remember when Timmy told me about his deal to drive for Stacy. He said the guy working on the car was Bobby Harrington. I had heard that name, and I was impressed.

Timmy said that as soon as he arrived in North Carolina, they were going to start testing for Daytona. This was November 1978, and the Daytona 500 wasn't that far off.

The weekend we were supposed to race, it rained. Timmy had qualified up front for the Grand American race, and I had qualified fifth or sixth. Not only was our race rained out, but the Winston Cup race the next day also was rained out, and we had to stay out there a whole week before the race could be run.

Timmy and I hung out that whole week together, goofing off, drinking a lot of beer, just having fun. Marc Reno was also at Riverside with Timmy and me that week. Ron Esau was driving Marc's car.

I remember that race as if it were yesterday. The track had dried, but there were no aprons and if you came off the track at all, you were in the mud. At speeds of over 150 miles an hour, it wasn't safe to be in that mud.

NASCAR officials determined that the race could begin. At the start Timmy was in front of me by three or four cars. Timmy and Glen Stewart were really hard racers, and going into turn five Glen got into Timmy a little bit, bumped him a little, and Timmy's right rear tire came off the racetrack and into the mud, and he lost control, slid and flew back across the track. That turn, turn five between five and six—I don't know how many feet from the track the wall is, but it's a long ways—and Timmy hit it hard, flat along the driver's side, and the impact was so great that the car caromed back onto the asphalt from a dead stop. Timmy never slowed down when he hit the wall on the passenger side, at the same place in the same manner that Joe Weatherly was killed in 1964. A body can't take a hit that hard.

When he hit I didn't think that much about it. We crash a lot in this sport. I went by. The caution came out. Ronnie Esau told Marc Reno on the radio, "Timmy is slumped over in the seat. It looks like he's hurt."

When I came back around to where he was, I went as slow as I could, looking. I saw he was still in the car and there were two guys inside looking at him. I couldn't tell if anything was going on. The next time I went by as the cars rode around under the caution, they had cut Timmy out of the car and placed him on a stretcher. I was thinking, He's probably all right, but I could see they were going to take him to the hospital, so I knew he had been hurt. The fourth time I went by, I saw that a doctor was pushing on his chest. That started making me a little nervous and worried. And then the fifth time I went by, he had been put in the ambulance, and they were taking him away. I didn't know anything more. Throughout the race nobody could tell me anything.

As soon as the checkered flag dropped, I came in. That's when somebody told me Timmy had died. My best friend. I could not wrap my mind around the fact that my best friend since childhood was gone. At such a young age, the death of your friend takes on a surreal quality. The culmination of all the events in the past year made life seem pretty suffocating. Everybody dealt with it differently.

Bill Gazaway was in charge of NASCAR then, and the first thing he did was issue a press release saying that Timmy didn't have his shoulder belt on. That was ridiculous. Timmy hit the wall so hard it might have been ripped off, but believe me, he had those belts on when he started the race.

None of us would forget that any more than we would forget to wear our helmet or start our engines.

Timmy's family was incensed, and his brother went down to the morgue and took pictures of Timmy's body to show the three-inch-wide bruises running down his body from the belts. He sent the pictures to NASCAR and demanded a retraction of that silly story that Timmy hadn't had his belts on. I know the family got a personal apology. I don't know if they got a public one. Back then, the sport was just trotting along. It wasn't like it is now. They were slow to make popular decisions then.

Timmy had been planning to leave the next day to drive to North Carolina. He was going to ride back to North Carolina with J.D. Stacy's crew and start Winston Cup racing. Instead, his family had to start making funeral arrangements. To this day I don't think any of us have really gotten over it. Timmy would have been a big Winston Cup star. I'd gladly trade all my victories for the opportunity to race against him today.

8

GONE TO CAROLINA

Once we were able to contact Dad, he could see how much we wanted him in our lives. I suppose Dad felt when he left he was doing all of us a favor. It was a hard time in his life, and he was working through it the best way he knew how. Interestingly, in some ways Mom seemed to be doing better than Dad. Maybe she felt she had to, since she had us kids around. Meanwhile, my dad grew lonelier, and my sister Tracy, who was still in high school, got in her truck and moved to North Carolina to be with him. My dad is and always was a proud man. He never came right out and asked me to move to North Carolina to be with him. Instead, Dad would say, "Ernie, it's really nice back here." But he didn't have to spell it out. I knew what he was really saying.

Dad would call and tell me how great the racing was in North Carolina. He was telling me that in Carolina they were racing four, five events a week. I started following Winston Cup racing a little bit, and it wasn't long before I was feeling pulled to the Atlantic side. I kept thinking, Ern, maybe what you need to do is go to the East Coast. Since it was difficult getting sponsorship money on the West Coast, I had only one reason to stay in California—my concern for my mom.

Mom co-owned an automotive repair shop she ran with a partner in Seaside. She did the books. Her partner fixed the cars. At the time it didn't look like she was going to move, but I also knew that Mom wouldn't hold me back if I wanted to go. It wasn't long before I told her I had decided to head east.

When Dad first arrived in North Carolina, he decided to try his hand at promoting races. He took over the old Concord Speedway and began putting on races. He enjoyed the promotional work, but he would be the first to tell you he was a better racer than promoter. While he worked at promoting the races, he also continued to drive in them. He took on a partner, and they had their own race car. Dad kept calling me: "Ern, you ought to come back here. You can race our car."

After I made my decision to join my dad and Tracy in North Carolina, I spent the next month getting things together. I had a little Dodge pickup truck. While I was working out of Ivan's shop building race cars, I built a trailer. I took an old pickup truck bed—just the bed—put on an axle and made a little trailer out of it. I had built a part of a race car and loaded it and everything else I owned on that little Dodge pickup truck and that trailer. The only money I had came from selling two race car transmissions to a racer for $700.

My diet, on my journey to the East Coast, was not one that is recommended by the American Medical Association. The father of one of my co-workers at Ivan Baldwin's used to get blocks of cheese from welfare. He offered me one of these blocks of cheese—his contribution to my trip to the East Coast. Needless to say, my uncle, who drove with me so I wouldn't have to drive by myself, and I went from the West Coast to the East Coast without spending much time in the bathroom.

Before we even got out of Modesto, we were stopped by the police. The California Highway Patrol said we couldn't move another inch until we installed a safety chain on our trailer. The cop ordered us to drive off the ramp and park.

I thought to myself, Man, we're going three thousand miles, and we get stopped twenty miles from town for no safety chain? I can't believe this. We had to walk to a parts store, buy a safety chain, and hook it up. Once we did that, we drove straight to Las Vegas, where we gambled a little bit, having a good time at Circus Circus.

My uncle and I figured it would cost about $600 to get to North Carolina, including gas, food, and motels. Before I knew it, I had lost $100 of my $700. I took $300 out and put it in my pocket. I told him I was going to gamble the other $300. My uncle said, "If you lose that, you're not going to have enough money for gas." But he was family, my dad's brother. I said, "But you'll loan me the money, won't you?" "Well, yeah." I knew he would. I probably should have asked him for advice rather than money, but at that age I didn't think that was what I needed.

I had just turned twenty-one, so I didn't know much about gambling. I started playing the slot machines, and quickly lost another $200. I had another hundred left, and after winning $40, we were getting ready to quit when my machine started clanging and dinging. I won $600, and I was in hog heaven. I'm a never-say-quit person, so I figured,

"Maybe I can win a little more." I took another hundred and played it. With the last dollar I had for the slot machines, I hit for another $300! It wasn't a lot of money, but I left Vegas a winner, and I sure had fun. Thank goodness I didn't have to borrow any money from my uncle.

We then drove nonstop from Las Vegas to North Carolina. We had a heck of a time finding my dad's house. I remember it was close to Thanksgiving, in late November and pretty cold. Once we arrived safely and my dad and my uncle had a short time to visit, my uncle was on his way back to California.

We arrived in Concord on a Thursday. On Saturday Dad and I went with his friend Haywood Plyor, who was going racing at a dirt track in Fayetteville. We loaded up the pick-up truck and towed the race car. This was the first time I had been to a North Carolina racetrack. It was cold, and I couldn't believe it when the spectators began piling up old tires and burning them to stay warm. As I watched the air grow thicker and blacker, I told my dad, "Man, those tires smoke so bad. You can't do that in California. It's against the pollution laws." It seemed to be a common event at the Concord track. Everybody was doing it. Dad could probably tell I wasn't adjusting to my new surroundings when I told him, "Dad, this isn't anything like California." He said, "Naw, it isn't, but the racing is really good here."

We went back to Dad's house, and I unloaded all my stuff. I parked that old car I had started building on the West Coast. Dad was working for Ed Negre, whom he had known on the West Coast, and doing a little driving himself. He and a man by the name of Jivey Simpson had become partners in the dirt car he was running. When I moved to North

Carolina, Dad wanted to see me drive their car. Jivey said, "Vic, how do I know that kid can drive?" He didn't know anything about me. He only knew what most people thought of the rough West Coast drivers. Dad said, "How do you know he can't?" Jivey said to me, "You're from the West Coast? You can drive?" I said I could. Jivey said to my father, "I don't know if he can drive, but I'm not going to spend my money to find out." Dad and Jivey ended up agreeing that the best solution would be for Dad to buy out Jivey's interest. Had Jivey asked me, I would only have been able to admit driving four times on dirt. Moreover, the dirt tracks on the West Coast are different from those on the East Coast. On the West Coast they are tacky, muddy. On the East Coast, like the racetrack at Timmonsville, where I ran my first dirt race in North Carolina, they are really sandy, very slippery. When they get dry, they are more like an asphalt track. I ran second that very first night. I went off the track a couple of times, driving in too deep and sliding off the track. All in all, though, I felt like it was a respectable effort for my first race in North Carolina.

At the same time I had to figure out how to make a living, which often can be the toughest aspect of racing. I was hustling, doing odds and ends, trying to find work building and fabricating cars. Dad had gotten to know some people at the Charlotte Motor Speedway and he did his best to help me find work. He put out the word, "My kid has moved here. If you have any side jobs, he could use the money."

My father got a call from Harvey Walters of the Charlotte Motor Speedway. Harvey said, "Can your son weld? I need someone who can do some welding." Dad said

I knew welding. "Does he have a welder?" Dad said, "No, but I've got a welder." Harvey said, "If he can weld, we have a project for him."

I went down to the speedway and met the men who had been hired to construct the grandstand seats and bolt them to the concrete grandstands. Four different seats had to be welded onto a mechanism that folds them up so you can sweep underneath them and then fold them back down. They hired me and two other guys—Jimmy Gee, the son of the famous engine builder Robert Gee, and another guy named Crony, a friend of Jimmy Gee.

It was the winter of '82, and the money was a godsend. We were paid by the piece—three dollars for building one section of seats; so if we built twenty of them in a day, that was sixty bucks. It didn't matter whether it was snowing or if the temperature dropped below freezing. Jimmy, Crony, and I would go out there and work. From the time I was very young the importance of being a hard worker was instilled in me, no matter what the task. Working hard and doing my best goes hand in hand with my competitive nature. Jimmy and I would have contests to see who could build the most sections in an hour. We could really turn them out. If you've been to the Charlotte Motor Speedway, chances are good you have sat on a seat built by Ernie Irvan. I would say that between the three of us, we built forty thousand seats. I ordinarily don't like to admit that in case one of them breaks.

Working with Jimmy Gee got me in the know of Robert Gee, one of the greatest chassis builders and crew chiefs in the history of the sport. Little did I know when I started out welding at the Charlotte Motor Speedway that I would come to meet a lot of other people in Winston Cup racing.

It's interesting to me how you can meet people, get to know them a little bit, and never realize how they might affect your life.

I was having a good time. Winston Cup racing wasn't something I was even thinking about. I was looking more to racing at Concord in the dirt. I ran my little pickup truck on the Charlotte Motor Speedway track one day when it snowed, and made some hot laps. You can have a lot of fun driving fast in the snow. At the time I was doing it, I had no idea I would ever be driving there for a living. It goes to show that sometimes you think your dreams are big, but maybe not big enough.

After building all those seats, I was in fairly good financial shape. I had saved enough money to finish the car I had started to build back in California. Dad already had a car, and I would kid around with him that my car was going to be better than his.

I started racing at Concord the following year in Dad's car, but Dad and I, having the same strong wills and our own ideas, got along about as well as we did back in California. We didn't see eye to eye a lot of times. He would want me to tighten a bolt one way, and I would want to tighten it another way. He would want me to make a spoiler one way, and I'd want to make it another way. It was typical father-son tension. If my father told me to do something a certain way, there is no way I was going to do it like that. But if someone else told me that something ought to be done a certain way, even if it was the way Dad did it, I'd be more likely to try it. We often drove each other crazy as only loved ones can.

Meanwhile, once Mom found out where Dad was living, they started talking on the phone more and more.

Eventually Mom decided to come to North Carolina to visit, and they seemed to take up right where they had left off. Both seemed content with their ways. They knew each other as no one else did. They concluded, "Is anyone else going to put up with us?" Happily, they reconciled, what looks to be permanently. So goes another chapter in the Irvan family soap opera. I can't imagine it would have ended any other way for them.

In 1984 I started running at Concord on dirt in a full-wedge Firebird. It looked like a big cheese wedge—but a fast one at that. I had built most of it on the West Coast, and finished it in North Carolina.

Still driving for my dad, but too much alike, we continued to fight like cats and dogs. That year I won two races and was running well, but I am sure our disagreements took as much of the pleasure out of our success for Dad as they did me. Finally, after one particularly bad argument, I decided it would be a lot better for both of us if I moved out. For three months I lived with Marc Reno and his wife until I could get on my feet.

Marc had moved to North Carolina from the West Coast about a year before I did. I knew Marc in California when he bought cars from Ivan Baldwin (in the days I was working for Ivan). Marc had been trying to buy a shop. He was one of those guys who could build anything and who always wanted to own his own race team. He'd had drivers on the West Coast, and we had hung out together there. But after he moved east, Marc and I got to be good friends. I began working out of his shop.

Marc was working a full-time job building a Winston

Cup car for Joe Ruttman, who was sponsored at the time by Pet Dairy. He was also building a car for a friend of his, Bud Reeder. Dick Trickle was going to drive it. Marc needed help, and I went down to the shop and started helping him build the car. The job gave me my first experience in learning how to build Winston Cup cars.

Marc also had been building a car to drive himself. While I was living with Marc, I convinced him to let me drive that car. We became partners—he paid the cost of building the car, and I drove for nothing and got 20 percent of the winnings. It was a good deal for me.

Once in a while Marc and I would take a trip to the Petty Enterprises race car shop in Randleman, North Carolina, to pick up motors. On one excursion, we ran into Robert Yates there. Marc begged Robert Yates, who was making their engines at the time, to give us some engine parts. Robert pointed to two motors that had blown up and said we were welcome to them. The pieces were in a pile. Marc and I found boxes, filled them with the blown-up engine parts, and hauled the stash back to our shop.

I had become friends with Keith Dorton, an engine builder who offered to build our motors. When I told Marc that Keith said he would build a motor for us for $600, Marc said he thought that was a good deal. Two weeks later Keith built the engine and presented Marc with a bill for $1,800.

Marc said, "Wait a minute, Ernie. What happened to the $600?" I told him, "It turned out that the engine needed more parts than we anticipated. The good news is that Keith said we can get the motor and pay him when we get the money." Such arrangements were rare. But that's the kind of guy Keith is. Keith, Marc, and I turned out to be great friends. Keith's generous and trusting gesture cemented our friendship. And we ran Keith's motor forever. I don't know how or why it managed to live so long.

For the most part, racing is a very expensive proposition. It was not that unusual that Marc's shop couldn't attract enough business to make the money we needed to finish the car. So we decided to work over at Tom Pistone's shop in Charlotte. Oh, man, was Tiger Tom a character!

Tom Pistone was a guy who always had grand plans that never seemed to pan out. He had raced thirty years earlier, even won a couple of Winston Cup races. After he retired he ran a race shop and had a parts business.

Tom was animated and talked fast. When he was trying to get Marc and me to come work for him, he would tell us, "If you guys build these race cars for me, we'll make a lot of money." He said, "I've got the jigs and all the rest of the equipment." That sounded good, but when we got there, we discovered that what Tom had was a whole building filled with outdated equipment. He didn't have anything to build anything! His welders didn't work. You could have built a Winston Cup car from thirty-five years before, something he drove, with his jigs, but you couldn't build a short-track car with that equipment. We decided to fabricate our own jig. The biggest thing for us was that Tom did have some money, which allowed us to get paid. And we ran our own little business out of Tom's shop on the side.

We started working at Tom's, doing his customers' cars and our customers' cars. Using one of Tom's blueprints, we also built our own car in about seven days. We didn't get it painted because we needed that money to race, but finally Marc and I were in a position to go racing.

Pistone, wanting to get in on the action, wouldn't leave us alone. As we were trying to finish the job, Tom was full of advice and his special brand of enthusiasm. He would tell us how he used to set the front end or say he was the best crew chief in the business. He would tell us how he had done this or that. Finally, we would have to set him straight and tell him that we just couldn't afford to do things the old way. He would get upset and start throwing stuff at us. Never a dull moment with wildman Tom. He was what you call "a piece of work," and we loved him.

We started racing at the New Concord Speedway (which is now the old one). We had built a brand-new car that consistently would finish first or second. Because we did so well, Pistone felt sure it would be good advertising for him. It may have been. Unfortunately it didn't translate into as many orders as he would have liked.

Marc and I finally quit Tom after about six months. We had built a brand-new race car, but didn't have the money to race it. All Marc could afford to do was rent out our car to any driver with the money to race it. A driver would get a sponsor and give Marc ten grand, and Marc'd run him for the year, maintaining the car. Marc made a few bucks, and it allowed Marc to continue paying me a small salary.

Meanwhile, in 1985 we raced our old car on dirt at Concord and were able to win eleven races. Neither Marc nor I particularly liked dirt. We liked the racing well enough, but we didn't enjoy the cleanup afterward. But we did remarkably well on the hard slick tracks. As naive as we were, we built an asphalt car and went dirt racing. As it happened, by the time the heat race came around, the track would be hard and slick and it was like racing on asphalt. I never pitched the car, never drove like a dirt racer. I'd drive it straight into the corner and straight out, while all the guys from the Carolinas, die-hard dirt track racers, would be driving around the track sideways. And while they were driving sideways, I'd be driving right by them.

I made one little 355-cubic-inch engine with those two blown-up motors Robert Yates gave us, and we outran all the 430-cubic-inch all-aluminum motors in cars driven by the likes of Freddy Smith, Willy Craft, and Jeff Purvis.

Freddy Smith was one of the best dirt racers who ever lived. I can't imagine how many races Freddy won during his career. Probably five hundred. It was a thrill being able to meet and run against him. He used to live south of Charlotte, at Kings Mountain, and I got to know his dad, Grassy Smith, who was a legendary racer in his own right. At times I would beat Freddy, and there were times when he beat me. We'd either run Friday and Saturday nights at Concord if they held two events, or we'd run Friday night at the Tri-County Speedway, a same-type track that got hard and slick.

What I discovered was that when the track got real dry-slick, I could run really well. If the track was wet and tacky, I didn't run as well because I didn't know how to throw the car sideways like the other dirt drivers did. Learning how to do that was a valuable experience. In my mind it is important for anyone who wants to do any kind of stock car racing.

During one highly successful period Marc and I went a month and a half running two or three nights a week, never finishing worse than second. With all the financial hardships, this was a welcome diversion.

■ ■ ■

At the beginning of that year Marc and I started with four wheels, four tires, plus the engine we got on credit from Keith Dorton. By the end of that year we had done well enough to build ourselves a bigger motor and sport a trailer with a rack full of wheels and tires on it. Marc was paying me $200 a week to work on customers' cars during the day, and I drove for 20 percent of whatever the car made in the races. Though we were making enough to continue racing, we weren't getting rich by any means. We put every extra nickel into running the car. We ran for three years that way, with Marc carrying the brunt of the cost of running the car while I made peanuts and worked my ass off to race.

Marc and I built the cars together, but once the car was done, I did about 80 percent of the maintenance work myself. Marc wanted me to drive more carefully, to preserve the car better. That was not my style. I had been a pedal-to-the-metal driver in California, and it was the only way I knew how to drive. The more I wrecked, the more he made me fix it up. There were times when we would have liked to strangle each other.

My approach had always been aggressive. I didn't believe in wasting a chance to pass someone if I had one. Nor did I care to wait a lap or two, or to wait five or ten seconds. My preference was to gain my advantage without warning. Actually it was quite simple. Either I moved ahead and the car I was passing moved aside to let me pass, or I would move ahead, risking that we both might get our cars bent up a little in the process. If someone tried to block my way, he could anticipate getting hit. The people who most influenced my style—Ivan and Dad—drove that way. I saw it as a method that suited me too. Pushing other cars out of the way, however, sometimes cost me as well. There were many times when I'd bang up the nose of my car that way. In fact, I can remember tearing the nose off the car so many times in our dirt car that one week Marc made me build three noses ahead of time. He figured since we were racing three times, in all likelihood I'd wreck the nose three times. This way we'd have the replacement noses in advance. We wouldn't have to build them every night between races. It was wise of Marc. It was a cure for me. After I built those noses and gained full appreciation for how much time it took to build them, I swore I wouldn't lose another nose, and I didn't.

We tried to run as many nights a week as we could. The more we raced, the more money we could make. We started doing really well once they paved the Concord track in 1985. After that, only Jack Sprague could beat me. Jack, who hailed from Spring Lake, Michigan, moved to the Concord track after they paved it. As victory often narrowed down to him or me, Jack and I got to be rivals. Our rivalry got to be pretty heated. When you run on a short track long enough, spending every week there, sooner or later someone will come along to challenge you. You'll find one driver who is your most consistently tough competitor every week. For me, Jack was that guy. We were friends, but on the track we ran hard against each other.

When Concord paved that track it was the best thing that ever happened to Marc and me. We knew how to run pavement. It was like coming home for me. Marc also knew a lot about pavement, knew how to build really good pavement cars. It was a great time to be partners. We were at the right place, at the right time, with the right people. It was only the local track, but I was making a name for myself, getting my name in the local paper and in the racing press.

Marc and I both were eager to move up to a higher level of racing. Unless you were fortunate enough to have a large bank account of your own, your chance for moving up would most likely come from someone with a car at the next level offering you an opportunity. I was winning a lot at Concord and had gotten close to Elmo Langley, who had driven for years on the Winston Cup circuit and was nearing the end of his career. Many times I tried to get Elmo to let me drive his car in a Winston Cup race just once. Elmo was our closest low-level Winston Cup driver, and he would let different people drive his car each week. Elmo knew I was a hot dog on short tracks, but he kept putting me off because we didn't have any money to offer him for the ride. In those days, it was more a rent-a-ride bargain than anything else. You could have been the greatest driver in the world, but if you couldn't pay Elmo to run the car, someone with money got it instead. Money was more important than talent. It had to be. There were many guys like Elmo, struggling financially to stay in the racing game. So Elmo would never let me drive his car. He came very close two or three times, but each time someone came in and offered him money, and we'd be out. Marc and I became angry and frustrated. We knew we needed a big break. As it turned out, the guy who gave it to me was none other than the Intimidator himself, Dale Earnhardt.

9

"DON'T EVER GET A REAL JOB"

By 1986, I was discouraged, ready to quit. Then I met Kenny Schrader. He had started racing in Winston Cup a couple years earlier. If Kenny had odds-and-ends jobs for Marc Reno and me to do, he'd say, "Hey, Ern, come on over. I've got a job for you to do. I'll give you fifty bucks." Marc and I needed the money, so we always went. Sometimes, when Marc and I were doing various odd jobs for Kenny and for Dale Earnhardt, Kenny would show up at Marc's shop. Invariably when we were done, we would go by Schrader's house and drink some beer and sit around shooting the breeze.

One day Kenny called and asked if I would help him unload his truck for $50. He was moving down to Charlotte from St. Louis. He had gone back and forth, but he was moving permanently. He wanted me to help him unpack, and I agreed.

When we finished we drove down to the corner store. Seeing as how I had just earned $50, Kenny suggested that I might want to buy him some beer. I didn't object, but now I was down to $40. The lack of money was really getting to me. I told Schrader, "Kenny, if I don't get something going in a Winston Cup car, I'm going to have to get a real job."

Schrader looked at me with great seriousness and said, "Ernie, I'm telling you, don't ever get a real job. Don't *ever* get a real job. I've done this my whole life and have never had a real job. I know you can do it too."

For reasons I'm not altogether sure of, that advice struck a chord with me. It inspired me to believe I really needed to keep at it—that I could do it too. Schrader hasn't ever forgotten the conversation either. Now that we're competing against each other all the time, he says, "Maybe I shouldn't have told you that." Thankfully, it wasn't too long after that before I got my first Winston Cup ride.

Marc Reno and I raced at night, and during the day built race cars for other people in Marc's shop. When we realized we couldn't get enough money together to buy a ride in Elmo Langley's car, the next logical idea was for us to build our own car.

Our first enterprise was to build a Busch car. The Busch races are on Saturdays. The cars have smaller engines than Winston Cup cars and are cheaper to build. Marc and I had always built everything ourselves, but we had no idea how to build one of those cars. We started by buying a five-year-old Frank Denny chassis Marc had found in California. It had never been used, but had been sitting outside in the rain all that time and was rusty as hell. It cost Marc $1500.

We then went around asking for parts and buying ones we couldn't get donated to our cause. We built the motor, and the first Busch race we tried to run was at Charlotte. First NASCAR had to okay you to run. The only reason NASCAR gave me the go-ahead on that race was because I had run Riverside when I lived in California, driving in Grand American races in a Camaro. Without those races under my belt, NASCAR would have required that I start out on one of the shorter Winston Cup tracks.

My dad was listed as the owner of the car, and Ted Proctor, who owned a beer distributorship in Salisbury, gave us $2,000 sponsorship money. Every bit helped.

I made the race, an accomplishment for us. But the motor broke which left us no better off than before.

We then decided to try a different route. We set our sights on winning a Road-to-Charlotte race at Concord. This was a promotion divined by Humpy Wheeler, genius promoter of the Charlotte Motor Speedway. Humpy wanted to attract local short-track racers to run on his track in a Busch race. The only trouble was, you needed to have a car that could run at Charlotte, and a lot of short-track racers didn't have the money or the inclination to run there.

Humpy devised it so that if you won one of the Road-to-Charlotte races at Concord or one of the other short tracks in the program, you got paid an extra $500 in winnings. Additionally, if you qualified to make the race at Charlotte, he would pay you an extra $3,000. That money could mean being able to at least buy new tires to race. Humpy's program really was important to the local drivers.

We entered our first Road-to-Charlotte race and were leading with five laps to go when our crankshaft blew out of the car. We were heartbroken. We were unbelievably disheartened about it when we were informed that the Ace

Speedway was holding another Road-to-Charlotte race the next weekend.

Ace Speedway was a muddy, sloppy dirt track. Though I had trouble driving on tracks like that, Marc and I decided to try for it anyway.

We arrived at Ace, ran like Jack the Bear, but finished second. We were down in the dumps, to say the least.

The local hero, whose name I can't recall, had won that Road-to-Charlotte race three or four times in a row, and he never went to Charlotte. He just wasn't interested. So his crew chief graciously came to us and said, "He's never used the invitation. You're welcome to it." So though we finished second, we got to go to Charlotte, and we made the race. Once again, our way of getting there wasn't the planned way; sometimes luck and a few generous people can take you where you want to go.

We went to Charlotte in the old car that I had brought from California and with which we built a Busch Grand National car. It was assigned number 09. We took it to Charlotte and qualified in the first round. We raced it, but unfortunately ended up breaking a motor. We made the needed repairs to get up and running again, and off we went to Rockingham. There, as luck would have it, one of our crew accidentally put his screwdriver through the radiator and we burned up the motor. Sometimes, as the saying goes, the only luck you can get is bad luck. Usually, though, it doesn't last terribly long.

Billy Ingle, who owned an alternator business and worked for Junior Johnson, decided he really wanted to buy our car. We felt we had done an excellent job building it, and it had come out pretty nicely. But after running only two races we decided it might be best after all to sell it to Billy. Our experience told us that instead of working at qualifying in the Busch series, we might as well shoot for the top. We took the money and used it to build ourselves a Winston Cup car. We figured that the only way I would get an opportunity to drive in Winston Cup was if we built a car ourselves.

At the same time Marc Reno's wife was working for Buddy Baker, who had the Crisco sponsorship. Somewhere along the line Marc, Buddy, and I established a good working relationship. In the summer of 1987 Marc and I made a deal to rent the Chevrolet we were going to build for ourselves to Patty Moise, a Winston Cup driver who had the Butter-Flavored Crisco sponsorship. She paid us to build it and work on it. We agreed to do the mechanics, work on the car, and make pieces for the car if she crashed. Patty wasn't running very well, but she had a deal, which was more than we could say at that time.

We bought the frame for Patty's car, and built the rest of the car. Watkins Glen was to be the first race in which she planned to run. We had almost finished the car when Patty came down to the shop to inspect the seat. She didn't hesitate to speak up about what she wanted us to do. In fact, the conversation digressed in much the same way as when my dad and I tried to collaborate, each of us with our own ideas. When Patty told us to move the shifter, put it "this" way, I lost it. I had listened as long as I could. I asked her, "Can you reach the shifter?" She said she could. Her reply to my remarks was sarcastic. She said, "Listen here, Mr. Road Racer . . ." She was letting me know that it was she who was the expert in road racing. I had yet to prove myself as far as she was concerned.

From then on, she called me "Mr. Road Racer." When I had won more road races than she did, I admit feeling more than a little satisfaction.

I was more than stinging from her sarcasm. It was frustrating to think that, with decent sponsorship, I could be driving that car—and just as competitively if not more so! I was unquestionably envious of her opportunities. I wondered often during those times why I couldn't get a deal like the one she had. It was like rubbing salt in a wound that we had to do what she asked.

So we built her a car and took it to Watkins Glen, and Patty wrecked it.

As the car was sitting in the shop wrecked, Marc and I decided it was time we raced it. There was no question we were capable of doing the work. We just didn't have the money. We decided then that if we could accumulate enough motor pieces, we could run in a Winston Cup race. It was so farfetched, but we had to try it.

We rolled up our sleeves and put this Winston Cup car back together. We straightened the front end, replaced some pieces, replaced the fenders, and did a lot of body work. Our goal was to go to Richmond and race in mid-September. Could we find a sponsor? It didn't seem likely. Neither of us had made enough of a name for ourselves—just like the thousands of other poor souls trying to climb the ladder to Winston Cup.

Ken Schrader stopped by at Marc's shop to drink a few beers with us. At that time Kenny was struggling up the ladder himself. Schrader and his pal Dale Earnhardt were daily visitors. They would come by, drink beer, and have a good time. Dale was driving back and forth from Darlington, a two-hour trip, and he would stop regularly at Marc's shop. When Earnhardt needed a trailer to haul his four-wheelers, he asked Marc and me to build it.

Dale, Schrader, Marc, and I drank beer and talked racing until two o'clock in the morning. While we were sitting and talking, Earnhardt noticed the car we were building and asked, "What are you guys doing with that?" Marc said, "We're going to put this car together and go to Richmond to race. We're trying to get enough money to do it."

Dale said, "Patty driving that thing again?" Marc said, "No, Ernie's going to drive it." Earnhardt said, "Ernie's going to drive it? He's a dirt racer, and Richmond is a little bit bigger than Concord, isn't it?" Dale knew I had raced Concord a lot. I said, "Yeah, it's a little bit bigger." Marc said, "Ernie's been doing really well on pavement." Dale asked, "Who is going to sponsor it? How are you going to get the money to do it?" We told him, "We're selling the dirt car. We're doing this, doing that."

Out of the blue Schrader said, "Hey, Earnhardt, you ought to sponsor this car." Schrader was probably thinking that his friend Earnhardt had more money than the law allows.

Earnhardt said, "Yeah, we'll put my chicken farm on the side of the car. It'll say, 'We lay them better.'" Schrader said, "Good idea, Dale."

When they were getting ready to leave, Schrader said to Marc and me, "We need to get Earnhardt to sponsor the car. Let me talk to him some more." Kenny told Marc, "I'll negotiate the deal—for 10 percent." We agreed. Marc and I had nothing to lose. Schrader said, "I'll have the deal by tomorrow." We were hopeful that Kenny could persuade Earnhardt to sponsor us. We wondered how much money Kenny would really be able to get.

Schrader went with Earnhardt and dropped him off at his house. The next day Kenny came back with the deal. Schrader said, "Earnhardt's going to sponsor your car." It was an understatement to say that we were elated. I said, "How much money is he going to give us?" Schrader said, "He's not giving you any money." Marc couldn't believe what he was hearing. He said, "You *have* to give us some money." Kenny said, "No, he'll give you the credibility." That shows how shrewd Earnhardt can be. Dale Earnhardt was one of the most popular and visible drivers in Winston Cup. He also knew we were in no position to turn him down. It wasn't like we had other offers on the table. Still, having his name used for our cause meant we would draw attention that we never would have otherwise.

Needless to say, we accepted Dale's deal. It was unique—no other Winston Cup driver had ever sponsored another Winston Cup car. Earnhardt was in the process of starting his Chevrolet dealership, so he had us paint DALE EARNHARDT CHEVROLET on the side of our car. It was great advertising for all of us.

We said, "What about tires and parts?" Dale said, "We have some used tires and some motor pieces. I'll give you that junk." To him it was junk! To us, it was like a lifeline. Anything he was getting from Chevrolet for free, such as ignition parts, he also passed along to us to help get the car completed.

We were really happy with this unique arrangement, feeling that with DALE EARNHARDT CHEVROLET written on the side of our car, showing everyone he was on our side, we were on our way. Everyone knew Earnhardt—a 1980 and 1986 champion who would win again in '87 and four more times after that. We had no doubts his backing would bring us the recognition and credibility we needed. With tires we got from Dale, in mid-September 1987 we went to Richmond to try to qualify in a Winston Cup race.

The entry fee was $200. You gotta have a car. In addition to having $200 and a car, NASCAR had to okay the driver too. I had already run two Busch races. Twice I had made the race and didn't crash or do anything that would jeopardize getting their authorization. Without much fanfare, but with plenty of enthusiasm, we were off to the races.

We didn't hold a press conference. There was nothing earthshattering about our presence. We just showed up. We unloaded at Richmond, pushing the car through the garage. That was the old Richmond track, a half mile. Once we pulled into the garage, people were quick to notice the big block lettering that said DALE EARNHARDT CHEVROLET. They knew Earnhardt was opening a Chevrolet dealership. The fact that Earnhardt would back someone inevitably begged the question, "Who's Ernie Irvan?"

It was all new to me and very exciting. All the best drivers were there, Richard Petty, Earnhardt, Rusty Wallace, Darrell Waltrip, Harry Gant, anybody you ever heard about. This was the moment I had been dreaming about and working toward my entire life. As part of our sponsorship deal, Earnhardt was also going to give us advice. He said to me,

"Get up there, make the race, and try to last all day."
Sounded like good advice to me.

We qualified twentieth in the first round, not bad considering. You didn't test in those days. You just showed up and qualified. Keith Dorton was still helping us. Keith had two used motors to work with, and he combined the parts at his disposal and added a few new ones to build us two motors. He also came to the race in case anything went wrong. Keith didn't get paid, just went with us to help. Keith, Marc, and I were beside ourselves about being in the race.

The harsh reality is that it's very difficult to compete at the Winston Cup level without money. It's hard to assemble good solid pieces without means. Used parts tend to break during a long race. As good as Keith Dorton was, he couldn't keep our engine together to the end.

Sunday morning we were inspecting the car when we found some trash in one of the air filters. We decided there must have been something wrong with the motor, so that morning we put the other motor in.

We started the September 1987 Richmond race. I drove car number 56. Dale Earnhardt, the defending Winston Cup champion, drove the number 3 Goodwrench Chevrolet. We started the race, and in those days they didn't have the radiator systems figured out. It had air locked—air got in it—and the engine overheated thirty-five laps into the race.

That was a real disappointment, but while I was out there, I didn't feel out of place. I wasn't overmatched. I wasn't intimidated. Believe it or not, I felt like I belonged. Richmond was bigger than any track I had ever driven on before. Though it was small compared to its size today, it still seemed big to me then. If I felt any nervousness or pressure at all, it was because I had DALE EARNHARDT CHEVROLET on the side of the car. Once I got out onto the track, though, and began racing, doing what I had been doing in one form or another my whole life, I was comfortable. I was also happy because for the first time I was running in a Winston Cup race.

Nevertheless, at the end of the day, it appeared that Marc and I still were nowhere. We didn't have enough money to run again. We had to park the car and try to figure out something later.

It's interesting to me how things can work: when I qualified twentieth and ran at Richmond, someone did notice. D.K. Ulrich had owned and driven his own Winston Cup car since the early 1970s. He was one of those independent drivers who never had much money, and as a result the vets wouldn't drive for him. If he had had the funding, a lot of people would have been honored to drive for him. He simply didn't. Without the necessary financial backing for success, his car never won a race. D.K. had other things going for him. He was a great guy, and he had a reputation of working very well with young drivers. Tim Richmond, Ricky Rudd, Sterling Marlin, Mark Martin, Morgan Shepherd, and even the King, Richard Petty, had driven for D.K. in a race or two. When D.K. contacted me about driving for him I was honored as well as excited.

One of the reasons D.K. gave me a chance was that Keith Dorton had been talking to him about me. I had been working at Keith's shop helping him build motors, and Keith kept telling D.K., "Man, I know this guy who's really good. He works with me a little bit, works at Marc Reno's, and I think this guy could do a really good job for you." D.K. was skeptical initially. Owners always hear this kind of talk about various racers trying to move up.

The other connection I had with D.K. was through the work Marc and I had done for D.K. He hadn't known anything about my driving, but was aware that I had raced. When D.K. failed to qualify for the Richmond race, he was hoping to find a driver who could do better.

Thanks to my arrangement with Earnhardt and after running well at Charlotte, I became a more suitable candidate for the job. D.K. contacted me and asked me if I wanted to drive for him at Martinsville and Wilkesboro. He said he wanted someone who could make the race and do a good job for him. Did I want to run? I answered, "Well, yeah." Hell, yeah. I would have at least two more chances driving in Winston Cup.

D.K. and I went to Martinsville, the first time I had ever been there. Martinsville was a lot like our old short tracks in California: no banks, real flat, real long straightaways for a short track. Not bad. D.K. said if I could drive his car in practice faster than he could, I could drive the car in the race. Like I said, I had never been to Martinsville, and he had been there a lot, but I had complete confidence in my ability and ambition and motivation to keep driving in Winston Cup competition. I managed to get around the track faster than he, and true to his word, he paid me 20 percent of the purse, not much money, but he also paid my expenses.

I managed to qualify twenty-seventh in a field of thirty-two cars. Believe it or not, we didn't think that was too bad under the circumstances. D.K. didn't have a sponsor, which meant there was no sponsorship money, and the cars we had to work with just weren't Park Avenue. I had made the field, which was all D.K. was worried about.

Everything was going well when two hundred laps into the race, I called D.K. on the radio. "D.K.?" He said, "Yeah." I said, "Man, my butt is burning." I'm sure he must have thought he misunderstood me. He said, "Your butt is burning?" I said, "My ass is so hot I need to get out of this seat."

The temperature in a race car can get pretty high. D.K. was probably thinking he really chose a new boy when I began complaining. He certainly didn't miss the opportunity to tease me. He said, "You wimp." I said, "I'm telling you, I can probably go another fifty laps, but my seat is on fire." D.K.'s girlfriend, Diane, got on the radio and said, "Donald will put his suit on." She called him Donald. That always floored me. Finally, D.K. said, "Okay wimpy, if you need, I'll go put my uniform on and finish the race." I said, "That's fine, because I'm not kidding about this seat being hot as hell." I had to get out even though my pride was hurting as much as my behind to know D.K. was thinking of me as a "Saturday night" racer.

About thirty laps later a caution came out. I pulled in, jumped out, and D.K. jumped in. My backside was blistered. As I was nursing my wounds on a throne of cold towels, D.K. couldn't resist another shot at me. D.K. said, "I can't believe you, wimp. You'll never make a Winston Cup driver if you can't stand a little bit of heat."

About a hundred laps later, D.K. called to his girlfriend, "Diane?" "Yes, Donald." He said, "You're going to have to get some cold towels for me. Ernie wasn't lying. My behind is burning too." He'd pull in, and we'd hose him down, squirt him with water on his seat.

Evidently the car had this old-time Banjo Matthews seat—everything D.K. had was kind of old—the bracket had broken, and it had collapsed down to the floorboard right above the tailpipe. D.K. finished the race and got out of the car. I felt a bit justified when D.K. had to drive home lying on his stomach in the van because he couldn't even sit down! If I was a wimp, we were both wimps.

We finished a remarkable fifteenth—quite respectable, we thought, considering our troubles.

Next up was Wilkesboro, also a track I had never seen. We qualified thirtieth, right on the bubble. I had run a lap of 20.006 seconds. Knowingly D.K. said, "We have to qualify again tomorrow. The time will never hold up."

I said, "Are you crazy? The time is always slower on the second day of qualifying (and certainly so at Wilkesboro). I don't know if I can go any faster."

D.K. repeated, "We have to requalify. If we're going to miss this race, we're going to go down fighting."

At D.K.'s insistence I ran again the next day. This time I ran a lap in 20.001 seconds. I went six-thousandths faster. D.K. was right: our first time would not have made the race. The new one did.

D.K. said, "I'm trying to condition you to do what it takes to be a good Winston Cup driver. I think we've built some character in you." I said, "What are you talking about?" He said, "I can tell now that you're going to be a good driver because you did the job and you didn't think you could." He was looking for a "never-say-die" attitude. He was telling me he was now seeing some of that in me.

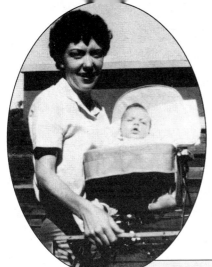

Mom and me. This was my first ride. *(The Irvan Collection)*

Here are my sisters Cheryl and Susan, my brother David, and I'm on the right. *(The Irvan Collection)*

In the pits at the Stockton Speedway in 1975. *(The Irvan Collection)*

Mom, Dad and I confer before a race. *(The Irvan Collection)*

As a teenager. *(The Irvan Collection)*

This is the car I drove for D.K. Ulrich in 1988.
(The Irvan Collection)

My big break was getting Dale Earnhardt to sponsor my car. It may be the only time a Winston Cup driver put his name on another car. *(The Irvan Collection)*

I was all smiles when I signed with Kodak in 1990. *(Photo by Don Grassman)*

Larry McClure *(l.)* always wanted me to stand on the gas. I was happy to oblige. *(Photo by Don Grassman)*

My first pole—at Bristol in April of 1990. *(Photo by Chobat Racing Images)*

Tony Glover and I were like brothers. *(Photo by Don Grassman)*

My first win came at the August race at Bristol in 1990. *(Photo by Don Grassman)*

Larry McClure and I celebrate our winning the 1991 Daytona 500. *(Photo by Don Grassman)*

The happiness is evident on everyone's face. *(Photo by Don Grassman)*

The Kodak race team cheers after victories at Sonoma *(above)* and the Daytona Firecracker 400 in 1992. *(Photos by Chobat Racing Images)*

A trophy for our big win at Talladega. *(The Irvan Collection)*

Our Kodak race team won at Talladega in July of 1992. At the time I could never have imagined driving for anyone else. *(Photo by Don Grassman)*

Davey Allison and I became friends at Loudon in June of 1993—it was the last race he ever ran. *(Photo by Don Grassman)*

Robert Yates hired me after Davey was killed in a tragic helicopter crash.
(The Irvan Collection)

Ford wanted me to challenge Dale Earnhardt's Goodwrench Chevrolet.
(The Irvan Collection)

The day Kim and
I were married.
(The Irvan Collection)

Our daughter Jordan celebrated her first birthday the weekend of my crash at Michigan in August of 1994. Few thought I would ever see her again. *(The Irvan Collection)*

A year after the crash at Michigan I visited with some of the staff who saved my life. *(The Irvan Collection)*

Dr. Farhat, Dr. Maino, Dr. Erlandson, and a grateful patient pose at a head injury foundation fundraiser. *(The Irvan Collection)*

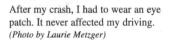

After my crash, I had to wear an eye patch. It never affected my driving.
(Photo by Laurie Metzger)

(Photo by Don Grassman)

As I was trying to focus on the race, I was mobbed by the press when I climbed into the 88 car at North Wilkesboro for the first time. *(The Irvan Collection)*

No one thought I'd ever race again. Wrong. *(The Irvan Collection)*

A pit stop during my first race back. I drove the 88. Dale Jarrett drove the 28. *(The Irvan Collection)*

Robert Yates *(r.)*, Larry McReynolds *(l.)* and I rejoice over the Loudon win. *(Photo by Don Grassman)*

I celebrate victory and life at Loudon in July of 1996. The feeling was indescribable. *(Photo by Don Grassman)*

Larry McReynolds and I hug after taking Richmond in September of 1996. That win proved that Loudon was no fluke. *(Photo by Don Grassman)*

Kim, Jordan, and I stroll before the Pocono race. *(Photo by Don Grassman)*

A tender moment before a tough race. *(The Irvan Collection)*

My victory at Michigan came three years after my crash. *(Photo by Don Grassman)*

Taking home the trophy at Michigan. *(Photo by Don Grassman)*

Michigan was the last race I would win for Robert Yates *(l.)*. *(Photo by Don Grassman)*

Jordan and I join in the festive celebration of the opening of the Fontana track. *(The Irvan Collection)*

Heading to driver introductions at Charlotte. *(The Irvan Collection)*

Standing with Jordan in front of the specially painted car to mark Robert
Yate's tenth year with Texaco. *(Photo by Chobat Racing Images)*

I joined the MB2 race team with a great deal of confidence. The owners and sponsers have been great to me. *(Photo by Don Grassman)*

Crew chief Ryan Pemberton and I have formed a close-knit partnership. *(Photo by Don Grassman)*

(Photos by Don Grassman)

M&M will be
my sponsor
beginning
in 1999.
*(Photo by Don
Grassman)*

The Blue M visits Jordan
at her school. *(The Irvan
Collection)*

Jordan gets to know baby brother Jared. *(The Irvan Collection)*

Jordan handles the refueling. *(The Irvan Collection)*

We're all smiles after winning the pole at Indy.

We ran the race, and we were running around twentieth, when I got a flat tire, hit the fence, and didn't finish very well. But it was important to D.K. that I get out there and race, do what we needed to do to attract a sponsor—and that was being able to make the race. So he was happy, though as far as I was concerned, we weren't running very well.

I had to tell D.K. I couldn't drive for him in two weeks at Charlotte. Marc and I were running our own car at Charlotte, again with Dale Earnhardt sponsoring the car. We did it because having Dale Earnhardt on our car was giving us great respectability and exposure with the Winston Cup crowd.

We checked in on Wednesday, and on Friday Dale sent word from Wilkesboro that we had to paint the car silver. Mind you, Dale hadn't paid us a cent. Marc said to Dale, "The car is already painted. We have to paint it silver now?" Earnhardt, who is as stubborn as I am, insisted. The race was Sunday, and on Saturday morning Marc went up to Wilkesboro to see him. Dale was firm. He said, "It has to be silver. I also want my signature on the car instead of block letters. This is what I want."

Well, D.K. didn't have a paint shop. We had to do it ourselves. Marc told Dale, "It's going to cost $1,700 in materials to paint the car." Back then we had sign painters. And you couldn't get decals quickly, had they been available. Earnhardt said, "I don't care. I want that thing painted silver."

We sat in the van and cut a deal right then. Dale knew he wanted the car painted, and he knew about how much it would cost. It was that simple for him. He said, "I'm going to give you guys three grand. That will cover painting the car." That was our first monetary sponsorship from Dale Earnhardt.

We worked on that car all weekend painting it silver. Our car 56 was the ugliest car you've ever seen, until they lettered it. Then it actually looked pretty good.

We were parked in the Charlotte garage outside because we didn't have any points. Next to us was A.J. Foyt, who didn't have any either. He too was only racing once in a while. A.J. was a kick. He was running some kind of fuel, and man, that fuel was burning our eyes. As our eyes were tearing, he was laughing. He was giving us suggestions too. He had an idea of who we were and what we were trying to do. Luckily for us, Foyt was in a great mood that weekend. He had gotten caught with a tiny little clutch on his motor, and amazingly, he was laughing about it. Marc and I were taking this all in. He was a veteran, one of the greats in racing history, and we were watching, trying to learn from a master.

Well, everybody used to drain their fuel tanks before they went out to qualify. As Marc and I were sitting there, Foyt walked over to his car with three gas cans to empty that car out. As we watched, we noticed he had drained gas out into two cans and then put one can in! We were baffled. It still didn't sink in what he was doing: he was running some sort of aviation fuel to qualify!

The next morning we came into our garage area, and A.J. started that thing up, had that car going. The exhaust of that car was pointed our way, and it was burning our eyes so bad we had to leave. I still don't know for sure that it was aviation fuel he was using, but I knew enough to be upset because Foyt chose not to share that little secret.

We made the race—a big deal at the time, because we probably shouldn't have. Fortunately, I was able to do a good job qualifying, finishing seventeenth. Earnhardt came over before the race, and offered some sage advice. He said, "Let me tell you one thing: what you need to do is stay out of trouble and run this whole race." I said, "Okay." He said, "If I drive by, and you've crashed and you're sitting down in the infield, I might just stop and whoop your ass." I said, "Okay, okay." This was Dale Earnhardt talking to me. I wasn't about to argue with him. To Dale, finishing is everything. To many people Dale is the Intimidator. Then and now, to Mark and me, Dale is our friend. He's a neat guy, as well as a great driver. Racing against him meant I was working toward the bigger dream.

We started the race, and I was just biding my time. I was running hard but trying to stay out of trouble. That was a little problematic as there were a lot of wrecks. It looked like Rick Wilson might have been responsible for one of them—something that happens to every driver at one time or another. About fifteen cars were already out, we were running around twentieth, and Earnhardt was leading, when Derrike Cope and he got tangled up, wiping his junk out. I went by, and couldn't resist getting on the radio. I said to Marc Reno, "Earnhardt's wrecked in the infield. You know, I ought to stop by and whoop his ass." Marc said, "Naw, you better just keep on going." I was feeling cocky because I knew I'd finish ahead of him—the Intimidator. Off the field he was our friend, but on the track he was a competitve driver to be taken very seriously.

Understand we were doing this on a zip budget. We had nothing. We were basically broke all the time. Any money we had we put into that race car. And here we were, running with the big boys!

What saved us, and I'll never forget it, Dale Jarrett was driving for Eric Freedlander. They pitted right next to us. Their engine broke early in the race, and they were done. They had three sets of scuffs that had two or three laps on them, and they asked Marc, "Do you want these tires?" He said, "Hell, yes," and that's what we raced on that whole race. Because we could only afford to buy our qualifying tires, and we had only one other set of tires. Once Jarrett fell out of that race and his team gave us those three sets of tires, we were able to finish well. We never could have done it without those tires. Those tires meant everything to us because there was no way we could afford to go to the tire truck. You just never know when those random acts of generosity will come along. It makes the job very gratifying.

It was a long race, six hundred long miles. With twenty miles to go, I began to pick up the pace. From halfway in the pack I started passing cars. A couple times off turn four I was a little sideways, and Marc started to get nervous. He radioed to me, "Ern, remember our goal. We've got to finish."

That was true. That was our goal, but sometimes your instincts just tell you that you can push the envelope. I was feeling good, and I thought I'd move up a couple of spots there at the end. I ended up finishing eighth.

People were incredulous. I had run faster than cars with million-dollar sponsors built in sophisticated race shops. Marc and I had built our car in a shed by comparison. But when everyone said, "Eighth? I can't believe you did so well," I thought, Eighth? That's junk. When I crossed the finish line,

I didn't feel that this was any big deal because I didn't have anything to compare it to. Shoot, most of the time when I had run on short tracks, I won, and if I didn't do so well, I finished second. I told everyone, "I should have won." They said, "No, Ernie, you don't realize how hard it is to finish eighth." I was so green. I had no idea.

The next year, when I knew a little more, it would have meant a lot more. I didn't have much Winston Cup experience, and it didn't take me long to realize that when you finish eighth in Winston Cup, you've done a great job. A lot of top cars had wrecked that day, and I had had the benefit of D.J.'s tires, and I was very fortunate to have finished so well. It was a 600-mile race, and it was a great milestone in my career.

As I said, we were doing it with mirrors. This was before the age of computers, during a time when you could write a bad check on Friday and hope to cover it on Monday. Before we went to Charlotte, Marc was $9,000 overdrawn on his bank account. (Marc says he doesn't know why he let debt run up like that. By way of explanation he says he can only attribute it to our love of racing. If we hadn't made the race, Marc would have had to borrow money to cover the deficit.) But with my eighth-place finish, we won a check for $9,100, and believe me, we didn't wait for the racetrack to mail it to us. We went and got it in person. It was my biggest payday. Of course, I had to wait a week or two for Marc's check to clear.

Marc and I decided to race at Riverside, California, in November because I had road-raced a few times earlier in my career and was familiar with the track. D.K. said, "Why don't we put my number 6 on your car, and I won't have to go." He agreed to buy the tires and helped us financially get to Riverside. He also gave us some gears and other parts.

We went to Riverside and qualified thirty-fourth. I was running pretty well in the race, about twelfth, when I broke an axle. We were running hollow axles back then, and they were brittle. This was only the second race for these axles, but during the race I ran off the track onto the dirt, and when I came back onto the asphalt, the axle snapped.

The caution came out, which was a break for us. We didn't have any spare parts, didn't really have anything. When we took the axle off, we saw that it had broken inside. Marc ran down the pits and located a piece of squarebox tubing. We knocked the broken piece out—it was fortunate for us that it came out—and Marc ran to the BSR parts truck and grabbed a new piece with a quick "bye," and then stuck the thing in, installed the new piece in the car, and I shot back out onto the racetrack.

I left pit road just as the leaders were coming out of turn nine. When they came around, they lapped us, which really hurt. If we hadn't gotten lapped, we'd have been a fifth- or sixth-place car. We finished nineteenth. We got the $3,500 show-up money, which wasn't much, but it paid our gas bill out there.

I got in the five races I could run and still remain a rookie the next year in '88. I was getting my feet wet. At the end of the season D.K. told me he thought he had a sponsor and asked if I would be interested in running for Rookie of the Year in his car. He was talking to Kroger, and they were interested in running a rookie. It was the kind of break I really needed. When D.K. asked me if I wanted to run for him in

1988, I said, "You didn't even have to ask me." It was a great opportunity. I had been waiting for it a long time.

In the meantime D.K. hired Marc Reno as our crew chief. Marc built a few cars to get ready, and D.K. agreed to pay Marc about $25,000 for his car that we had run at Riverside and two engines. It was a nickel on the dollar for the stuff, but Marc wasn't making anything on the deal. What he was doing was taking a big chance supporting a friend. Marc actually closed down his shop to be my crew chief. His pay was less than what he was making at his shop. With D.K.'s financial condition, Marc worried all year long whether his paychecks would be good or not. I knew Marc was making a big sacrifice for me. Again, it was one of those incredibly great gestures that make life worth living. In addition to the car he bought from Marc, D.K. bought two or three other people's cars, after which we were off to Daytona to run for Rookie of the Year. My strongest competition that year was against Kenny Bouchard and Brad Noffsinger.

We were at Daytona practicing, working hard at trying to qualify for the '88 Daytona 500. That was an eye-opener for me. This was the first year of restrictor plates, which were mandated by NASCAR to slow the speed of the cars. These plates, which cut down the intake of air into the engine, have reduced speeds by as much as 20 miles an hour. Even with that plate, a fast time was 190 miles an hour. When I got running out there, I was going 184 miles an hour. I said to Marc, "I'm really glad they got these plates on because 185 miles an hour is pretty sporty. I don't know about that 210 miles an hour they had been running." Marc laughed.

We were in garage 13—a garage I haven't visited since. We kept trying to loosen the car up to go faster, always trying to get speed. We were set back a little bit when I spun off turn two. Luckily I didn't hit the wall, but then I hit a car going slowly on the bottom of the track. It did a lot of body damage.

They towed us in. We congregated in the garage and started working on the car to fix it. Once we got it patched up and ready to go, I went back out again. No sooner was I warming up on the apron, than right about at the tri-oval Bobby Hillin and Richard Petty collided, spun out, crashed, and ran into me. Amazing. For a second time, the car was a mess. Butch Mock and his team were laughing at our rotten luck as they called the wrecker driver. We weren't having a very good time at Daytona.

Again we did the only thing we could do: we returned to the garage and fixed up the car again so we could run in one of the 125-mile qualifying races. My time in qualifying hadn't been very good. To make the Daytona 500 I needed to finish in the top 15 in the 125.

We started the 125 in our Richmond car. Going for Rookie of the Year, it was critical that we made all the races. With seven laps to go we were running along in fourteenth, and I was sure we'd make the race.

Phil Barkdoll was behind me. I was trying to bide my time, stay out of trouble. Ah, the best laid plans. Phil's plans were different than mine. He took a more aggressive approach. He ran right into the back of my quarter panel going into turn one. I spun—and that close to the finish, I was bumped out of the Daytona 500. Had it not been for that encounter, I think I would have made it. What an eye-opener! You learn in racing that there are times you do well when you have no right to, and there are other times when things go wrong and that isn't right either. Racing is ironic that way.

Whining or crying about it wouldn't bring the race back. It was pretty depressing luck though. Our time wasn't fast enough, and we ended up not making the 500 that year. That was pretty much the start and finish of my Rookie year. In a nutshell, not making the 500 ended up costing me the Rookie of the Year award. I finished behind Ken Bouchard as a result. That was my first Daytona 500. Three years later I would return to win it. But at this time I would have told you, This race is impossible! You can see how depressing the whole thing had been.

In fact, that first full year with D.K. was a year of gaining experience and eating humble pie. Even at the worst of times, though, I was happy to be Winston Cup racing. I knew I had to pay my dues. D.K. was doing the best he could with the little money he had from Kroger's. Where he had maybe $500,000 for his race team, Earnhardt and Hendrick and Junior Johnson had $3 million to spend, the best of equipment, the best of everything. It can be very easy to start comparing what other guys are able to put into their race cars and teams with what you don't have. If you spend too much time dwelling on it, you might lose sight of your ambitions, abilities, and any other assets you may have and start the "if only I had . . . then I'd be as good as—win this or that."

Instead I've learned that wisdom comes from failure, as well as success. So it's important to roll with the punches but learn from them as well. Winston Cup racing can be a very short life. You've got to be able to take the good with the bad. And be careful not to get hung up on the bad.

We finished eighteenth at Atlanta, twenty-fifth at Rockingham, and then went to Darlington where I had to perform in Darlington's rookie test. Darlington is one of the hardest tracks to run, and this would be the last year when they would hold their test for rookies. Darrell Waltrip and a few of the other interested Winston Cup veterans would watch the rookies go around the track to see what kind of groove they were in.

D.K. wisely advised me, "It doesn't matter how fast you go. All that matters is that you don't hit anything." He made it clear that it wasn't a very good idea to crash the car on the rookie test. I was confident during the test, and we ended up running twenty-second in the race.

Your rookie year is pretty important. It is your time to gain the respect of your fellow drivers and of the racing industry in general. DALE EARNHARDT CHEVROLET helped us gain the kind of recognition we wanted. Automatically, we earned a certain amount of respectability as a direct result of our association with Dale. Those associated with racing knew that Dale very carefully would choose who he would back. Having Kenny Schrader as my friend and talking me up the way he did helped immensely too.

At the same time it is also essential to earn that respect on the track. NASCAR is very diligent in its efforts to make sure the rookies understand how important it is not to drive overly aggressively, not to be a menace. As a young and ambitious driver, I listened; however I was still green enough to think it wasn't necessary to be lectured to like a schoolboy.

NASCAR held a rookie meeting before every race. Dick Beaty, who was basically in charge of the races for NASCAR, and some of the Winston Cup drivers would remind us of practical things on which we should remember to focus. I remember Darrell Waltrip gave us some very good advice, telling us about the tracks, reminding us what to be concerned about, not to take anything for granted so nothing would jump up and bite us. It was before the Darlington race that Darrell was very adamant in his advice that we be sure to "Race the track. You don't need to race everybody, just the track." It was sage advice. Too bad I was too young to really hear what he had to say. Today I would listen. Back then I felt like I could "whup" up on everybody with no real repercussions.

But I was brash then. I had won a lot of short-track races and felt I knew what I was doing. I had run up front when the car was right. At Bristol in April I ran really well, ran with the leaders. This was not a good year as far as tires go. Hoosier tires came in to challenge Goodyear, and they made the tires too thin. I blew out the right front tire, crashed, and finished twenty-sixth.

I tended to wreck because our equipment wasn't as good as what it might have been. I felt I had to drive harder than other drivers with better equipment to overcome the distinct disadvantage. Sometimes the wrecks were my fault. Often they weren't. When you're in the back of the pack, you tend to get caught up in wrecks caused by other guys driving harder than they should or taking risks they shouldn't be taking.

In my first race at Talladega in May I was in a wreck. At Charlotte I was in a wreck. We then wrecked at Dover, and just two races later at Pocono in mid-June, I was involved in a crash on the opening lap in which Bobby Allison almost was killed.

D.K., in an effort to get me to see how advantageous it was to finish a race, started making me work at the shop to fix the cars. Like Marc Reno used to do, D.K. figured if I had to repair them after I wrecked them, I might think twice about taking unnecessary chances when I was running in the back of the pack.

I wasn't finishing a lot of races. At Michigan in late June we finished the race fifteenth, my best run up to that time. It was a decent finish for a rookie. If you finish anywhere in the top twenty, that's an achievement. Considering the equipment we had and everything else that went with the D.K. package, it was a respectable finish. In fact, had we finished in the top ten, we would have felt like we had won the race.

It was fortunate for me that I had Kenny Schrader to talk to about what I was going through. Before Kenny drove for Rick Hendrick, a full-blown operation, he had driven for Junie Donlavey, who had a program a lot like D.K.'s. Junie didn't have a lot of money, didn't have a lot going on, so Kenny knew exactly where I was coming from. At the same time Kenny would tell me how unbelievable the Hendrick operation was. Hendrick had started only a couple of years earlier, but he had unbelievable resources, deep, deep pockets.

D.K. ran as best he could, and the one advantage to that was that D.K. didn't put extraordinary pressure on me to run with the leaders. I could learn at my own pace, though there were races when I tried to go faster than I should have with the cars I was driving.

I finished twenty-ninth at Watkins Glen, thirty-third at Michigan, running as best I could, happy even just to be making the race each week. I hadn't forgotten how hard Marc Reno and I had worked just to get into races. I knew how lucky I was, getting the opportunity to run each week.

We finished fifteenth at Bristol, a moral victory, then finished pretty far back at Darlington and Richmond. Whining and excusing aside, it is extremely hard to run with the leaders when your race team has very little money.

D.K., in fact, ran right at the edge of solvency. He sometimes had to juggle to make it from one week to the next. It must have taken a major effort for him to stay afloat. You can only imagine he did it out of his deep love for racing. When it's that tight financially, a lot of sacrifices are made along the way. Many of those sacrifices have nothing to do with newer or better parts for the car.

Back in January D.K. had promised to pay Marc Reno for Marc's car and two engines, but come August he had not yet gotten paid. In anger and frustration, Marc quit. That money represented everything Marc had invested in racing, and he was scared stiff that D.K. wasn't going to pay him. Marc had been happy to make sacrifices for me, but he hadn't bargained on doing it for D.K. Like all of us, Marc was suffering financially, and he decided he had no choice but to leave the race team and reopen his body shop. Marc was surprised and pleased when soon after he quit, D.K. paid him in full. Marc never did hold anything against D.K. He knew how hard it was to race without money. It was unfortunate that Marc had to quit the team in order to get his money.

After Marc left, Bob Johnson came to work for us as

crew chief, and he helped us finish eleventh at Martinsville. But every time we had a good week, it was followed by a couple of disastrous weeks. Looking back on it, I can see that I was part of the problem.

I finished twenty-sixth at North Wilkesboro in October even though I was driving the wheels off the car. During the race Harry Gant came along and passed me, going on and spinning the tires sideways. I thought, In five laps, I'm going to pass him back. I couldn't believe it when after another thirty laps, here came Harry again, and he put another lap on me. I thought to myself, How did he do that?

The next week Harry and I were talking. I said, "Man, Harry, how did you do that?" He said, "You know, boy, one of these days you're going to be able to do that, but what you've got to realize is that you are only out there racing the leader. You shouldn't be out there racing everybody else. You're wasting your time and energy concentrating on every position. You need to stop doing that. If you're jacking around, racing somebody for fifteenth, the leader will be getting farther away. What you need to do is set your sights on the leader."

He added, "If you remember that, sooner or later you'll be a good Winston Cup driver." That was some incredibly shrewd advice. It's one of those treasures I pass on to today's rookies.

Essentially what he was trying to tell me was that I needed to be more patient, that if your car is really better, you'll go from thirteenth to twelfth without having to race door handle to door handle to get there.

Harry said, "Ernie, it's a 500-lap race. You really have to concentrate on running 500 laps, not 250." It has been invaluable and unforgettable advice that has stayed with me to this day.

The rest of the season left me finishing between fifteenth and twenty-sixth. I finished 59 points behind Kenny Bouchard for 1988 Rookie of the Year. Perhaps if I had made the first Daytona race I would have beaten him. Then again, I also might have won it if I hadn't crashed so often.

10

Nineteen eighty-nine started about the same way 1988 finished. We went to Daytona and had motor trouble the whole time we were down there. The car ran sluggishly until the Richmond race, where I finished ninth, my first top-ten finish for D.K. It was my second time to finish in the top ten. (I had finished eighth at Charlotte in the Marc Reno car that Dale Earnhardt sponsored.) That one had come easy. This one had been hard. It had taken a while. This time, I savored the moment and appreciated the achievement.

After a couple of subpar runs, we went to North Wilkesboro, where we were actually a top-five car. I'd run up front, eventually head for the pits, and drop down ten spots every time I had to pit. Then I'd maneuver back to the front. I finished the race in tenth. Once again people expressed their amazement we were running that well. The next few races we weren't able to pull off those same victories.

Hurricane Hugo struck the Carolinas with devastating force a few days before the Martinsville race. I was living in a mobile home on Sapp Road in Charlotte with my first wife and son. I'm not going to say very much about her because the outcome of our relationship hurts me to this day. I will say we were both very young, and I'm not really sure what compelled us to get married in the first place. She was a nurse's aide, and I felt like a local hero, getting written about in the paper a lot. Very quickly she discovered that because I was really just getting started in Winston Cup racing, my work schedule was seven days a week until midnight working on the cars and going to the races on weekends. Anyone in the business can tell you racing can put a strain on even the best marriage. You have to have a patient and understanding wife. It would not be long before I would find out that the racing life was too much for our relationship.

But at the same time, as Hurricane Hugo was leveling trees all around us, we were still together. Late afternoon of the storm, she took our boy and left for higher ground. I wanted to stay put. I was supposed to leave for the racetrack early the next morning. I didn't get much sleep, but I felt that someone needed to stay and keep an eye on our property. Those storms can create incredible damage.

Martinsville was two hours away. When I got up to leave around 5 A.M., downed trees were blocking my driveway. There was disaster everywhere. It wasn't as bad as on the coast or in Charleston, South Carolina, where the hurricane hit full force. When I got up, trees were still flying. I didn't know whether our mobile home was going to get up and fly away too. I had to find out if qualifying was still on at Martinsville. With the winds and debris all around, I wasn't all that surprised to find that my telephone lines were gone. I decided to go over to my parents' house to call from there. I wanted to check on them anyway. After cutting up a few fallen trees, I managed to get out. When I managed to get through to somebody who could give me the scoop on qualifying, I was told, "We're checking in right now." I hung up the phone with a renewed sense of urgency and determination to make qualifying despite the obvious setbacks.

My brother-in-law, who was a truck driver, D.K., and I were the only ones from our race team to make it to Martinsville. The term skeleton crew took on a whole new meaning. The three of us worked to get the car through tech inspection. We practiced, set our own shocks and springs, set the car up the way we thought best, and were elated when we qualified thirteenth.

After actually making it to qualifying and then having to do double duty as driver and crew member, I was feeling pretty good about the general momentum of things. I had an idea about how I wanted the next day's setup. Bob Johnson, the crew chief, had his own ideas. Looking back, it's easy to see how quickly our discussions escalated into an argument. He was just trying to do his job. I was trying to go with my instincts. As I said, he had his own ideas and I had mine. Unfortunately, we were not on the "same page" and didn't slow down long enough to figure out how to get there.

As I recall, we ended up using the setup I wanted to see. Happily, we finished sixth in that race. We had a lot of witnesses to our success, not only on the track, but in the garage as well. Other crews and drivers saw our rag-tag crew hustling up to make it on the track. They noticed and let us know they really respected our efforts and the character it took to try under the trying conditions we were thrown into.

Based on the coverage we got from the press, they

noticed too. I was delighted when they asked me for an interview. It was a moment of success that was made better by the sharing of it.

That sixth-place finish at Martinsville was the highlight of our second season. It's hard to be consistent when the equipment breaks or if the pit stops aren't always positive or if you have an emotional cloud hanging over your head. Still, we finished the '89 season with an eleventh-place finish at Atlanta, not bad for a race marred by the death of Grant Adcox.

In '89 I ended up making 35 percent of $150,000, which wasn't bad. In fact, for the first time I was making a living. And I wouldn't have to get a real job, as Kenny Schrader had counseled. I was feeling okay about things, but I would have felt better had D.K. found a solid sponsor for 1990. At Atlanta D.K. had told me he hadn't found a sponsor, but he kept saying, "I'll be able to get a sponsor," and I had no reason to doubt him. If there is one trait of mine that I am very proud of it's loyalty to those who have been good to me, shown me kindness, treated me with respect. I will treat you the same way. D.K. had shown me all of those things, and I felt a huge debt of gratitude toward him and wanted to stay with him as long as I could.

Not finding a sponsor was not helping either one of us. D.K. might have felt okay about that. I don't know. Though I felt this loyalty toward him, I was pulled by the unsettling notion that my career could be in that kind of limbo if I stayed with him. Maybe in the scheme of things, D.K. was doing what he did best—giving people a boost up and seeing if they could take it and keep going. Again I couldn't say for sure. As far as my immediate future, I felt it would have been foolish to have waited much longer than the first week of 1990 to find out whether or not he could secure a sponsor.

When D.K. called me in early January 1990 to tell me the situation hadn't gotten any better, I became really concerned. I had no idea whether another race team would even hire me. For a couple of months I didn't know whether or not my driving career in Winston Cup was over.

I really didn't want to leave D.K. I loved him, but I eventually had to come to terms with the fact that he just didn't have a deal. By mid-January I had talked to car owner Junie Donlavey a couple of times and told him I'd consider driving for him if he could get a sponsor.

One day around that time I was at Marc Reno's when Kenny Schrader came over to visit. "You doing anything tomorrow?" he asked me. "Nope." "Okay, how about riding with me to St. Louis to drive my truck home?" Kenny knew I was the sort of person who'd accompany a friend at the spur of the moment. I gladly went along.

It was at Kenny's shop in St. Louis that Junie called me. Junie knew Schrader. Kenny had driven for him and told me he was a great guy. Junie asked if I was still available to drive. He said he had lined up a big-time sponsor called True Cure, an automotive product. Junie said he had a contract, but that the representative from True Cure hadn't signed it, and he wanted to make sure I was going to be available. I told him I would be. Junie said if I drove for him I would get a salary as well as a percentage. I was thrilled to know that I would be racing, that I wouldn't have to take odd jobs on the side to pay the bills.

Kenny and I returned to the Carolinas a couple of days

later, and I met with Junie and the head of True Cure. While I hadn't met many sponsors previously, the True Cure representative didn't inspire me with confidence. I just didn't have a very good feeling about things. Unfortunately, at that time, I knew it was my only option.

Meanwhile, the executive from True Cure kept saying he was going to send the money tomorrow. It was always tomorrow. But True Cure didn't pay Junie a penny.

We went to Riverside, and the True Cure representative continued to assure Junie all was well. We went to Daytona. We painted the car with True Cure on it. Still Junie didn't see any money. Junie finally set a deadline. He told True Cure: you need to come up with the money you promised by a certain date, or I'm taking all the decals off the car. The deadline came and went and Junie never got any money. True to his word Junie did what he said he'd do; he took off the decals. Facing a season with no sponsor was devastating to Junie and me. This situation was no better than what I had with D.K. It was a real strain and put Junie in a very tough spot. Junie made a last-minute one-race deal with Bulls Eye to be our sponsor for the Daytona 500 in 1990. Their car hadn't made the race, and we didn't have a sponsor, so Junie structured a deal with them.

We ran thirteenth, a pretty good run for us considering the turmoil of the last thirty days. Dale Earnhardt led that race but had a tire go down on the white-flag lap, allowing derrike Cope to win the Daytona 500. No one expected Derrike to win that day, but it's always hard to predict the outcome of a Winston Cup race. I was an acquaintance of Derrike's. On the West Coast I had helped build a few of his cars when I was working with Ivan Baldwin.

After Daytona, the True Cure executive told Junie he was going to send the money "next week." We went to Richmond. Once again the undependable executive never sent any money. It was Junie's home track and I wanted to do well, and I was running twelfth when the clutch started slipping and our day was over.

At Rockingham we couldn't get the car to turn. Junie and I were trying to loosen it up, but nothing seemed to work. I kept trying to describe what the car felt like, saying, "Junie, it pushes." In practice I spun coming off turn four, and Junie, a cool old guy, said, "Well, I think you got it loosened up now." We laughed. He was, and is, a great person to drive for. I crashed during the race and finished poorly. I was disappointed for Junie, but in truth we just couldn't seem to make the proper adjustments that were essential to get good performance from the car. It's hard to explain but it just never felt "right."

After the Rockingham race I got a call from Larry McClure, co-owner of the Morgan-McClure racing team out of Abingdon, Virginia. Abingdon is a small town just north of the North Carolina border. Larry co-owned the number 4 car sponsored by Kodak. Morgan-McClure was a relatively new team. Larry had hired drivers Mark Martin, Rick Wilson, and then Phil Parsons, who had just started driving for them. But three races into the '90 season Larry decided that his team wasn't making headway, that Phil's style of driving wasn't what he was looking for to fill out his team. Larry had higher expectations than Phil was able to deliver at that time. Phil had had some eye surgery, and everyone was saying he couldn't drive because of his eyesight. I think it's fairer to say that Larry ended up letting Phil go after only three races because he wanted a driver whose style was more like Rick Wilson's. Rick had left at the end of the previous season to go to another race team.

I had become friends with Tony Glover, Larry McClure's crew chief, while I was driving for D.K. and Junie. Tony and I both came from a similar background. His father, Gene Glover, had been the 1979 Late Model racing champion. We both had been around cars all our lives, and we both wanted the same thing: to become successful in Winston Cup. Glover had worked for Petty Engineering, but when his grandmother became ill he decided he wanted to return to east Tennessee to take care of her. He asked Larry for a job in 1984 and has been there ever since.

Near the end of the '89 season Tony and I happened to be sitting around talking about what we loved best—racing. I told Tony I would very much like to drive for his race team. I said, "Glove, if you get me a ride in the 4 car, I'll make you sandwiches for life."

Tony did help me get that ride, but it had nothing to do with my making him sandwiches. It was about business—driving fast, hopefully faster than anyone else on that racetrack.

Larry and Tony both told me later that they had been interested in me even before he hired Phil. But as fate would have it, at the time when Larry was choosing between Phil and me, Phil had won a race at Talladega. Kodak decided to go with Phil because he had received some media attention. As for his driving style, Phil was laid back. He was the kind of driver who waited for an opening and then made his move. He didn't like to force the action. His philosophy was to stay out of trouble and finish the race. I'm not exactly clear on why, but when Phil got behind the wheel of the Kodak car, he had trouble doing that. He went to Daytona, didn't run very well, and wrecked, the first car out of the race. At Richmond he wrecked once in practice and once in the race. At Rockingham Phil finished fifteenth, and by then Larry was very unhappy. He decided the chemistry between him and Phil was wrong for the race team. He felt he had a better race team than what was being demonstrated on the racetrack.

A shrewd and complicated businessman, Larry McClure may carefully consider some things, but can surprise you occasionally with his snap decisions. That interesting combination has helped him become as successful as he has. He's not afraid to say he's not happy with something and then promptly fix it—not tomorrow or the next week, but now.

Larry McClure is also a very gutsy man. Still, the idea of telling Kodak that he no longer believed Phil was best for his race team after only three races could not have been easy for him, especially after Kodak had made a large investment in Phil Parsons souvenirs, such as shirts, jackets, posters, and mugs. According to Larry, when he told Kodak he wanted to change drivers, they said, "If that's what you want to do, do it." He was relieved and very appreciative that a sponsor would trust him and support him as fully as it did.

In 1989 the Morgan-McClure team had been on the brink of success with Rick Wilson, a very aggressive driver. They had finished second in the Firecracker 400 at Daytona, fourth at Martinsville, and at the time Rick announced he was leaving the team, they were eighth in the points standings. Tony and Rick had become very close. Tony had spent a lot of time helping Rick curb his aggressive tendencies and stay calm out on the racetrack, and they had worked well together. When Rick left, there was a void. It was a difficult spot for easygoing Phil Parsons. Both Larry and Glove wanted the old chemistry back or something close to it.

There was no denying forever that Larry preferred someone with a more aggressive approach. He got together with Glove, engine builder Runt Pittman, and his brothers, and decided the person who might fit their bill was me. I couldn't have been happier with their timing.

Larry called me at home and wanted to know if I'd drive up to his shop in southern Virginia and meet with them. When I met with Larry, he said his race team was going to Atlanta to test and I was invited to go with them. We entertained the idea of my driving the car in a couple of races to see how things worked out. If I did all right, I'd have the job. Junie Donlavey still didn't have a sponsor. He understood this was a good opportunity for me and encouraged me to take it. I was elated. My dad had to pick up some parts in Atlanta, so I showed up to test in my dad's van.

Tony Glover is the type of crew chief who likes to build rapport quickly, and he really knows how to roll out the welcome mat. Dan Donnelly worked on the Morgan-McClure race team and had a side business making T-shirts and hats. Tony had Dan make up a dozen black hats that said, "Go get 'em, Ern" on the front. When I arrived, he passed them out to me and the rest of the team. Tony really knows how to make a guy feel at home.

The weather in Atlanta was rain and more rain, as Atlanta often is. It would rain and then quit. I couldn't have been more anxious to get out on the track. This was the first car I would drive in Winston Cup that was well funded.

On the third day, the sun finally came out. Water seeped out of the racetrack in four or five spots at each corner. I wanted so badly to crawl into that car that I rode a tractor in turn one, blowing air on the track to dry it off. It dried enough so that there were only streaks of water coming down the racetrack. I kept nudging Glove to let me go out there. I had been waiting for this moment for three days!

At this time Geoff Bodine was driving the number 11 car for Junior Johnson. Bodine went out, ran a few laps, and returned to the pit. His time was 31.50.

Glover said, "Just go out and warm up." I did, and the car felt great. It was a treat for me, really. I said, "Glover, it doesn't feel that bad." He said, "Try to run me a couple laps." On the very first lap I ran a 31.10, just blistered that track. Glove was standing on top of the truck and saw how deep I was running in the corners. I could hear his excitement on the radio as he talked with Larry.

Glove told me to come in for a plug check. He said, "Come in, we'll look everything over." And then it started to sprinkle again, and the rest of the day was canceled. But Larry and Glove had seen enough. Glove told me later, "I was glad it rained, because I was afraid you might kill yourself trying to get that ride."

When Glove told me my time, I told him, "I can go faster than that."

Larry McClure told me exactly how he wanted me to run at Atlanta: "Ernie, I want you to drive the wheels off this car.

That's why we're hiring you. If you wreck it, we'll fix it." After all the years of working to buy parts and spending my time fixing my car if I wrecked it, this was an incredible luxury. For the first time I could drive a car with nothing to hold me back.

We had a short practice session on Saturday before the race. It didn't last more than thirty minutes, but we were running very fast. At the time the tracks didn't have monitors to report everyone's lap times like they do now, so if you weren't timing a particular car, someone might be fast and you wouldn't necessarily know it. Tony Glover told his wife, "Ernie Irvan is going to take them tomorrow like Sherman took Georgia." She was surprised to hear that because Tony rarely boasts before a race. He knows that overconfidence can jump up and bite you. She told Tony, "I'm surprised to hear you bragging that way about a driver I've never even heard of."

Because it had rained, we didn't get to run qualifying times, and I had to start thirtieth because that's where the car was in the points standings. Larry told me, "Run as hard as you can." I did what he said, playing catch-up in a race that ran under green the whole way. Had there been a couple of cautions earlier in the race, we might have won it.

I got up to third, and a caution came out with only a few laps to go, and everybody pitted. It was a dogfight to the end, and we finished third. That was a great run for us. Dale Earnhardt won, Morgan Shepherd was second, and my buddy Schrader finished fourth, right behind me.

The run that day gave me great confidence. I had never been in a well-funded car. Nobody really knew whether I could run up front or not. I felt my performance that day let those who were watching know that if I had the right equipment, I could get the job done.

It was great for Larry McClure as well. Larry doesn't show a whole lot of emotion. Still, he was pretty pumped up. After I finished third, Larry looked shrewd and was credited for having the courage to make a tough decision. We were all satisfied. Larry McClure signed me up for three years.

We got pretty cocky, and that's not something you need to be when you're heading to a tough racetrack like Darlington. Our whole team was that way. It just seemed contagious. We thought we could conquer the world, and when we qualified third, our confidence grew. We were pumped up. We all believed without a doubt that we had a legitimate shot at winning any race.

We drove to Darlington to test and really ran well, way faster than anyone else testing. When we went out to qualify, we were a thrilling third.

Early in the race I went from fourth to second and was trying to pass Geoff Bodine for the lead—after all, my car owner had told me, "Drive the wheels off the car," and so I went for the lead, got side by side with Bodine, and as I was coming down the straightaway, I spun coming off turn four and came down the racetrack backward. I managed to control the car, didn't hit anything, and went on. I didn't lose a lap. Tony Glover later paid me a compliment that meant a lot to me: "That day I knew you were a race driver, because while you were spinning, you were driving that car."

During that spin the left front tire went flat, and when the car dropped down we broke an oil line. We didn't know it when it happened, and so I went back out on the track for another ten to fifteen laps when smoke began to appear. We pitted and went behind the wall, and we lost about ten laps before we could fix it. Larry, crew chief Tony Glover, and I still felt we could come back and win the race. We were all relatively new to the game.

Our outsized confidence told us we could win, but looking back, we weren't being very realistic or smart. Why not come back from ten laps down? We had finished third at Atlanta. We had qualified third for this race. Larry's exact words to me were, "You go out there and make these laps up. We can do it."

I am sure Larry had no idea the kind of effect that would have on a young, up-and-coming hotshot who tended to get carried away. I went back out, and I was having a good ole time. Though I was ten laps down after two hundred laps, I had no intention of being a backmarker. In my mind, I was the hard-charging new kid who was going to show 'em.

Glove says sending me back out there was the worst mistake he ever made in racing. But hindsight is almost always 20/20. There was another caution, and we started at the front of the inside line of cars. Ken Schrader was leading the race, and so I was starting next to him. Glove wanted me to go to the back of the line, but Larry said, "Nah, we have a good car. Let's put him up front and try to get some TV time."

From ten laps down I yelled to Kenny that I intended to run hard, but I doubt he heard me over the roar of the engines. Well, Schrader acted like Schrader, and raced me like it was for the Daytona 500. If you know Darlington, you know it's not safe to run side by side. That's when accidents happen.

We ran door handle to door handle for three laps and during that last lap Glove was screaming at me to back off, warning me, "Something is going to happen." I was coming off turn four, trying to get by him, and I lost it and spun, and Schrader lost it, and man, there was a hellish pileup. There were wrecked cars everywhere. A whole damn load of them. We wiped out about half the field! It was in that wreck that Neil Bonnett suffered severe head injuries and was taken to the hospital pretty messed up.

I came in, and they were working on the car, and it was junk. I didn't yet know what Neil's injuries were. I was still considering how nice it was to have my team owner think that I could make up ten laps in a NASCAR race. As a race team, we were doing exactly what we wanted, racing hard to make up the laps and win the race.

After the wreck, Larry McClure came over and I said to him, "You told me to drive the wheels off of it," and we laughed. Larry was really enjoying himself. It was the first time Larry had a winning combination. It was plain to see he was *very* happy.

At the same time a lot of other people were upset—drivers, owners, and reporters who complained that I was driving over my head, but I didn't pay any attention to any of it. Sterling was in the wreck, and he was mad. Dale Earnhardt was very upset. Neil Bonnett and he were tight. We never really talked about it, but I could feel what he was thinking: if you hadn't been so reckless, Neil wouldn't have gotten hurt.

We made a really bad mistake. We shouldn't have done it, but we were immature. The race team wasn't used to running well and having a fast car. Like many owners, Larry

McClure was anxious for success. His team had never won a race. Larry pushed me. If he had pulled the reins back, I'd have driven more calmly. But it didn't take much, then, to push me to exploring the edges. Larry and his crew hired me because they saw how hungry I was for victory, and I liked them for the same reason. Plain and simple, we became too ambitious and aggressive after finishing third at Atlanta and qualifying third at Darlington. We knew we were a really fast car in the race. When Larry asked for more speed, I was happy to give it to him; what we got was a huge pileup that ended up with drivers being injured.

I got the blame, but I had been doing exactly what I was instructed—what we thought best at the time. Looking back, I believe some of the criticism may have come from the fact I was from California, that I wasn't from the Carolinas. You like to think something like that doesn't matter, and perhaps they don't think it really matters. But it was difficult for me to believe it when I kept hearing, "You're from California, and we don't care how you did it in California. We care about what you do here." A lot of times it doesn't matter if you're black or white, but there can be automatic prejudice if you're black. It doesn't matter, but it does matter. Nobody will say that, but it's the reality.

The McClures also were outsiders. They were from Virginia. That's not as bad as being from New York like the Bodines, but it's still not the Carolinas, and the McClures were known as nonconformists. They didn't fit in very well with the usual Winston Cup crowd either.

Looking back, that was not the way we needed to be racing. Had we been more experienced, we would have looked at it and said, "We're ten laps down. Let's not worry about it. We're pretty much done. Let's just bide our time, pass when we can," but that's easy to say now. It's real easy to play Monday morning quarterback.

In 1990 Larry McClure, Tony Glover, and I went on to have some great runs. After Darlington, we went to Bristol, Larry's home track. Abingdon, Virginia, home of the Morgan-McClure race shop, is only five or six miles across the border from Bristol, which is in Tennessee. Going to Bristol, I was facing a lot of personal and professional criticism for causing the pileup at Darlington. I had to suck it up, do my job, and keep my mind on business. We went out during qualifying, and we sat on the pole. It was my first pole in just my second qualifying effort in the 4 car. I hoped it was the best way to answer my critics. Winning that pole was extraordinary, something you shoot for your whole life, and when you finally accomplish it, it's awesome. Everyone was elated.

We have two races when we go to the racetrack. We run to get the pole, and we run to win the race. There is a lot of company in trying to get the pole. You always shoot for the pole because if you shoot for twentieth, you might miss the race. If you shoot for the pole and end up twentieth, you get to run in the race.

A pole is financially rewarding because you then qualify for the Busch Clash, a special race for pole sitters. That's also good for your sponsor. It's a great race to be able to run in. It's also bragging rights that you beat everybody, that your car was the fastest that day for those two laps. Winning the pole that day meant the Morgan-McClure race team had gone from struggling and not running very well to being a competitive force in a very short period of time.

At Bristol they dropped the flag to start the race, and I took the lead in our Kodak-yellow Oldsmobile. I led the first sixteen laps, when a caution came out. On the restart, leading the race, I came out of turn two and I spun out, which can happen at Bristol. I wasn't hit. The car just spun. At Bristol, you can spin out at any time. In fact, I spun coming out of turn two in three different races and each time hit the inside wall. And at that time I only drove at one speed, flat out.

Right after my incident Dale Earnhardt spun coming off turn two, and later Bill Elliott did the same thing, except they really tore their cars up. I was lucky, but Glove was still mad at me that day for running too hard. He hardly could talk to me. When I went back out, I was three laps down, and I made up the three laps. This time, though, I was a lot more patient when I tried to pass. I didn't want to repeat what I had done at Darlington. Once I was back on the lead lap, I asked him, "How's that?" He said, "Hell, I'm still mad at you. You should be a lap ahead of everyone."

We got back to the fourth spot, and we were on our way to having a really good run when right near the end Dale Jarrett ran us over and we wrecked.

I had a couple of good runs at North Wilkesboro and Martinsville, and then in May at Talladega, I finished fourth. I was gaining consistency. I began finishing in the top ten in race after race.

What really stands out about the 1990 season was that in the first eight or nine races I never qualified worse than seventh and usually started in the first two rows. At the same time, despite my newfound success, other drivers were trying to talk to me, sitting down with me and giving me advice about what they saw as my overaggressive driving style. Darrell Waltrip was one. He said, "Ernie, you have to take your time. You don't have to conquer each racetrack the first time you're here. Just be patient." Richard Petty also sat me down and told me essentially the same thing.

We went to Sonoma for the Sears Point race, and at that time we really didn't have a very good road race car. At best, it was decent. On the way to the race, I told Glove, "I want you to know, I'm not very good at Sonoma. I'm just a fair road racer, and I don't really like the track." I told him I knew we had a great qualifying streak going, but I wanted to warn him about my lack of road racing experience. Glove reassured me. He said, "If we can somehow get through Sonoma and Pocono, we'll get back on our qualifying streak." And lo and behold, we went to Sonoma, and we sat on the outside front row after we qualified second, and at Pocono I sat on the pole by three-tenths of a second! I was learning about not being too cocky.

I led the first two laps, but the car didn't run very well, and then at Michigan we had a good run all day long. We had been top five all day. I was running third to Bill Elliott and Earnhardt with fifteen laps to go when Elliott blew an engine, leaving the race to Earnhardt and me. We had a fair battle, and late in the race I was even leading, and that was the closest I had ever come to winning a Winston Cup race. I held Earnhardt off for seven laps, but with six laps to go, Earnhardt bumped me a couple of times, got me loose, and coming to get the white flag Earnhardt got by me by rubbing against me in such a way that he slowed me down without having to slow down himself. He passed me, and I couldn't catch him. Sometimes, you can gain a lot of wisdom from your failures.

Earnhardt is a driver who doesn't give you an inch. He has a groove around that racetrack that is second to none. He is tough to pass, no matter how his car is handling. This is particularly true at Michigan. I might have won had I gotten into him and sent him into the wall, but at that time in my career, if I had done that, the other drivers, owners, and NASCAR would have hung me from a tree.

I finished second, and Tony and the crew were tickled to death. Tony was jumping up and down. I came into the pit, and Tony was getting ready to congratulate me, and I told him, "That will never happen again." Tony said, "What do you mean, Ernie?" I said, "He'll never use that move on me again." Earnhardt had really taught me something, and it had cost me a win. But I was learning.

The next race was at Daytona on July Fourth, and at the start of the race I was caught up in a huge wreck initiated by Greg Sacks, who was stuck in the middle of a three-abreast situation with Richard Petty on one side and Derrike Cope on the other. The inspectors had caught something Sacks had in his car, and it slowed him down quite a bit, and to make up for it, he was driving very hard. From behind him I could see his car bouncing like a pinball from the inside to the outside, and I knew that soon there was going to be a wreck. What a mess! It took them a half hour to clear the wreckage. After that, no one was left to challenge Earnhardt.

As an indication of our progress as a race team, Larry McClure changed from driving Oldsmobiles to running a Chevrolet. Larry owned a Chevrolet dealership, and for several years had begged Chevrolet to sponsor his team, but until his team was more successful Chevrolet wasn't interested. When we started finishing well in '90, Chevrolet had a change of heart. Their executives said, "Okay, we'll pay you to race one of our cars, but you have to make the switch by the Bristol race."

We went to Bristol on August 25 and raced under the lights. It was our first race in a Chevrolet. We started off running well, until the car started to get loose. I called in and pitted on a caution, and Tony and his team worked on the car, and when I went back out it was better, though still not great. By this time Glove and I had become like brothers. We were very close. I was moaning and complaining about the car, even though at about halfway through the race we were in second place. The caution came out, we pitted, and after I went back out, I continued to talk about how bad the car was handling.

Tony said, "Ernie, look out front of the windshield and tell me what you see." I said, "Dale Earnhardt. That's it." Tony said, "What do you see behind you?" I said, "A bunch of cars." Glove said, "Things can't be that bad. You're second. That means there's only one car better than you." He was right about that. I had to laugh. And I stopped complaining.

When Earnhardt had a tire go down, we took the lead. There was a caution with about fifty laps to go, and Rusty and I took on four new tires. To the end we raced as hard as two competitors could race. He was under me, on top of me, but he didn't get by as I led for the remainder of the fifty laps to the checkered flag.

It was a good race for Rusty and me. He is a great competitor, and he raced cleanly. Thankfully, I ended up with my first win with Glove and Larry and the rest of the Morgan-McClure team.

Glove was particularly proud that we had won. He told me that from the time he got into Winston Cup racing and got to be a crew chief, all he wanted out of life was to win one race. For many frustrating years, he felt he might never get that opportunity. Then when we started running together, he saw that everything seemed to be clicking and that he could be hopeful things could go really well. He vowed that when that opportunity came, he was going to make sure he didn't mess it up. That night, Glove did everything right. I can remember back then people made fun of Glove for yakking a lot on the radio during the race, acting like a football coach sometimes. For the last seventy-five laps of that race Glove kept telling me, "All right, Ernie, no one can beat you. Just don't screw up." Every lap he said the same thing: "Just don't screw up. Keep on doing what you're doing. Don't worry about Rusty. He can't beat you. Nobody can beat you. You're the man." He was my personal cheerleader throughout the end of that race. When we won it, no one was happier than Glove. His wife and dad were there, and he was just brimming with the enjoyment of our victory—as were I and Larry McClure, who had waited as long as Glove had to earn his first win as a car owner. I was as happy for them as I was for myself.

It's sweet to win at Bristol. If I were to win at Bristol today it would mean a hundred times more than what it meant that day because I've been to Bristol many times since winning that day, and I haven't won since. I've finished second, but other than that, it's been tough to even finish a race there. It is tough to stay out of trouble with so little room to pass.

After the victory it appeared that some people were beginning to appreciate that I wasn't going to be one of those drivers who would show some sparks and talent and then fade away. Believe me, drivers who have won a race are given a whole lot more respect in the garage than those who never have won. A lot of people in the garage area started looking at me differently.

Chevrolet was very high on me and so was Kodak. The demand for their souvenirs increased, and Kodak was beginning to see results from their participation in Winston Cup racing. My hard-driving style was making me, Kodak, and the Morgan-McClure racing team a lot of fans. We were loving it.

I won a total of six races with Morgan-McClure. In retrospect, we'd probably have gone even further if we could have curbed our excesses. Larry continued to be a gas pedal instead of a brake—again his style matched mine perfectly then. We should have tried to gain our successes in a more politically correct way. We all felt we had a lot to prove. It was important to Larry that people see he made the right decision by getting me to drive his race car. The part about Larry I truly appreciated was his sense of loyalty. No matter what I did, right or wrong, he was there behind me.

I started out the 1991 season in great emotional upheaval. I was living a nightmare out of a bad country and western song. I'm not really sure why I married my first wife in the first place, but it wasn't long before we started not getting along. I'm sure that my being away from home, in the shop, or at the track had a lot to do with it. Her seeking solace in the arms of another man also played a part.

We were married for three years, and we had two kids. When she filed for divorce in 1990, she was seeking to take the house and what seemed like about everything else I owned. She also was seeking child support. I moved out and was living in a studio apartment.

My general approach, when my life is in turmoil, is to focus on something else to take my mind off what is bothering me. Naturally, I focused on racing. As far as my future in the sport was concerned, as of the 1991 season, I was feeling a lot of confidence.

The race team was supposed to leave Abingdon midday for the drive to Daytona to start the season. Back then we drove to most of the races. I called the shop and asked Glove what time they were going to leave. He said, "We should be finished by noon." I was driving my Camaro, a black convertible, from Concord down to Daytona. I said, "Meet me in Concord, and you can ride with me."

The motor came in late to the shop, and so Glove didn't reach Concord until about ten at night. He got in my car, and we stayed up all night long, riding and talking.

I was extremely angry with my wife and felt very alone, except for my great friendships with the members of my race team. I was particularly close to Tony Glover and his family. We had a wonderful rapport and a warm friendship. Generally I'm not one to spill my guts very quickly, particularly if I'm having a rough time, but I was close enough to Glove to share some of the hurt and pain caused by my failed marriage. We were such good friends that we could talk about most everything.

Glove and I both grew up wanting to work on race cars, loving racing, and both of us had a great deal of ambition. When we tested at Daytona, we felt we got everything out of our car that we needed to. Prior to qualifying we had everything going for us. We believed that not only could we win the 1991 Daytona 500, but that we also had a shot at the Winston Cup championship.

I qualified second to Davey Allison, the driver for Robert Yates, one of the best engine builders in the business. Davey beat us by one hundredth of a second. We were in the hunt. We knew we were fast.

We were entered in the Busch Clash, which you qualify to run if you or your car won a pole the year before. It's an invitational, doesn't count for the points, but you can win some good purse money and give your sponsor important exposure.

The race is run in two segments. At the end of the first segment the field is inverted, the last-place car starting first, the first-place car starting last. We finished second in the first segment, behind Earnhardt. I was beating on his bumper, tap, tap, tapping the back of his car as we crossed the finish line.

For the second segment, I went to the back of the pack. In the first turn I dropped my left wheel off the apron and broke a rotor button, which retarded the timing of the car and caused us major problems. We didn't know what had happened until the race was over. As a result we didn't finish well and went home disappointed.

Next came the two qualifying races for the Daytona

500. I started on the pole for the second 125-mile qualifier after running at over 195 miles an hour, and finished second to Earnhardt in the race. Earnhardt led most of the way, but I was drafting with him most of the time. Right at the end I tried to pass him, and he blocked me, and I ran into the back of him. Earnhardt being Earnhardt didn't wreck, and I was on his bumper as we crossed the finish line.

After the qualifying race Richard Childress came up to Larry McClure and told him Dale was mad. Childress said, "Ernie was beating on Dale's car." Larry said, "That wasn't the way I looked at it. Looked to me like Dale was blocking him." Larry added, "Dale's a big boy. He'll get over it." Larry was impressed that under our pressure Dale was bitching about how we were treating him.

We didn't want Dale mad at us. A mad Dale is a dangerous Dale. So after Larry and I discussed it, I went over and talked to Dale to try to smooth things over. After the Darlington wreck, it was best that no one hold a grudge against us.

We had been fast all week, but people didn't know it. The press wasn't paying much attention to us. Earnhardt and Davey Allison were the favorites, and you could never count out Junior Johnson's two cars.

Tony, Larry, and I went to dinner the Saturday night before the big race. We were discussing our strategy, rehashing everything. I looked at Tony and said, "Glove, if it comes down to me and Earnhardt, I'll win it." Glove said, "What do you have up your sleeve?" I said, "I have something planned for him. I will pass him, and he'll never know what hit him." Glove asked me, "How are you going to do that?" I said, "Just watch. You'll find out."

We started the race, and we were really fast. All day we worked to get the car to handle and be able to run wide open. We led some, and we ran second or third a lot. Midrace there were a lot of green-flag stops, which shuffled everyone around. In the end, it came down to fuel mileage.

That year NASCAR instituted odd-even pitting rules, which really made things difficult and confusing.

Larry had wanted me to find a drafting partner, but it seemed that no one wanted to work with us. During our first pit stop under the green, one of my tires went up on the yellow blend line, which you're not supposed to do, and NASCAR penalized me, made me come back in, and we lost two-thirds of a lap on the field.

It didn't matter. I had the fastest car that day. In fact, Glove was amazed to discover that I could run faster by myself than the cars with drafting partners. I had so much car I could come up on any car being drafted by another and get by him by myself. By the end of the race I had made up the two-thirds of a lap.

With about twenty-five laps to go, I had gotten back to midpack when a caution flag came out. We returned to the track in fifth place, and with ten laps to go we had to make a final pit stop to get some gas.

Tim Morgan, Larry's business partner, was the gas man. He was screaming that Glove had held me too long in the pits. We came back out, and we were now second only to Darrell Waltrip. Darrell wasn't running that fast, but he had gotten excellent fuel mileage. Without another caution Darrell stood to win the race. But Richard Petty crashed on the backstretch, a yellow came out, and the field closed up.

Glove needed to know if the crew was sure we had

enough gas to finish. The answer came back, "Yeah, we have enough gas." We were able to stay out on the track when everyone else came in to pit for gas. We had pitted in a different sequence than a lot of other cars. It was a crucial moment when Darrell finally had to pit; we were then able to take the lead.

With twelve laps to go, Dale Earnhardt passed me and took over the lead. Then, behind us, a big crash took out Darrell and a bunch of other cars. Earnhardt had lost the Daytona 500 the year before when he blew a tire on the last lap. This was the one race he had never won, but in 1991 we were figuring this would be his year.

With ten laps to go, we had a restart. Earnhardt was leading, and I was running second. He jumped me on the start, had a lead of ten to fifteen car lengths, and I thought, "It's going to be hell getting by him now."

Davey Allison and his 28 car came flying up behind us. I figured I could get past Dale because I had done it before, but I wasn't sure about Allison. He had qualified on the pole. Still, during the race we had been faster.

As I was drafting behind Dale going down the back straightaway, I had it all planned. Back then everybody passed going down the backstraight. I decided to do it differently. With three laps to go, I got a run on Earnhardt coming off turn four and had such a slingshot on him at the exit of the tri-oval that I was really coming fast. It was as though Earnhardt didn't know I was there. I don't know whether I caught him asleep or whether he just couldn't keep up with me, but after I dove down inside, I blew right by him going into turn one.

Davey, who was running third, drove to the outside of

Earnhardt. In my rearview mirror I could see Davey and Earnhardt side by side behind me, Earnhardt low and Davey high, as I stretched away from them. Then suddenly, Earnhardt got loose, spun, and banged into Davey, who spun off turn two, got tangled, and they both wrecked. The caution came out with two laps to go.

I couldn't believe my luck. As soon as the yellow flag began to wave, I knew the race would not get restarted before time ran out, that I had won the Daytona 500. The realization that I would win the Daytona 500 was incredible. It was one of the most exhilarating moments of my life. I also marveled at the fact I was even participating in the race. Not too many years before I had gone to Daytona for the very first time to work as a mechanic. I was over-whelmed.

After the caution flag came out and victory seemed to be mine, I looked in the direction of my pit and could see Glove and the guys jumping up and down, celebrating. Because the race was under caution I was crawling around the track. Then I heard the engine cough. Going into turn two, I said into the radio, "Glove, I'm out of gas." I couldn't believe it.

We seriously questioned whether I had enough fuel to go the five miles to the finish line. I was running out, and at the slow speed under the yellow I was having a fuel pickup problem on the high banking. It's easier to pick up gas going at fast speeds. Time elapsed very slowly. It felt like an eternity. Glove told me, "Ernie, weave the car back and forth." I dropped down and ran on the apron.

While everyone else was in a panic, believe it or not, I felt calm behind the wheel. I didn't worry for a second. If the car ran out of gas, it ran out. There was nothing I could do to change that. I knew then that my worrying wouldn't help.

We made it, though. The engine sputtered as my car crossed the finish line. It was a tremendous win for me and the Kodak race team. At the same time, because I was so inexperienced, I failed to appreciate the moment as much as I could have. When I won I did what I had been doing all my life—focusing my attention on what was next, figuring out what loftier goal I could attain. I'm sorry I didn't spend more time reveling in my victory, but I had only raced at Daytona five or so times. I hadn't lost it twenty times like a lot of the drivers. Dale Earnhardt, for one, had lost it twenty times before he finally won. He's a driver who can tell you what winning the Daytona 500 really means. I didn't have enough experience to appreciate my monumental achievement. Derrike Cope had won it in 1990 when Dale blew a tire on the final lap. That was a defining moment for Cope that continues to help him secure rides. I realize now that winning the Daytona 500 is very important for your career.

My mom and dad had driven to Daytona Beach for a trade show, and they attended the race. That night we had a big party at a local restaurant, and spent the night. I drove back home the next day in my Camaro with the Daytona 500 trophy propped up proudly in the backseat.

When I arrived home in Charlotte, I went back to my studio apartment. I turned on my answering machine, and I was amazed at the number of calls from friends and from TV and radio reporters wanting interviews. We didn't have a lot of PR help back then, and so I called a couple of the stations myself and went down for interviews. From there I stopped over at Sandwich Construction, the local Charlotte hangout for the Winston Cup set, and Chris, the owner, and everyone else who was there when I walked in proceeded to have a darn good celebration party. We drank Dom Perignon and had a good time.

It was late when I went back to my studio apartment, folded the bed from the wall, and went to sleep.

11

The Tuesday after winning the 1991 Daytona race, I appeared on *Late Night with David Letterman*. Going on Letterman was an interesting experience. I had never been on national TV before. I was surprised to find that they have a producer interview you for a long time so Dave's writers can find things about you that might be funny. It surprised me how hard Letterman and his staff have to work. It all looks so impromptu on TV.

I spent some time in New York, did a couple of other shows, and during the week I received a lot of gifts and telegrams and letters of congratulations. Despite all this attention, it still hadn't registered that I had actually won the Daytona 500. It was only when I arrived in the garage area before the Richmond race that I realized the full impact of winning that race. In the racing business the garage area is where all your friends are. What meant the most to me was going back to the racetrack and having a lot of guys come over and say, "Congratulations." That's when it all sunk in.

At the same time, even though I had won the Daytona 500 and everyone now knew we had a fast car and I could win races, the jury was still out on whether our race team could do it week in and week out.

We could. After two top-ten finishes, we went to Bristol, where I finished second to Rusty Wallace. We ran a very competitive race.

Back then, the rules called for odd-even pitting. Although Rusty and some of the other cars were able to change tires, we weren't allowed to come in and change them. Then with about eighty laps to go, it rained, and the race was halted. Rusty was behind me, but with his new tires he knew he was going to be tough to beat.

While we were sitting in the drivers' lounge, Rusty and I were bantering back and forth. Rusty and I always have had a good relationship. We both come from short-track racing, and he used to live in Concord near my house, and every once in a while we'd fly to races together. He kept telling me, "If you don't get tires, you're going to be junk." I told him, "No, Rusty, I'm not gonna be junk. Even with my old tires, I'm going to run the wheels off you."

The rain stopped, and we got back to racing again, and still we couldn't pit, because if we did, we'd have to go to the back. Rusty, on his new tires, ran right to the front. It took all my driving skill to keep up with him.

With fifty laps to go, I was on Rusty's bumper, running just as hard as I could run on those old tires. It was certainly the hardest I have ever run at Bristol.

With one lap to go, Rusty was in front of me, and I was running just as fast as he was, and I was working on him real hard, trying to pass him. It's really tough to pass at Bristol, and Rusty was closing the door on me big time. Going into turn three, he drove down low to cut me off. This time I drove right into the back of him. I didn't want to clean him out. If I had wanted to, I was positioned in such a way that I could have. If I had hit his left corner or right corner, I'd have wiped him right out. But I knew if I hit him from behind in the middle of his bumper, he might drift up the track, giving me a chance to get by him.

I tapped him, and he began to drift up the track never losing control of the car. I got under him coming off turn four, and as we came across the line, he was fifteen feet in front of me. After racing hard for fifty laps, he beat me out, getting me back for beating him the year before.

In May 1991 we traveled to Talladega. I won the pole, and I was sure I would win the race. I was hard-charging Ernie Irvan, and if you were in my way, well, you'd better move it or lose it. Looking back on it, I think I drove overly aggressively, and that was a lot of my problem. It wasn't long before our race team was becoming marked. My yellow Kodak number 4 Chevrolet was making everyone nervous. I was ten points behind the points leader, and that was making people take notice too.

Talladega is a big, big racetrack, and the cars reach speeds approaching two hundred miles. Recklessness is not encouraged or admired. Being relatively new to Winston Cup racing, if someone would have told me at the time that I was driving recklessly, I would have figured he was saying that only because he couldn't catch me. I had won a lot of short-track races during my career moving other cars out of the way, and I had won a lot of other races with my daring. I saw no reason to change my style for the Winston Cup circuit.

Midway through the Talladega race, a caution came out, and we pitted. Everyone knew we had a fast car, so the other race teams were going to try to work against us as much as possible. On a restart, Kyle Petty went to the inside, and Mark Martin went to the outside, which left me in the middle. The middle is not an enviable spot. Once all the other drivers line up behind the other two cars, you find yourself all alone and getting passed by just about everyone else in no time flat. That's exactly what was happening to me. An experienced driver will be patient until he is able to wedge himself back into line.

As we were driving through the tri-oval, Glove said to me, "Ernie, just be patient. You have a good enough car. Even if you go all the way to the rear, you can come back to the front. Be patient. Be patient." But at that time in my career, I wasn't apt to listen to talk about patience.

As we were coming off turn two, I decided to squeeze between Kyle and Mark. There was just about a car width between them, and I was sure I could get between them and make a clean pass. You can do that all day long if you do it successfully. The problem is that if there's a wreck, there's hell to pay.

I made my move. Mark was to my left, and just as I stuck my nose in between him and Kyle, they unexpectedly closed down on me. Neither of them had enough room because the nose of my car was already between theirs. I had only advanced about a foot when Mark hit me. I doubt he even saw me. When Mark hit me, I slid up the track and hit Kyle, and Kyle hit the wall hard and broke his leg. Mark went up in the air over my car. I wrecked, and behind us was a junk pile. Davey Allison crashed, along with Dale Jarrett, Terry Labonte, Chad Little, Greg Sacks, and a couple of others.

No one said anything to me after the race, but there was a lot of sniping from other drivers and owners in the newspapers. Davey was upset, but I didn't pay much attention because Davey often was vocal. Everyone pointed fingers at me, even though at the time I felt that Mark had squeezed me too hard, causing me to hit Kyle and start the wreck.

In all honesty, I can say after many more years of experience that I should not have been in that place. I should have used better judgment and not gone there. After the race, I received a lot of strong criticism and bad publicity. It seemed to become personal.

We went to Charlotte the next Saturday for a Busch race, and during the driver introductions, the fans booed me something terrible. This was my hometown, and I was really hurt by it. I got into my car with tears in my eyes.

All of a sudden I was Ernie the Villain, something I had trouble with, considering how well we were running week after week.

I was consistently in the top five. At Sonoma I finished fourth to Davey, who was leading when Ricky Rudd hit him from behind, spun him out, passed him, and won the race. Ricky is very adept at public relations and is very shrewd about not emphasizing that he is a hard charger. When Ricky hit Davey on the last lap, to me that's racing, something that Richard Petty and David Pearson used to do to each other every once in a while, and what Earnhardt does all the time. But at the end of the race NASCAR decided that Ricky was wrong to have done that and awarded the race to Davey. When NASCAR ruled that Ricky had driven recklessly and penalized him by taking away his win, Ricky was furious.

We continued our top-ten consistency and almost won at Pocono. This time it was Dale Earnhardt's generosity that stood in our way. I led, and even though we could see that rain was coming, we had to pit because we were running out of fuel. We went in, and Rusty stayed out, and after he ran out of fuel, Dale pushed him to victory. Dale was four laps back. He couldn't win, and he was helping a friend. That's why Dale did it.

During that race I was involved in an incident at the front of the pack. Hut Stricklin was leading, and I might have gotten him loose—Hut said I hit him, but I didn't—and then Hut and the King became involved, and Richard spun and wrecked—it was a no-no to get tangled up with the King—and the cars began to pile up. My car didn't have a scratch, but I landed the blame for the pileup.

A lot of people are quick to place blame on somebody, because they figure it has to be somebody's fault. It was my turn to assume the blame. After the crash at Talladega, things seemed to be getting out of hand. It seemed as though even if I were nowhere near a wreck, everyone was saying I was at fault. If I was anywhere on the track when cars started spinning, it seemed I was sure to be at the root of it.

Some of the drivers were really upset with me that day. Darrell Waltrip didn't mention me by name, but he told the press, "Isn't there anyone out there who knows how to drive a race car? No one will give anyone a break out there."

The press followed suit when they pushed the envelope by asking, "Is Ernie Irvan safe?" "Does he do things that aren't the NASCAR way?" This was not the kind of media attention I had hoped for. I expected something a little fairer. I wasn't angry so much as disappointed and frustrated.

Since I started driving the 4 car I had been called into the NASCAR truck quite a few times by Dick Beaty, who would lecture me about my driving style. He was getting a lot of pressure from the other car owners to slow me down. They wanted me to straighten up. Felix Sabates, for one, would crucify me any chance he got. Dick didn't tell me how to drive. He was more subtle, saying, "Ernie, you have to be more cautious when you're passing."

The criticism was costing us the driving championship. It's tough to drive hard when you're worried that you're going to hear about it if anything happens within ten car laps of you. You have to pay attention to the other drivers and to NASCAR.

I knew I had to do something. The criticism was bothering me something awful. I may have had a reputation for racing with reckless abandon, but I wasn't made of stone.

The next race was at Talladega in late July. A few days before the race I was summoned by Richard Petty. Richard had talked to me before, and again he wanted to tell me how important it was to be patient out on the racetrack. He said, "Ernie, you have to earn respect. You can't take respect. You have to earn it." After I spoke with Richard, I was really feeling the negative pressure coming from my peers. Boy, everyone except my Morgan-McClure teammates, who still wanted someone to stand on the gas, was sending heat my way. It wasn't long before I started questioning myself. I was trying to be objective when I asked myself if there was any truth to the charges that these crashes might be my fault. Darrell's snide remarks really made me reevaluate things. I thought it was important that I consider things truthfully and as objectively as possible. If you're only involved in accidents one time out of nine, you can't say that's a trend. If you're involved in an accident seven out of nine times, then you really have to question how you're driving. I felt pressure from everywhere.

After the Daytona 500, I had really enjoyed the camaraderie in the garage. The idea that other drivers considered me to be a menace on the track was difficult. In the papers they were calling me "Swervin' Irvan," which really made me (and still makes me) furious. I knew it was all coming to a head, and I had better do something. I was on the verge of earning my stripes in Winston Cup racing. But I was also on the verge of getting shut out of it. NASCAR was mad at me, and it's their ballpark and ball game, and if you don't play by their rules, you don't get to play. I knew which way I wanted to end up on that seesaw.

I went to see Dick Beaty, who was in charge of NASCAR's officiating. I said, "Dick, somehow I have to change how I'm treated, and the things I do in the Winston Cup garage." Dick said, "I don't know what you need to do, but I think you're right."

After our meeting I decided that I better apologize to the other drivers if I wanted to continue in Winston Cup racing. The next day I went to Dick with my idea: "What if I came to the drivers' meeting and told everybody how I feel?" Dick said, "What do you mean?" I said, "I need to turn over a new leaf. I need to start doing things differently. I can't go to each person's truck to apologize, so maybe I can do it at the drivers' meeting." Dick said, "Nobody has ever done that before. Let me check with Bill France and Les

Richter and make sure they're all right with it." He checked and said I could do it.

Apologizing was very hard for me, and at the same time very simple. I knew if I didn't do it, my career was in jeopardy. I stood at the drivers' meeting and expressed how sorry I was about the way I had acted on the track. I admitted to being overly aggressive. I said I needed to straighten up, needed to respect my fellow competitors more. I said, "Hopefully, everybody'll give me another chance. I'll prove to you that I'll do what I'm saying, and I apologize."

After I walked out of the meeting, I felt better. Some drivers seemed surprised, if not shocked, that I had done that. Others were skeptical. "Yeah, right. Uh-huh."

Darrell Waltrip called me over to his truck. He said, "That took a lot of guts. The thing is, if you say that but if you don't follow through, that will be pretty stupid." I respected Darrell Waltrip. Darrell's a neat human being and he's been a lot of help. Richard Petty also spoke up. The King stopped me and repeated what Darrell had said: "Okay, boy. You said that in the drivers' meeting, but if you don't put it out on the racetrack, then it ain't nothing."

I told myself that words were cheap, that I'd better live up to what I was saying. I was determined to go out and show people that I meant what I said.

My public apology turned out to be a turning point in my career. The press appreciated it, and so did the competitors. My career definitely took off when I changed my whole outlook. And looking back, more than anyone else I have Dick Beaty to thank for that. He must have called me into his trailer seven times, chewing me out but talking to me like a human being. He would say, "Man, you're one of the drivers who can make a big mark in Winston Cup driving. If you'd just slow down to go faster." I owe Dick Beaty a lot for his invaluable advice, encouragement, and patience.

During the Talladega race, I was involved in a ten-car wreck when Buddy Baker hit me, but this time everyone went out of their way to say I had nothing to do with it. I was just riding along, and Buddy ran into me. I couldn't and wouldn't complain. The rest of the year I stayed out of trouble.

For the next race we went to Watkins Glen, a road course. With twenty-two laps to go, I passed Kenny Schrader to take the lead and never again was headed. Mark Martin and I had a good battle at the end. He could have wrecked me if he had wanted to, and you might think the natural move would have been for Mark to clean me out, but if you remember, this wasn't too long after Ricky Rudd had run into the back of Davey's car at the end of the Sears Point race and was penalized for it. With Sears Point in the back of everyone's mind, Mark stayed behind me and finished second.

The other thing that happened that day was that J.D. McDuffie was killed early in the race. I didn't really know J.D., had just spoken to him a couple of times, but he had been in the sport a long time. Out of respect, when I got to the Winner's Circle I dedicated the race to him. It was the right thing to do.

Two weeks later I finished second to Harry Gant at Darlington. Funny thing about Darlington: I've never won there, but I've finished second several times. Harry then won the next three races in a row at Wilkesboro, Dover, and Martinsville. Harry is just a neat person. I still wonder why he isn't in racing. Harry's a lot of fun, and if you need someone to throw a roof on a house, well, he can do that too.

It is very possible we would have won the racing championship that year if it hadn't been for two unfortunate incidents. Very early on in the Wilkesboro race I rubbed up against another car, knocking the fender into the tire. Before I could come in and pit, the tire blew and I hit the fence in turn one and crumpled the car. I finished dead last.

The crusher came in the next race at Charlotte when Kerry Teague spun in front of me. I tried to get by him on the bottom side, but he collected me, and we wrecked. If it hadn't been for those two races, I would have been in the points hunt. We went to Phoenix and finished sixth behind Davey, and in the final 1991 race at Atlanta, I finished second behind Mark Martin, a great way to end the season.

Considering what I went through in my personal life in '91, it was a very rewarding season. I finished fifth in the points standings and our race team earned more than a million dollars in purses, a terrific achievement for a race team in only its first full year of competition. By year's end, we were feeling really pumped up. Nineteen ninety-one had been some roller coaster, starting with the win at Daytona, sinking to the depths at Talladega, where everyone considered me a menace, and then I came back the next week at Pocono, winning the race, but more importantly, with everyone talking optimistically about the "new" Ernie Irvan.

As a race team, we were really pumped. We felt that if we could only eliminate the DNFs ("did not finishes"), we would have a shot at winning the racing championship in '92.

12

During the years 1991 and 1992 I experienced a period of extreme highs and lows in my personal life. After bitterly splitting up with my first wife, I met my present wife Kim in late March 1991 at a barbecue. She had grown up in Concord and had taken a sales job right out of college in Savannah, Georgia, for an import-export company. Her girlfriend Gena, who knows everybody, introduced us.

Kim and I got off to a slow start. At the barbecue I spent most of my time talking to one of her girlfriends. I think Kim may have been a little suspicious of me. It was Kim I really was interested in, and I sent her flowers at work. Shortly after that, we started dating. It wasn't long before I asked her to marry me, and we set a date for November 21, 1992. Pete Vargas, who had helped me work on my cars in California and was a close boyhood friend, was my best man, and Tony Glover and Larry McClure were part of the wedding party. It was a great way to start the Christmas season.

The low point emotionally occurred when Kim, who has uncanny instincts where human nature is concerned, strongly suggested that I consider testing the parentage of my younger son. After hearing stories about my ex-wife, Kim had a hunch that it would be wise to test for matching DNA. She had heard rumors that my ex-wife had been seriously involved with someone else. Eventually Kim helped me to see how important it was that we find out who, in fact, was the boy's true father. I had raised the two boys as my own, and part of me didn't want to know, but Kim helped me see how unfair it was to everyone involved not to know the truth. When the results came back, I was crushed to learn I was not the father of the younger boy. Kim then encouraged me to have the older boy tested, and it turned out that I wasn't the father of that boy either. I was devastated. The feelings of betrayal, anger, and shame were more than I imagined they could be.

My older boy was five, the younger one just an infant. The whole situation placed me in a terrible position. I felt it would be best for the boys to be raised by their natural father, and so, not wanting to make the situation any harder than it was, I stepped aside and let my ex-wife and the father of the children raise the boys. It was clear now, he was their father, not me. You couldn't have written a soap opera during that period of my life that was as confusing and complex as what I was going through. It was not an easy time in my life. I spent a lot of time feeling confused and hurt. Consequently, I was a bundle of emotions all through the 1992 season. Sometimes it was hard for me to stay focused. Too often I had difficulty concealing my irritation and controlling my anger. In '92 things just did not go as smoothly as Larry McClure, Tony Glover, and I had hoped they would.

I was glad to get back to racing, and it was rewarding to

return to Daytona in February 1992 as the reigning champion. Everyone automatically assumed that I was going to be the car to beat. Unfortunately, you can never live off what you did the year before. When we tested, we were fairly competitive, but not as strong as in '91. It was another year, another car, a different set of specifications. That's the way it is in Winston Cup racing. Nothing is ever the same from year to year, and if you don't adapt as well as the next team, you find yourself running behind.

We started Daytona Speed Weeks by finishing second in the Busch Clash, a race for pole winners from the year before. The way it works, you race ten laps, and when the race is over, the order of finish is inverted. Geoff Bodine, who finished far back in the opening segment, beat me in the twenty-lap finale.

After the '92 Busch Clash, I ran in the 125-lap qualifier and finished third behind Dale Earnhardt and Mark Martin. Any time you run in a 125 and you have Earnhardt in there, it's tough to win. Dale beat Mark when he tapped his quarter panel and sent him spinning off the fourth turn. Mark was furious. If there is one race in which Dale dominates, it's the 125-lap qualifier. It seems like he wins it every year. However, if there's one race he hadn't been able to win, it was the Daytona 500 itself.

I started the 1992 Daytona 500 in seventh place, and after a rain shower, the green came out to start the ninetieth lap. Bill Elliott and Sterling Marlin, who were driving for Junior Johnson, were leading the race. As we came down the straightaway, I made a move to catch Elliott. I was on the inside and Bill was on the outside when Sterling, who was right behind Elliott, snuck in between us going down the straightaway. I had about an inch on either side. And at 200 miles an hour, that's not a lot of room.

As it turned out, it was not enough room. The three of us bumped each other around, and Sterling wrecked, Elliott wrecked, and I got hit in the rear quarter panel, not enough to put me out of the race but bad enough to take my car out of the running. What really angered me was that after the race Elliott blamed me for the whole thing. Just when I thought we were all through with that, he said, "Every time something happens, Ernie is right in the middle of it." I didn't see it that way at all. I was spitting mad, but it was done and over with. After the race Junior Johnson was very vocal about his opinions on the matter, though, and it was Sterling's name that came up most often then. Junior was hot that both his cars were knocked out of the race. At the end of the season Junior let Sterling go. Davey Allison won the race, establishing the 28 Texaco car as the team to beat in '92.

Bill Elliott then came back and won the next four races. He won at Rockingham, Richmond, Atlanta, and Darlington. Tim Brewer was his crew chief, and they were a very good team. Not only that, but Elliott's Ford had a cambered rear end that no one else had, and it took a few races for the other teams to figure out what he was doing. Once everyone else figured it out, that was the end of Bill's dominating streak.

In 1992 I drove in the Busch series races on Saturday as well as in Winston Cup. At Atlanta I started the race about fifteenth, and five laps into the race, a car spun in front of me in turn one. Trying to avoid it, I got sideways, and was just about finished spinning when another car came along,

never even lifting, and smashed into me going wide open. I
suffered a broken collarbone. The injury, coupled with my
emotional state and too many engine failures, really hurt our
season in '92.

The next morning I got out of the hospital, went to the
track, and started the Winston Cup race. I would be in a lot
of pain for about a month, but I started the race because I
didn't want our team to lose any points. We knew the shoulder was going to be all right in another week or so, and there
was no race scheduled the Sunday after Atlanta. After I ran
one lap, Bobby Labonte took over for me, and though we
didn't finish very well, we did get some points on the day. By
the time Darlington rolled around, I was fine. I just wish my
car had been in as good shape as I was. The car didn't work
well, and again we finished in the back of the pack.

Alan Kulwicki won the Bristol race, ending Elliott's
string. Once again, at Bristol I crashed. It seems that almost
every time I race there I crash. Bristol is a great racetrack, a
lot of fun to race on. You have to be on your toes the entire
race. It's just hard to stay out of trouble the whole day. You
can be running in turn one, and there may be a wreck in turn
three, and heck, it's only seven seconds before you get there.
Even though you have a spotter, seven seconds gives you
very little time to react. You try to slow down, but the cars
are spinning every which way in front of you, and it
becomes a matter of luck whether or not you get swept up
in it. Davey and Elliott were involved in separate crashes.

After one mediocre finish, we were even worse at
Martinsville when we broke an axle. It seemed we just
weren't getting the job done and were having trouble all the
time. We just weren't hitting it like we needed to.

Tony Glover and I were getting along great, but we were having trouble pinpointing the problems. A lot of times things happen, and you just can't pick out what really is the problem. It's like going to the doctor with a cough and an achy feeling, and the doctor says to you, "You're sick, but I'll be darned if I know what you have."

Our first good performance in '92 came at Talladega. I was the pole sitter, though I can't say that I took very much credit for that. When the car is right at Talladega, the driver doesn't have to do very much except steer a little. At Talladega you could take just about anybody and in a matter of a few days have him qualify the car on the pole if the car is good enough. It's not very tough to do. When the race gets started, of course, it's a different deal.

Davey Allison's Ford won the race, and I finished fifth in a Chevrolet. Davey was really coming on for the first time, making himself felt out there on the track. It helped that Davey was driving a Ford because the Fords really had it all over the Chevys then. Even Dale Earnhardt, Mr. Goodwrench Chevy parts, didn't have what the Fords had. Toward the end of the race Davey ran off and hid while Bill Elliott's Ford blocked Dale from getting by him. All the reporters wrote that Elliott was blocking Dale because he was trying to keep a Chevy from winning. The fact of the matter was that Elliott wasn't doing anything more than trying to finish second. He didn't want to finish third, and he was fighting to keep Dale from passing him. It may have looked like he was blocking for Davey, but actually he was blocking to make sure he would finish second. You always read in the papers about these conspiracies out on the track. The truth is, most of the time, they are not conspiracies at all.

■ ■ ■

I believe I might have won the next race, the Coca-Cola 500 at Charlotte, if I hadn't had a carburetor malfunction. To this day I am also convinced that Dale Earnhardt pulled a fast one when it looked as if he didn't go the required speed on pit road.

All day the car I had to beat was Earnhardt's 3 car. Dale was at the top of his sport. You might beat him one week, but he and his crewchief Kirk Shelmerdine made a team that was hard to beat. It seemed that his car handled well every race. They had a great driver and a great crew. They were competitively tough every week.

In the Charlotte race I had to come back from two laps down. Eleven laps into the race my engine was misfiring badly, and when I came in Glover and the boys somehow figured out that the problem was a bad carburetor. They fixed it in no time, and when I went back out there, the car still didn't have all the power it should have, but considering that the bad carburetor had almost cooked the engine completely, I couldn't complain. At least the car was handling really well, which was crucial, and I was able to make up the two laps on the field and go to the front.

I was leading the race, with Kyle Petty behind me and Earnhardt third, when with about fifty laps remaining Kyle and I pitted at the same time. We took four tires and fuel, and so did Petty, whose crew managed to beat ours, and so when we got back out there Kyle was a few car lengths ahead of me. Dale pitted a lap later.

He was three seconds behind us, and he made a pit stop in which he was timed at about the same time as us and Petty. But when Dale came back out, he had the lead by a little over a second and went on to beat me by that one second.

I couldn't figure out how Dale could have been ahead of me if our pit stop was 20 seconds and his pit stop was 20 seconds. One minute I was in front, the next I'm not. Circumstances point to one thing pretty clearly. There was only one way Earnhardt could have made up the time: racing over the 55 speed limit coming in and going out of the pits. Otherwise, where did he gain all the speed? How could he have gained any time on us otherwise? None of us could figure it out.

Felix Sabates, the owner of Kyle's car, complained to NASCAR about Dale's failure to obey the pit road speed limit. Kyle had finished behind me in third, and Sabates wanted Dale disqualified, which would have been fine with me. It would have given me the race. But Sabates didn't get very far in his protest. Glove also saw that Dale had sped down pit road big time, and he complained a little too, but no one listened to us either. It was a race I should have won, but when our protests were denied, we could do nothing about it. Once again, there was no use crying about it.

Two weeks later at Sears Point I drove one of the best races of my career. Tony Glover says it was the best performance he ever saw a race driver make in Winston Cup, because Sears Point is a road race—it's very hard to pass on that track—but after I was black-flagged by the NASCAR officials and made to go to the back of the pack early in the race, I was still able to come back through the entire field and win! I have to say that all these years later I can still bring to mind the thrill of winning that race.

We started on the outside pole, which was odd by itself. The pole sitter, Ricky Rudd, had the option to choose whether he wanted to start on the inside or outside, and for some reason he chose the outside. That left me basically starting on the pole, even though he won it, and him starting second.

We were running in line coming for the green flag. They threw it, and I took off. Well, Ricky never gave it any gas. I think he figured out he was getting beat on that start so he just decided not to take off. That made it look as if I had jumped the start. NASCAR black-flagged me.

When I came back around, Glove said to me, "All right, Ernie, you have to come in for a stop-and-go for jumping the flag." I had never seen that happen before. I'm still puzzled, and it happened a half dozen years ago. I never said a word. At that point you don't have time to argue. You just do as they say. So the next lap I came in straight to the pits, and after they held me, I headed back out, but as I left the pits my transmission got stuck in fourth gear. Caught in gear, I had to ride around slowly until the next caution and come back in again. We jacked the car up and popped the transmission out of gear. When I went back out, I was dead last. Sonoma is only a 72-lap race. It was a quarter of the way over.

Despite our predicament, Glove never gave up hope. He kept telling me, "Ernie, we can win this race." I said, "Glove, you're crazy." I ran a few laps, passed a few cars, ran a few more laps, passed a lot more cars, until all of a sudden we were in fifth place! Turns out, Glove wasn't really that crazy after all.

I came in for our last pit stop, and after going back out,

I ran down the last four cars one at a time, just blew them away. I went from last to first and never put a scratch on that car. We had a great car that day. We didn't win it on pit stops, didn't win it on strategy, didn't outsnooker them. We just outran them. When your car is running is good as that one was, you can do that. It was an amazing victory, one of the most incredible wins of my career. It shows what determination and perseverance can do, both for the driver and for the race team.

Alan Kulwicki won the next race at Pocono, heating up the points race among Alan, Davey, and Bill Elliott. Going into Michigan in mid-June, Davey had a small lead over Elliott who had a fifty-something point lead over Alan. In the race among these three, I was pulling for Davey because it's always fun when a driver wins a championship for the first time. Before the year was out, though, I would cease rooting for Davey.

For the June race at Michigan, Davey had the pole and I qualified sixth. On the second lap, without warning, Davey moved up the track, ran into me, and knocked me into the fence. His explanation was that he had slipped in some oil.

We put the car back together as best we could, and I went back out to finish the race. I didn't know it, but CBS was scanning my conversations so the folks at home could listen in and hear what Tony Glover and I were saying to each other. I said something unkind about Davey, and it went out on the radio. They then went over and interviewed Davey, and over the radio with millions of people listening, including our race team, Davey swore he never touched me.

Davey changed tires during the first pit stop, and my team went over to the Texaco pit area and inspected the right front tire they took off Davey's car. It had my yellow paint all over the tire. Glove called me on the radio and said, "Davey said he never touched you, but his whole right tire is yellow." Imagine that.

The situation was not helped when Davey won the race and my car limped along way in the back.

The next day nine race teams went to Indianapolis to test for the very first time—we tested for Goodyear on Monday and Tuesday. I finally saw Davey where we both tested our tempers. He said, "Man, I never even touched you." I said, "Davey, did you see your right front tire?" He said he hadn't. I said, "It had yellow paint all over it. My yellow paint." He said, "No, it didn't." I said, "Davey, why do you have to lie?" Then I told him, "Davey, sooner or later I will get even." He mouthed off something. I said something. Larry McReynolds, Davey's crew chief, stepped between us and kept things from getting hotter.

At the time it seemed as if Davey was everybody's fair-haired boy, the white knight in contrast to Dale Earnhardt's black knight intimidating image. But anybody can tell you that Davey was no choirboy. He was as tough as nails.

The next race was the Daytona Firecracker 400. Nineteen ninety-two was Richard Petty's last season, the last time he would run at Daytona in a career that began back in 1959, and on the first day of qualifying Richard almost won the pole. Pretty exciting not just for the fans, but for many of us in the industry. Richard is well liked and everyone was sentimental about his last go-round. Right to the end Richard had the pole, until Sterling beat him out. Boy, did everyone give Sterling a hard time on that deal!

Once the race started Richard actually led the first five

laps. Unfortunately for him, the day was hot and his car wasn't handling very well. The heat must have really bothered him that day because after eighty laps he had to get out of the car. It was great to see Richard riding up front, if only for a short period of time. The fans really look up to him, and the racers do for sure. It's hard enough to win one Winston Cup race, let alone two hundred, as he has done.

I had a great-handling car the whole day and beat the pole sitter to the finish line. Everything went the right way. As a driver it's important to maneuver at the proper time, make the right moves. In a restrictor plate race, however, there is just so much maneuvering you can do. Daytona is a lot different from Talladega, where there is a lot more strategy involved. At Talladega, we race side by side for two hundred laps. At Daytona, when it starts getting hot, we don't run side by side very much at all. It's a race where your car has to handle right to win, because as soon as your car starts acting up and you have to lift, you'd be surprised how fast those other cars start zipping past you. I've said it all along: at Daytona if you have a good-handling car and you can keep it wide open, you have a good shot at winning the race. That's what happened that day.

The next race was Pocono, a track that is hard on engines. I had to drop out early with a bad valve. It's just so tough to make the motors last there. When they go, there isn't anything you can do about it.

After we dropped out, I left the track and went to the airport to fly home. The plane had just left the ground when I heard on the radio that Davey and Darrell Waltrip had gotten tangled up. Davey's car had flipped several times. When the medical crew got to Davey, they could see he was badly hurt. Davey underwent surgery for a broken arm, a broken eye socket, and a skull fracture. It was the fourth time that year Davey was hurt in a bad crash. This time he had cut Darrell off. In many ways Davey ran along the same path as I did during that time. He and I both seemed to be trying to straighten things out on the track and off the track in our personal lives without much success. I can't help but wonder if our troubles were coincidental or whether they were the direct result of trouble on the homefront.

At Talladega I was as dominant as I had been in the previous Daytona race. Things didn't look very promising at the start of the race, though. I had a flat tire, and then suffered a penalty for driving too fast down pit road, the same sin we had previously suspected Earnhardt of getting away with. I almost went to the back of the pack. But my Kodak Chevrolet was so smooth, I was able to get back on the lead lap in no time at all.

With eleven laps to go, I hooked up with Ricky Rudd, who was a lap down but willing to help because we were both in Chevrolets. Together, my car in front and Ricky's behind me on my bumper, we went flying by Sterling, who would then come in second.

I came in first, Sterling came in second, and Bobby Hillin, filling in for Davey, who actually started the race in great pain in a cast, finished third. That second place finish to Sterling may have been an unnecessary gift from Hillin. Davey, who ended up spotting for Hillin, advised Bobby to. "Just stick with the 4 car because he'll take you to the front." I never found out for sure the reason he chose not to hook up with me. Instead, he went to the outside as I moved to the inside and that decision, pretty much, secured his third-place finish.

Bobby also made the independent decision to pit earlier than he was advised. Sometimes the drivers do that based on a variety of reasons. That day, Bobby was told to pit when I pitted. Again, I don't know why he didn't. Luckily, everything seemed to be going smoothly for us that week, and not pitting at the same time did not have the same significance it might have had, had we not been running as well.

Our next race was at Watkins Glen, where we would, should, and could have won, but there's not much you can do about scheduling the weather to suit your racing agenda. We had a great car again. When the rains came, washing out the rest of the race, Kyle Petty was in the lead, Morgan Shepherd was second, and we finished third. That was how the race concluded.

An interesting note, I think, about Kyle and about racing is a lot of fans felt that Kyle was going to be a big career winner like Grandpa Lee and his father Richard. Undoubtedly, they are a tough act to follow. Kyle is still hard at work on his career, which he takes very seriously. For Kyle, or any driver for that matter, you have a tougher go of it when you don't start by getting your feet wet as a short-track racer. Kyle began at a relatively young age driving in Winston Cup without having a chance to fine tune his skills on a short track. Like me, I know that's how guys like Rusty Wallace and Jeff Gordon also get started. All of us who started short-track racing had to learn how to run in close quarters with competitors, how to quickly outmaneuver and outfox the other guy. I also believe you can watch every race in the world, but you won't learn how to race just by watching. You only learn by hands-on racing. In short-track racing you have to adapt quickly, learn and master the track and the other drivers because there's no time to make up for any errors. Can you tell how strongly I feel about the experience of short-track racing?

The next week we went back to Michigan, where there was more heartbreak for the Allison family. During practice Clifford Allison, Davey's younger brother, was killed before a Busch race. I didn't know Clifford, but the deep sadness that ran through the entire garage area had a very strong presence. Any time we lose a fellow competitor, it's tough. However, this was Bobby Allison's son, and we all knew Bobby had been through so much in the last couple of years. He had almost died in a crash that would end his career. Then Davey almost died in the terrible crash at Pocono, and now Clifford was dead. It didn't seem right that one family should suffer so much tragedy.

The afternoon Glove arrived at the track, my father went to his room and told him what had happened. I remember they sat and talked a long time about it. Dad was terribly upset, as were we all.

A distraught Davey started the race. I wanted to go over and say something to him, tell him how bad I felt, but he and I weren't that close at the time, so I didn't. Davey drove an entire race for the first time since his crash and finished fifth, an incredible performance considering he was all smashed up and that his brother had just been killed. We finished fourth in front of him. Harry Gant won by conserving fuel and having to stop one less time than the rest of us.

Michigan is one of those tracks where you can do that. He was featherfooting, not running as hard as he could, and he got away with it because there were no cautions to mess up his strategy. One caution at the wrong time, and all of a sudden your fuel savings are thrown out the window. Harry got lucky, though, and was able to carry out his plan.

At Darlington, Davey Allison was kept from winning a million dollars when after almost twenty years of trying, Darrell Waltrip finally won there, with the help of the rain, which came just in time. I finished far back with transmission problems.

At Richmond I was the pole sitter, and I led the race at the beginning. Toward the end of the race the car's performance seemed to deteriorate and I finished eleventh. That is also what I placed at Dover after Rusty went three abreast and clipped me. Normally, Rusty doesn't wreck you much, but he nailed me that day. I was leading the race, and we had a restart. My car was running on the outside, and I was next to Brett Bodine, who was a lap down. Rusty decided to make it three wide, and there was a collision, knocking all three of us from contention. Rusty said Brett should have backed off the gas, and knowing Brett, I'm sure he had something to say about Rusty as well. All in a day's work as they say.

At North Wilkesboro, Davey Allison and I got into it again. Davey was leading. I was a lap down, and I was trying to get my lap back. I was up under him, trying to pass him, and he was blocking me.

We came off turn two, and I hit him, sending him completely sideways, and me sideways as well, and we came back together, hit again, and it cost Davey the race. Robert Yates, the owner of Davey's 28 car, was standing on top of the pit box, and when we collided he forgot he was up there, and he stepped forward and fell to the ground. He was furious with me, as anyone can imagine.

I ended up getting my lap back, and finished sixth, with Davey two laps behind me.

We went to Charlotte in October and finished sixth to Mark Martin, who outran Alan Kulwicki by a couple of seconds to win the Mello Yello 500. Alan had wrecked at Dover, was two hundred points behind Davey and Elliott in the points race, and no one thought him capable of getting back in the hunt for the driving championship. But he did. Alan was an amazing guy. He had high standards and an independent streak you had to respect. A couple years earlier Junior Johnson offered him $1 million to drive for him. When Alan turned it down, I thought he was crazy. Alan knew if he took Junior's million dollars, he would have to do it Junior's way. Alan didn't want that, no matter how much money he was offered. Ninety-nine guys out of a hundred would have taken the money. I certainly would have. Not Alan. No way.

At Rockingham, I had a car that performed really well and finished second to Kyle Petty. Kyle was unbeatable on the track that day. He sat on the pole and led almost every single lap. Try as I might, I never was able to catch him. It was one of the best races I ever saw Kyle run. Rockingham seemed to be the hot track for him for a number of years. In all my years driving Winston Cup, I've only met up with Kyle a couple of times, but I don't know him that well. Socially speaking, I know he sings and plays the guitar. I can't carry a tune.

Meanwhile, that year Kulwicki finished behind Elliott

and Davey at Rockingham. Alan was still in the points chase, but he was fifty points down. I didn't think Kulwicki had a prayer to win it.

The second-to-last race of the 1992 season was at Phoenix. Early in that race Bill Elliott's car started smoking, and he finished way back. I crashed and finished even worse. Davey won the race, which made him the favorite to win the points championship over Alan, who finished fourth. Alan was thirty points behind Davey going into the last race of the season at Atlanta. Elliott was ten points behind Alan.

Most of the people in the garage area were rooting for Davey or Alan, while not many were looking in Bill's direction. Bill had already won a championship. For those of us in the garage area, it's generally pretty fun to see a driver win a championship for the first time. I personally was rooting for Alan because I admired the fact he had done things his own way. I also have a tendency to root for the underdog. No one thought Alan would win it. Even though Alan could seem strange and hard to get to know, he also was very focused, and you could never count him out.

The final race at Atlanta was a real spectacle. Not only did the fans come to see who would win the racing championship, but it was also Richard Petty's last race in a career that began in 1959, the year I was born.

All Davey had to do to win the points championship was to finish fifth, but Davey and I seemed to have magnets for each other, and about three-quarters of the way to the end, I blew out a tire coming off turn four, spun, and collected Davey up in the wreck with me. His fans said I had wrecked him. To his credit Davey never felt that way. He knew I had blown a tire and there was nothing I could have done about that. I had crashed into the wall pretty hard and was taken to the infield care center, and Davey wouldn't leave until he found out that I was all right. We may have a very tough sport, but we are all very sentimental when it comes to each other's well-being. We all do care about one another.

The King went out of contention in a burst of flames when he crashed and his car caught on fire. Rather than quit in the middle, the Petty Engineering crew patched up the car, and Richard got back out there and cruised at half speed until he passed the checkered flag that ended his long and illustrious career. I gave him a lot of credit for sticking it out.

We're going to miss Richard being out there. The sport owes him a great deal. During the years when the car companies were out of racing and no one had much money, the force of Richard's personality kept the sport going. He would stand for hours and sign autographs, pose for pictures, and sit for interviews when there was little else to write about. And that is why Richard will always be the King.

Bill Elliott won the Atlanta race, but because Alan led one more lap than Bill, Alan received a five-point bonus and won the driving championship over Elliott, by ten points. If Elliott had led just one more lap, he would have won it again. I was very happy for Alan. He had worked so hard to prove he was as good as he thought he was. He put his money where his mouth was.

All in all, I don't think we had a bad year. We won three races and finished in the top five only nine times (which showed our lack of consistency). However, Larry McClure and the crew and I ended the year on a friendly note, even though we had had some disappointing engine failures and I was involved in some wrecks. I knew I needed to be a more consistent driver. We also knew we needed to make better pit stops. Larry and I sat down and tried to figure out what we could do to be better in '93. We tried to analyze it by asking the question, "If we could make a perfect team, what could we do?"

We were able to address most of the problems. The one subject that was a particularly uncomfortable topic regarded changes in the crew I thought might help. Unfortunately, some of the crew I thought ought to be reevaluated were part of Larry's family.

Larry was very good to me, but he made it clear that blood was thicker than water, and his obligation to his family came before everything, including our success as a race team. If I felt our jackman wasn't as good as he might be, for example, well, I'd have to live with that. I did.

13

We started the 1993 season the same way we ended the season before: I crashed. Two weeks are spent down at Daytona testing and practicing and running in the Busch Clash and the 125 qualifiers, so you do get some racing in. It is the 500 that everybody's shooting for, though. On race day we started out with a really good-performing car. We made our last pit stop under the green, because we knew the car was quick and efficient, and pitting would not be necessary again. As I went back out, a slower car ran into the back of me and knocked me out of the race. I knew the car was running well, so it was seriously disappointing when I ended up thirty-seventh. That's where I had to start in the points race, and it's very difficult to win after starting out in a hole like that. I couldn't have felt more frustrated after starting out with a good shot at the race and the beginning of a good points standing.

Dale Jarrett beat Dale Earnhardt to win the 1993 Daytona 500. Jarrett was running on the high side and Earnhardt was running down at the bottom, and as they came around for the last couple of laps, Jarrett was able to keep his line in the corners while Earnhardt would slide up the track. As a result Jarrett was able to get by him and win the race. It was hard to believe that Jarrett had a better handling car than Earnhardt. It was harder to believe that Earnhardt had lost the Daytona 500 again. It's the only race that Earnhardt consistently lost, and it was understandably a really sore subject with him. Not having won the Daytona 500 since 1991, I'm beginning to get itchy, and I can really appreciate how he was feeling.

At Rockingham I finished third behind Rusty Wallace and Dale Earnhardt, the two favorites to win the points championship in '93. Rusty is partners with Roger Penske, a smart individual who can take a financially troubled company or an interesting idea and make something out of it. Together Rusty and Roger make for a very tough team. As the driver, Rusty is just about as focused as any team owner would hope for. From time to time Rusty and I catch up on what each other has going on.

In mid-March everybody in the racing industry packed up and went to Atlanta, only to be present in time for a blizzard that dumped more than a foot of snow on the racetrack, forcing the track officials to postpone the race. When the race was finally held, I had the race won, but Morgan Shepherd managed to run the last 105 miles without a pit stop and barely beat me out. It was the fourth win of his career—three of them had been in Atlanta. The Wood Brothers had hit on the setup they needed to run well on that racetrack. At that old Atlanta Speedway, Morgan Shepherd was as good as they get.

Two weeks later, at Bristol, a nightmare occurred that shook the entire sport. It was nighttime, and I was sitting in our motor home at the Bristol track right up in turn two. It was pretty foggy, and we were watching TV. The local newscaster broke in and said there had been a plane crash. He didn't say who or how. But when they said a plane had crashed at the nearby airport, I thought about many of us flying in and out. I shivered involuntarily as I considered that it could be someone on the race team.

The next morning I learned that Alan Kulwicki's plane had crashed and he and three others from the Hooters company had been killed. The news stunned everyone. Alan had worked so hard to get where he was. When he started out he had one car that he towed behind a makeshift trailer. From there, he became Winston Cup champion, a remarkable accomplishment for one so insistent on doing things his way. Loners don't usually end up winners in NASCAR, but Alan was the exception. That he never got to take advantage of all his success was very sad for all of us.

I wish they had canceled the race. That would have been right. There were a lot of tears that day. It didn't seem appropriate to be there, and I know everybody felt the same way. We just wanted to go home and pay our respects. That day there were many of us out there driving with no heart in it.

I remember when the cars lined up for the race, Kulwicki's orange-and-white Hooters car wasn't one of them. The afternoon before the race everyone watched as the AK Racing transporter—with a memorial wreath on the grille—made two laps around the soggy Bristol track and then drove off as we all bowed our heads in silence. It was gone for good. It was tough for everybody.

In that Bristol race I crashed, as I often do there. Bobby

Hillin and Dale Jarrett came together, spun, and that wiped out seven or eight cars, including mine. Rusty won and Dale Earnhardt came in second, which seemed to happen a lot in '93, but there was no spirit of competition that day. Alan was too much in our thoughts.

We were having a terrible year when we arrived in early May at Talladega. I was running fourth, behind Earnhardt, Rusty, and Mark Martin when with two laps to go it began to pour, bringing out the black flag. As the rain fell, we pitted on the front straightaway. Tony Glover, my crew chief, knew we had been lagging in the race for the points championship and was pleased that our performance would improve our standing. He said to me, "It'll be a pretty good day. Just bring her home, and we'll be in good shape. If we finish fourth, we'll change some spots and points."

Glove seemed satisfied, but I was angry. I wanted the race to resume. I was determined to win it. When they finally announced they would restart the race, in effect setting up a two-lap shootout, Glove said to me, "Keep your nose clean and we'll come out of here smelling like a rose." Glove and I had the kind of relationship that made long conversations unnecessary.

I said, "Hey, Glove." He said, "Yeah." I said, "Did you come here to run fourth?" He said, "Nope." I said, "I didn't either. I came to win."

The race was restarted with three laps to go. When we came around for the green flag with two laps left, Rusty and Earnhardt went to block each other. Mark Martin made a move to the outside of Rusty, and Rusty squeezed him into the wall. I came from the top of the racetrack down across Mark Martin and was able to clear both Mark and Rusty, leaving only Earnhardt standing in my way of victory. I continued to the low side, and in the first turn Dale and I banged on each other. Ultimately I was able to muscle past him. I had my foot all the way down on that gas pedal and I had no intention of lifting.

Jimmy Spencer, who drafted behind me, was second when Rusty, running hard to catch me, ran into the back of Spencer's car, then hit the side of Dale Jarrett's car in turn three. Spencer stayed in shape and ran behind me as I went across the finish line. Rusty, in an attempt to keep Earnhardt from passing him, tried to shut the door on Earnhardt, but Dale rammed Rusty and sent his car flipping end over end in a terrible crash. Rusty broke his wrist and messed up his face. Rusty tried to be diplomatic about it and assumed all the blame, but that was just Rusty being the nice guy he is. Sterling was angry because the other guys had tried to wreck him. In my opinion he was lucky to have finished second after all that slamming and banging. I can tell you for sure I felt lucky. I had managed to come out ahead of a lot of drivers for whom I have the greatest respect. It was also fortunate that NASCAR didn't call the race with only three laps to go, which they very well could have done. Because they decided to let us finish, the fans saw a heck of a show, and my standing got a desperately needed boost.

In mid-July we traveled to Loudon, in New Hampshire. It was the first time we ran on that track for a Winston Cup race. I had run one Busch race there and really liked the place. Loudon's a great track, and I seemed to be able to make my way around pretty well there.

When I arrived in the garage area I discovered that

Davey Allison and I were parked right across from each other. The day before the race, I happened on Tony Glover and Davey Allison sitting together talking. Glove and Davey were close friends, and it was uncomfortable for Glove that Davey and I never hit it off. When I came over, Davey and I said hi, and I sat down beside him, and we started talking as though there never had been any tension between us.

Davey and I decided that since we were going to have to race against each other every week, we ought to make an effort to get along better. We didn't say it in so many words, but that was the outcome of our conversation. Davey and I talked about race cars and anything else that came up. We were surprised to find we actually enjoyed each other's company. That night at the Goodyear dinner Davey came over and sat down with me. I can honestly say that at Loudon we really became good friends. The next day before the race we even rode in the same truck together during the drivers' introductions. Although I didn't know it, it would be the last race of Davey's life. I am very grateful that I was given that opportunity to become friends with him and to see him in a different light.

After racing at Loudon, we flew home to North Carolina. Michael Waltrip's pilot invited me to fly with him, and we went up for a spin in the little plane. We soared around, and he showed me the countryside around Mooresville, just north of Charlotte. After we landed, while I was driving home, I heard on the car radio that there had been a helicopter crash at the Talladega track and Davey had gotten hurt. Davey had tried to land his helicopter in an enclosed area and the back rotor had hit the fence, tipping it over on Davey's side. Red Farmer, an old friend of the

Allison family, was riding on the passenger side, but Red hadn't been hurt too badly. Davey, however, suffered severe injuries.

For me the timing of it seemed strange: as I heard the news I felt amazed at the coincidence that I had gotten to know Davey, and then two days later he was in the hospital on life support.

The next day Davey died, and once again, all of NASCAR deeply mourned, as did many of those who tuned into the news that night.

Davey's funeral was held in Hueytown, Alabama, the hometown of the Allisons, and the service was attended by hundreds of distraught mourners. Everyone was somber and sad. The Allison family has been in Winston Cup racing a long, long time, and Bobby and his wife have made a lot of friends over the years. I had always made a habit of not going to funerals. Before this one, I had attended one, my best friend Timmy Williamson's, after he was killed in that terrible crash at Riverside years before. I always intended the first funeral I would go to would be my own—albeit unwillingly. When Timmy died, I knew in my heart I had to go. Interestingly, I felt the same way about Davey. It was hard to believe we wouldn't be seeing that dynamo any-more. Davey always seemed such an important part of the sport. He consistently ran up front and helped to make us all more competitive. It was so difficult to believe that a guy so full of life was being buried that day.

More unbelievable is what the Allison family has been through. The year before Clifford had been killed at Michigan in a crash. Now his older brother was being put to rest in a quiet, tearful service. Bobby and Judy had lost both of their children, and their lives would never be the same again. As often happens, Bobby and Judy split not too long after Davey died. The grief probably was more than their marriage could bear.

From the funeral we went to Pocono for the next race. It was there when I went out onto the racetrack that I was hit with the full realization that Davey wasn't coming back. The 28 car wasn't even there. Robert Yates didn't run his Texaco car in the Pocono race. When I lined up for the start of the race, there was a huge void without Davey. It was very difficult for a lot of us to continue.

Late in the evening before the day of the Pocono race, around eleven, I got a phone call from Lee Morse, who worked for the Ford Motor Company. Lee said, "Ernie, what are the chances of your getting out of your contract to drive the 28 car?" The question caught me completely off guard. Even after I learned of Davey's death I had never thought about stepping into his now-vacant spot. I said, "I'm pretty happy where I am." Lee argued that making such a move would be a big help to my career. He said the 28 car was the premier Ford team, and my 4 car would never be the premier Chevrolet team because Earnhardt's 3 car was that, if not the Hendrick cars. He said, "You can be the top guy with Ford Motor Company. The 28 car is our premier car. We feel it would be a great opportunity for you." He said, "We need someone who can challenge Dale Earnhardt head to head in a Ford, and you're the person we think can do that. It's tough having to fill Davey's position, but the long and the short of it is, it has to be done and you're the guy the Ford Motor Company wants."

I had no idea I would be getting such a call. Lee didn't talk salary but it was all positive, all about what Ford could do for me. I said, "Let me think about it." I told Lee I had a contract to drive the 4 car another year after this one, and I would have to get out of it. He said, "If we can figure out how to make it work, would you be interested?" I didn't tell him no.

My wife, Kim, and I must have lay awake half the night talking about what I should do. I didn't know much about the 28 team. I knew that Davey had won races, but that was about all I knew. I knew they had a good program, a strong sponsor in Texaco, and the Ford Motor Company seemed to be a fine manufacturer. Lee had told me they'd love me to sit down and talk with them. I asked Kim, "Do you think there'll be something there?"

The next day I talked to Mark Martin about the offer a little bit because we were close and I valued his opinion. I didn't say the opportunity had been offered. I just said, "*If* the opportunity to drive the 28 car became available, what would you think?"

Mark said, "It would be awesome. They've got decent money to back up their program, and they are the number-one Ford team. It would be great for you. If they offer you that, I don't think you can turn that down." He went on to say that with the deal he had driving for Jack Roush, he wouldn't make the move, but reiterated that if they were to offer it to me, it would be the thing to do. It seemed the more I talked about it, the fewer reasons I could find to turn it down.

Still, I thought it was important to find out as much as I could about the race team. I didn't know anything about

Robert Yates, the owner, or the team. Before this, I had no real association with the Robert Yates organization. I remembered that Robert had helped Marc Reno out a number of years earlier by giving him some engine parts, and I had talked to Robert a couple of times at the racetrack. When I was checking around, I could find no significant drawbacks that sent out red flags. All the feedback was positive. Kim, whose intelligent and analytical approach I respect, reminded me that I had been with the 4 car several years and still saw no real changes being made that we felt were necessary to produce a successful team. Additionally, I was not getting the kind of money I thought I should.

My wife had one major reservation about my taking it. She was concerned that whoever got in that car would have to contend with being the first one to take over after Davey. She was worried that Davey's image would be greater in death than in life, and I would have to compete with that. Whoever drove that car would have to be very careful about the grief many still felt over the loss of Davey. We knew that some people might prefer to see that car retired in much the same way some of the great basketball players' jerseys are retired along with the player.

Eventually, though, we kept coming back to our ultimate goal—to be on the team where we felt we might get the best advantage to win. I felt that Davey's whole team, the Robert Yates team, was very consistent and could be that team.

We went to Pocono with the offer from Ford on my mind.

■ ■ ■

From the day Davey died, Robert Yates was inundated with phone calls from racers wanting Davey's ride. Road racers, a motorcycle racer from Alaska, other Winston Cup racers, anyone who considered himself a motor sports personality, called asking for that ride. Robert didn't know what to do, and it was one of the reasons he didn't run at Pocono that weekend. Larry McReynolds, Robert's crew chief, told Robert to bide his time. He said, "If we're patient and don't choose someone too soon, the type of driver we're looking for will come our way." Robert decided he would hire drivers on a race-to-race basis until the "right" driver came along. For the Talladega race he hired Robby Gordon, a young driver with little Winston Cup experience.

When Lake Speed became available, Robert put Lake in the car for a few races. Lake had been trying to run his own program and was struggling, and this gave him the opportunity to have a more secure ride, if only for a few races. In the meantime Lee Morse was talking to Robert and Larry about me. Robert asked Larry, "What would you think about hiring Ernie Irvan?" Larry said, "I think Ernie is exactly who we should be looking for. He's young, energetic, he'll stand on the gas, he drives the car hard, and that's what we're used to. That's what we want in a race car driver." Robert then told Lee to talk to me and get the ball rolling.

At the same time Robert sat down with his entire crew to discuss the possibility of my driving for their race team. Larry McReynolds saw that some of the crew were skeptical. He knew they were thinking of my reputation for tearing up equipment, for getting into scuffles on the track—one of those heated arguments had even been with Davey—and a few still felt I had cost them the 1992 racing championship when I crashed at Atlanta and collected Davey and wrecked him too.

Larry McReynolds spoke up for me. He told them the truth, that a flat tire had caused me to crash in Atlanta that day and Davey was just a bystander. "Ernie spun out and we got into it," Larry told them. At the end of the meeting the crew gave their nod of approval to making me their new driver. Still, McReynolds could tell there were some who had reservations but were keeping quiet.

When Robert Yates called me a few days after my conversation with Lee Morse and wanted to know if I was interested in coming over to his race team, I was able to tell him I wanted to make the switch. Robert made it clear that he didn't want to have to buy out my contract. Robert told me, "The car is available if you can make it happen." He offered me an enticing and rewarding salary. He also explained what benefits I could expect. It was the number-one Ford team. I'm not so sure it isn't still the number-one financed Ford team. Larry McReynolds, who had a great reputation for working with other people, was the crew chief. They had all the makings of a great race team. All that was left for me to do was figure out how to cut my ties with Larry McClure.

The next step was my going to see Larry McClure. I told Larry that after the season ended I wanted to get out of my contract. What Larry said was unprintable. He became very upset.

I told Larry, "This is an opportunity I should take. It's not something anybody planned. Davey died, and someone has to drive the car, and I feel it would be a great break for me." I said, "You gave me a good shot, but things are not moving up to the next level."

In truth, it really didn't matter what I said. It was like going through a divorce that one party doesn't want. Larry may have known what I was saying was true, but he didn't want to hear it.

I said, "We've always said, if you didn't want me driving for you, then I don't want to drive for you, and if I didn't want to drive for you, you didn't want me to drive for you. You've always said that. I feel this is an opportunity I can't turn down. How can we make it happen?"

Larry said, "It's going to be tough to make it happen because we have sponsors." I said, "Okay, what can we do?" We didn't seem able to hit on a quick agreement.

I called Robert Yates and told him, "We want to do it. I'm not sure how we're going to be able to do it, but let's go to the next step." Robert said, "The next step is to get the people from Texaco to sign off on the deal." I said, "Let's do that before we do any further negotiating with Larry."

Robert Yates and I flew on a commercial plane to Houston and met with the Texaco people. Everything seemed to go well. Before they made their final decision, they wanted to meet me face to face and have a chance to talk to me.

I needed to have further discussions with Larry McClure. I told Larry I wasn't looking to make a move until the end of the '93 season. I had one more year on my contract after that. He said, "I'm not sure I'm going to let you out of your contract." This was in July. I said, "Larry, I am giving you plenty of time to get another driver. You know I'm being more than fair with you."

Larry said, "You are going to make *x* number of dollars on your contract with Yates, so if you pay me *y* number of dollars, I'll let you out of your contract." Using his mathematics, Larry's y turned out to be a demand for a million dollars!

I said, "Larry, this is buying blue sky. It's not right." Larry was playing hardball, and I felt he left me no choice but to bring up an issue that had been a sore point between us the whole time I was with him. I said, "What about all the money you owe me for souvenirs?" That figure worked out to be about a million dollars!

We started arguing, and like a messy divorce it just did not go well. It ended with my hiring a lawyer in Tennessee. It got uglier than I thought possible or would have liked.

I told Larry, "No matter what, next year get yourself another driver."

Making all of this harder was that as a race team the 4 car could still run like nobody's business on any given day. We went to Talladega on July 25, and Earnhardt and I had a finish that brought the huge throng of people in the stands to its feet. It was in that race that Neil Bonnett, coming out of retirement to make his first start in three years, had a terrible crash, flipping over cars and knocking down the wheel fence, which forced a halt to the race for over an hour. Bonnett, who had been a TV and radio announcer during his retirement from racing, had a camera in his car and was taking his fans for a "fun ride" when he lost control of the car and smashed it up. Fortunately Neil wasn't hurt too badly.

When the race resumed, Kyle Petty had the lead, Earnhardt was second, and I was third until about four laps to go, when Earnhardt made his move to get past Petty, and

I went with him. I was surprised Dale didn't wait until later in the race, but I knew that as soon as Dale went, I had to go too. I rode right on his bumper until I got to the backstretch of the final lap, and I made my move to get past him in an attempt to win the race. The rest of the way we were side by side and neck and neck, never separated by more than a foot or two. It was a seesaw battle, Dale in front, then me in front, then him in front, as we flew past the checkered flag. Even though I was only eight or nine inches behind him, I knew Dale had beaten me. It was the closest finish in the history of motor sports.

Then, as often happened on the 4 team, we were mediocre or worse in several races. Our lack of consistency only served to reinforce my belief that I should leave the 4 team.

After I received the offer from Robert Yates, I talked about it quite a bit with my crew chief, Tony Glover. We had been close friends, and Glove didn't want me to leave either. I explained to Tony what I felt needed to be done to improve the 4 car. I also didn't think the needed changes in personnel would ever be made because it involved family. Glover finally had to concede he saw my point, though he was mad and hurt that I was leaving. Both of us had been sure we would stay together until we won a championship, and that was not going to happen now. Glove was heartbroken, and I hated not being on his team. I would miss him and the easy way we could talk. My timing, from his perspective, was awful. During that time Glove and his wife divorced, and the day I called and told him I was going to drive for Robert Yates, his mother passed away. I felt very bad about leaving Glove.

Once Larry McClure realized I was leaving, the atmosphere in the shop turned ugly and for several weeks stayed that way. Larry and I wouldn't talk to each other. It was a bad situation, though I can honestly say the unpleasantness never affected the way I drove the car for him. I ran one final great race for the 4 team at Talladega. I battled Earnhardt down to the wire before finishing second. Tony Glover wasn't there for the race and had to watch it on television. It was the morning he buried his mother.

I was visiting Michael Waltrip's house at Lake Norman, where Michael and I were riding around on our waverunners, when I was summoned to the phone. The message was that Larry McClure didn't want me driving for him at the upcoming race at Darlington. I was asked to call him back.

I walked into Michael's house and called Larry. He said curtly, "If you still want to, you can drive the 28 car this weekend." Larry apparently had received some kind of financial payment from Ford and Robert Yates. During that last conversation, I could hear Larry's anger toward me. He felt I had betrayed him. In many ways I had residual feelings that he had not done all that he could or should have done for me either. For a long time Larry and I harbored feelings of animosity and bitterness toward each other. Thankfully, in our case, time has had a healing effect, and we're friendly once again. Things had been said that shouldn't have been. Words were spoken out of anger and not necessarily for any other reason. It's much easier to put things in perspective with the passage of time.

I called Robert Yates. It was a few days before we were supposed to go to Darlington. I was happy to relay to him:

"Larry has just released me from my contract. I can drive for you this weekend." In his brief and effective way Robert said, "Come on."

I went to Darlington not knowing whether we were going to make it happen in time or not. I was very enthusiastic about moving over to the Yates team, and I couldn't wait to drive that 28 car. With the release signed about an hour before practice, I officially became a member of the Texaco/Havoline race team. Larry McReynolds, the crew chief, had been warned by a lot of people that I might be tough to handle, but Larry had confidence in his ability to work with drivers. There was some talk that the Morgan-McClure team had been wild, but that was exaggerated. If some of the Yates crew wondered whether I would fit in, they sure didn't act like it.

They immediately made me feel like one of the guys. Pretty quickly, me, Larry McReynolds, Raymond Fox, and Raymond Beadle and just about everybody who was there on the race team seemed to be communicating well.

I got into that 28 car for the first time. People often asked me whether I felt Davey's presence or in his shadow in any way. I can't say that I did. In fact, the first time I went out to practice, it was like I had been driving that Texaco Thunderbird for a long time. I felt very comfortable with the car and the team.

I went out and ran that first practice at Darlington, and as I came in Larry McReynolds bent down at the door to talk to me. I think both he and I could feel a bond that seemed easy and as if we had worked together for a long time. It certainly didn't seem like our first day together. I think Larry felt comfortable with me from the start, and I with him.

It was early September when I went out to run at Darlington. The track was abuzz with the news I would be driving the 28 car. We qualified tenth, which wasn't great, but the Ford handled a little differently than the Chevrolet I was used to driving, and it took a little getting used to. At that time the motors ran with such an insignificant difference that you couldn't really feel it. Simply put, if the car handles well, it handles well.

We got going during practice, and then right at the start of Happy Hour (the last hour of practice of the day) I went out and blew a motor. I thought to myself, I guess we're going to start the race tomorrow without any practice. Boy, was I wrong! The crew jumped in and took out the damaged motor and put in a new one in fifty minutes, giving me an important ten minutes of practice. I was really impressed with the team. They too had a lot to prove. Most memorable, though, was how well I worked with crew chief Larry McReynolds right from the beginning.

The day of the race held a great deal of excitement. Lee Morse of Ford had said more than once that one reason he wanted me driving the 28 car was that I was to be the Ford driver who would challenge the great Dale Earnhardt. Trying my best to live up to those expectations, at the Darlington race, Earnhardt and I had a shoot-out that was a classic.

I would pass him down the front straightaway, and he'd run right behind me down the back straightaway and go into turn three and slingshot past me, and I'd pass him back down the front straightaway, and we did this for four or five laps. It was fun to know the crowd was going crazy!

That's what the whole picture and sound was, what many fans came to see: Earnhardt was the dominator, and Ford wanted someone who could be competitive with him. Well, I was certainly willing to try for Ford.

We led a lot of the race, and I think it was one of the best races they ever ran at Darlington. With my crew sitting on the front stretch watching, Dale was second or third, and I was right behind him. I got a good run off turn four, and I got up underneath Dale's rear bumper. For just a second I lifted Dale's rear wheels off the ground. I never said a word about it on the radio. But after the race, Larry said to me, "You were dogging Earnhardt pretty good, weren't you?" I said, "Did you see that? I tried to make sure I did it right where you could see it." I wanted them to know I was going to be the hard charger they were expecting.

Earnhardt and I raced side by side for quite a while, until we wore ourselves out. Mark Martin ended up passing us both to win his fourth race in a row. Dale finished fourth and I finished right behind him.

We went to Richmond right after that and blew up, and Doug Yates, Robert's son and the man who built the engines, said, "Ernie, I'm real sorry. Normally my stuff doesn't blow up." I said, "Doug, that's all right. Sooner or later, I'll crash, and we'll be even." Sure enough, I qualified second at the next race at Dover, but crashed in the race.

When we went to Martinsville, I started on the pole, and Geoff Bodine won the outside pole. Geoff had just bought Alan Kulwicki's race team including all his cars, and Geoff's car was painted just the way it had been when Alan was driving it, with the Hooters owl and the orange-and-white colors. Geoff was sitting where Alan used to sit. I, of course, was sitting next to him in the car that had been Davey Allison's for many years.

The year before it would have been Davey and Alan in the front row. Their cars were still there, but they were gone. That was a little eerie. It was also sad for all of us.

Although my positioning at the start of the race was a little ironic, I had a great car at Martinsville that day. It ran like a top, and when I pitted it seemed like I never lost a spot the way I did when I drove the 4 car. We led four hundred of the five hundred laps that day and crossed the finish line ahead of Rusty and Jimmy Spencer.

It was my first win for the Robert Yates racing team—in only my fourth start. I couldn't have been prouder of my performance or my decision to switch race teams. Winning that race at Martinsville was significant in many ways, not just for me, but for Robert Yates as well. He had never won at Martinsville.

A very poignant moment came for me after I took the checkered flag, came back around, and was driving down pit road toward Victory Lane. It seemed that nobody else was there when Bobby Allison walked halfway out on pit road and gave me a thumbs-up. It meant so much to me that he had seen me win and wanted to congratulate me.

I didn't want people to think I was trying to replace Davey Allison. No one could do that. In fact, out of respect, I refused to wear the same design Davey had worn on the driving suit.

Before the race I had bought a T-shirt memorializing Davey, and that morning I put it on under my uniform. It was my intention if I won the race to make it a tribute to Davey. This was no PR stunt. It came straight from the heart.

After I won, I got out of the car in Victory Lane, knelt down and undid the top of my driver's uniform so that the words on the shirt, "In memory of Davey Allison," could be seen. I was feeling very sentimental. A lot of people thought I did it because it was a politically smart move. Anyone who knows me well enough can tell you I rarely do anything political. I'm simply not that calculating. I just felt like it was the right thing to do to express my sentiments about my friend and his untimely death, and to show I would never forget who drove the 28 car before me.

After that race things continued to go well. At Wilkesboro I won the pole. At Charlotte I qualified on the outside pole. To give you an idea of how well and quickly the Texaco/Havoline race team and I clicked, this was the fourth race in a row in which I was sitting in the front row at the beginning of the race! Before the Charlotte race everyone was expecting another Wallace-Earnhardt duel. That wasn't the way things worked out. In all the years I have been racing, my car that day was by far the most competitive piece of equipment I have ever driven—to this day. Driving that car to victory took very little work because our crew had her dialed in. NASCAR had just made some rule changes—it announced a five-and-five rule—the rear spoiler had to go down and the valence had to go up, and Larry and the crew got it just right and we murdered them. We qualified on the outside pole, and led 328 of the 334 laps. The only laps we didn't lead were after cautions when we made pit stops.

During the race Larry McReynolds held his breath only one time. We had a 15- or 16-second lead midway through the race when a caution came out, killing our advantage.

When they restarted, Earnhardt was on my bumper, and when we came back around Earnhardt went by us, causing Larry a moment of concern. The next time around I was able to put a half a straightaway lead on him, and Larry was able to relax.

Our hearts skipped a beat halfway through the race when the engine started skipping. There are three ignition box switches, and I just switched them all, and luckily the trouble stopped. We were running so strongly even after, with a 14-second lead over Mark Martin, NASCAR announced there was oil on the track and threw a caution flag. It could have cost me the race, but there was no help for it. When the caution came out, we pitted and went about our business. Nothing changed. There was no one out there who was running close to us that day.

During the latter part of the race, Larry didn't have a lot to say except to remind me not to race the lapped cars and to slow down if I needed to in order to pick the right time to go by. Larry had had a lot of dominant runs with Davey—the World 600 at Charlotte and Michigan races in 1991—but Larry has always said that this was the most dominant car with which he was ever involved.

With two races left in the season, we went out to Phoenix. The day before the race Mark Martin came over to Larry McReynolds and me. He said, "I am just not running well." Larry asked him what his problem was. Mark, who was also in a Ford, described what he and his team were doing. Quickly analyzing the situation, Larry told Mark he thought their setup might be soft. We told him how we liked things set up.

Apparently Mark listened. Several times during the first part of the Phoenix race, Mark and I swapped the lead. Whoever was running behind often ended up being a little stronger. I led most of the race, but halfway through Mark took the lead from me. I had two hundred miles to catch him, but was never able to pull it off. We ran nose to tail that whole two hundred miles! I could get under him, but he would never let me on the outside, which was the faster groove. I had several opportunities to lay into Mark's car a little bit and spin him, but I had promised the other drivers to be more responsible, and when you trade paint you risk spinning yourself out. I had reached the point in my career where my decisions were becoming tempered by more than just the immense desire to win. Out of respect to Mark and the potential consequences, I did not try to run him off the track. A year earlier, I might have been more interested in pushing the envelope. I'm beginning to appreciate that skill can often compensate for the times when being daring can be too costly.

It was a good race and after listening to our advice, Mark won it. I came in second.

Larry McReynolds noted my newfound maturity and congratulated me on my performance. Larry said, "I'd rather finish second than be penalized five laps for rough driving." It always makes the crew happy when you bring your equipment home in one piece. That was another reason I was satisfied that I chose not to collide with Mark and send him spinning.

The final race of 1993 was at Atlanta in a race Rusty won. It was Rusty's tenth win, although he didn't win the championship. It was Earnhardt who won it for what would be his sixth time.

Before I started driving the 28 car, we had no idea we could run as well right off as we did. We ran eight races, won two, sat on two poles, and were consistently strong. Robert and Larry were great about giving positive feedback. It was gratifying that they thought our team was humming along so well, especially after having to recover from the untimely death of Davey. Overall, the 28 car finished twelfth in the points standings, which was respectable. More importantly, that first season with the Yates team seemed to be on the right track. Going into 1994 we seriously believed we had a legitimate shot at the championship. Our race team was about as high as a group could be. Larry McReynolds advised the crew that to keep the momentum going into the next season everyone would have to work hard throughout the winter, which is just what they did. The team worked to stay focused and to make the race cars as efficient as possible all winter so we would all have a decent chance at the championship. Between the crew and the good working relationship that Larry, Robert, and I had quickly developed, I felt that 1994 just might be my year.

14

ON TOP OF THE WORLD

During the winter testing that led into the 1994 season, no car was faster than my number 28 Texaco/Havoline Thunderbird. Everything seemed to be running as smoothly as I could have ever hoped. My dream to make a successful run for the championship seemed just within reach. As a team we all could feel everything humming along at a finely tuned pitch. No one or nothing associated with our car seemed out of sync.

If I had to point to any black cloud on the horizon in 1994, it was the coming of a new tire war, this time between Goodyear and Hoosier. Goodyear had been the tire of choice for years. In 1994 Hoosier challenged Goodyear's dominance.

Whenever we see a new tire company come in, those of us in racing hold our breath. Competition is good in anything we do, but there is something about competition with two race-tire companies that doesn't seen quite as beneficial. They try to outdo each other, sometimes stepping in the danger zone. They don't do it on purpose. However, often the result is that durability is sacrificed for performance. The bottom line—drivers end up getting hurt.

You might get a tire that sticks a little better, but sometimes a tire company will go right to the edge of safety with the strength of the tire. If the strength of the tire is insufficient, you can just about count on a higher chance of blowouts. Those blowouts can be deadly. It can also be an expensive proposition. The race teams will feel obligated to test both sets of tires to make sure that one brand doesn't offer a substantial advantage over the other.

The Robert Yates team never did use Hoosiers. Like many teams, we remained loyal to Goodyear. I don't know if it was out of superstition or something else. My guess is, the biggest reason so many teams didn't switch over was more because of the old adage "If it ain't broke, don't fix it."

In January '94 Neil Bonnett was driving on Hoosiers while practicing the first weekend for the Daytona 500, when something went wrong. He smashed into the wall and was killed. I was out on the track when he crashed, but I can't say what happened to Neil that day. It was hard to tell, really. Maybe it was the tires. Maybe Neil just lost it. It was a very windy day, I remember, and maybe that had something to do with it. Who knows? He crashed head on into the wall. Neil was a nice guy who had been another member of Bobby Allison's Alabama Gang, and a close friend of Dale Earnhardt. He had a great career as a television commentator when he decided he wanted to go back to racing again. His death saddened everyone. We all wished he had stayed up in the booth. Later during practice, another driver, Rodney Orr, was killed in a wreck. Again, who knows if the tires had anything to do with it? It is just kind of eerie that when there's a tire war going on, drivers die.

We went to Daytona with our Goodyear tires to qualify. After running 195 miles an hour, we sat on the second row. The pole was won by Loy Allen, one of those drivers who has never made it in the sport but who has run a few Winston Cup races. When Alan Kulwicki died, the Hooters company wanted Loy to drive the car. Loy's father was going to help buy the race team, although Alan's father ultimately sold it to Geoff Bodine instead.

A friend of mine, Mark Smith, was building Loy's motors. Mark is one of those mechanics who knows how to put together a good package. So though it was surprising that Loy Allen won the pole, at the same time I could see how things were in place that could make that a possibility.

When the race began, I was in the hunt all the way. Our car was running very well, but we were just on the loose side (on the turns the car would ride up the track). We kept tightening it up, but we could never get it tight enough.

I had led a lot of the race, and Sterling Marlin had run right with me the whole time. Then late in the race, about lap 150, I got loose coming off turn four—they had an in-car camera in our car, and the car was running sideways, about to spin, when I used all my driving skill to keep the car from spinning out of control and hitting the wall. I was able to save it, though I had to drop back six or seven spots.

I told Larry McReynolds I was loose, but I didn't make a big deal out of it because we were running under the green. Larry told me, "Ernie, I don't know if we're going to get the chance to adjust it." I knew I'd have to drive the best I could without the car feeling exactly as I would have liked it. The bottom line—I would never quit trying to get that lead back.

I made my way all the way back to third behind Mark Martin. With three laps to go Sterling Marlin led, and I was running not far behind, right behind Mark, ready for Mark to make his move and take us to the front. Sterling, who was in my Kodak 4 car, was very strong. I figured that if Mark and I could hook up, we could run faster in tandem than Sterling driving by himself. I anticipated that once Mark and I drafted past Sterling, I would find a way to get past Mark. Unfortunately for Mark and for me, Mark ran out of gas.

I made a try at Sterling one last time. After I came off turn four, I could see I wouldn't be able to catch him. I told Larry on the radio, "He's got me beat. I can't do anything with him." It was frustrating after having gotten so close. There just wasn't anything that I could do. We knew we had given it our best shot.

When I talked to Mark Martin right after the race, he said he had been trying to stretch his fuel mileage right to the end, and it hadn't worked out. It was Sterling's first race in the 4 car and his first win after nearly three hundred starts. I was very happy for him, as I was for the rest of the Morgan-McClure team. Tony Glover told me later that after I left, he had dedicated himself to beating me. When Sterling won, Glove felt vindicated. Despite the lingering resentment from their team, it was good to see both of us doing and running well. In many ways it was hard to lose to my old team, but my confidence in my new team was exciting. In my heart I knew that a lot of good times were in store for the Robert Yates race team.

■ ■ ■

In early May we traveled to Talladega, Davey Allison's backyard. Before the race Robert Yates and Larry McReynolds were concerned with the reception we would receive from the Allison fans. These were knowledgable fans, and they were aware that Davey and I had had our differences in the past. I suspected that some of them still might harbor the erroneous belief that I somehow had cost Davey the 1992 racing championship when I crashed at Atlanta in the final event and knocked him out of the race.

Robert told Larry, "This is going to be the true test. We don't know whether these people are going to cheer us or throw chicken bones and beer cans at us." We all hoped for the best but braced ourselves for the worst.

I went out to qualify, and when the PA announcer said over the loudspeaker, "The 28 Texaco/Havoline Thunderbird driven by Ernie Irvan," the fans cheered very loudly. I couldn't have been more appreciative.

When I won the pole, the fans were so excited I thought they were going to tear the Talladega grandstands down. It seemed as if those fans shared my feelings about winning the pole in Alabama. I had always honored Davey. My thoughts from the start were, "I'm not here to replace Davey Allison. I'm here to continue the job that Davey started. Nobody is going to replace Davey." I always believed that was true and I would like to think the Allison fans knew I was sincere and that was why we were all in the same corner. Whatever the reason for their support, I was deeply gratified by their encouragement.

Even though we qualified fastest, the crew was not happy about the effort it took just to qualify well at Talladega and Daytona. Just setting up the car to qualify two laps at Talladega and Daytona required an incredible number of tasks in a relatively short time. To get ready for the race itself meant switching a lot of that setup around.

We didn't win the Talladega race—we finished third to Junior Johnson's two cars, but we had a very satisfying day and we would go on to win the next race in mid-May at Sears Point.

We built a brand-new car for the Sears Point race. Larry worked closely with Riley & Scott Engineering out of Indianapolis, who helped do the design work and created the geometry of the car. The week before the Sears Point race we had taken the car to Road Atlanta, where we tested our road course cars. While I was out on the track testing the brakes, I spun out. Fortunately I didn't hit anything. It would have been difficult to get the car repaired or replaced in that short a time. Everyone in the crew breathed a sigh of relief when the car stopped spinning. It was still intact.

We had had an excellent test at Road Atlanta and were feeling very confident when we arrived in California in mid-May for the race. At a practice session before qualifying I was out running the car when I found myself in competition with Mark Martin. Mark is a very respectable road racer. Competing with him is very effective in terms of knowing where you sit in the scheme of things. It's also just plain fun because he's so good. You can imagine then what a pleasure it turned out to be when, as one of the last cars to go out and qualify, I was able to run a decent lap and take the pole at qualifying.

We were getting incredible performance from our cars. In fact, during the race, we were still using the Goodyear tires, despite the seductive enticements from Hoosier to switch over. That day in particular, Hoosier had the relatively faster tire. Nonetheless, midway through the race, I had a 20-second lead over Geoff Bodine, who was using the favored Hoosier tires.

I would go through turn one, and I could see Geoff coming through the esses, and I would gauge myself and how I was doing by what Bodine was doing behind me. For five laps in the middle of the race I slowed just a little, and Bodine still wasn't gaining on me. Ever vigilant, Larry noticed. He radioed me, "Ernie, is everything okay?" I told him it was and what I was doing, that I was just running as fast as I had to. When I sped up again, I checked to see what Larry thought. "It's faster now, isn't it?" I said. Larry chuckled. It was one of those days when the car was dialed in and everything was just right. Those days are damn good.

I led almost the whole way. The only other driver to lead was Earnhardt. He got by me once, but on that day, ours was the dominant car. It was one of those days when I felt a powerful sense of destiny—that in our car, during that year, we would be a force to be reckoned with.

Though it was only May, we had already won on an intermediate track, a superspeedway, and now a road course. As long as we kept our nose clean, all of us felt we had a legitimate shot at winning the Winston Cup championship. At that time all we thought about was being competitive with Dale Earnhardt. We had no idea that tragedy would want to intercede in such a nasty way. We felt confident we could make it as far as Dale was concerned.

We went to Pocono in mid-June, and I had a terrific duel with Rusty. I was ahead nearly the whole way when Rusty won a one-lap shoot-out to beat me. Then Rusty won again at Michigan, his third win in a row. It's what I said before about Rusty: he wins in streaks. It's funny how he can go weeks without winning, and then suddenly pick things up and win four in a row.

When we went back to Daytona for the July Fourth race, I finished second to Jimmy Spencer. It was our guess that he must have had fifty more horsepower than we did. Spencer was driving for Junior Johnson, who all of a sudden got awfully good in the restrictor plate races. The Daytona track gets very hot and slick in July, and handling becomes a big issue. I was running all over Jimmy in the corners, and then he would kill me in the straightaways. One time I came on the radio and said, "Larry, he's backing off in the corners, but as soon as we hit the straightaway, he pulls ahead of me four car lengths." That was a telltale sign that maybe they had a better car than we did.

Spencer may not have been aware of whatever Junior and his crew were doing, and it's always possible they weren't doing anything at all, but it was very interesting that the car could be so bad in the corners but beat us so thoroughly on the straightaways, especially with the horsepower we had with the Yates engine.

Spencer stroked the whole day, just rode along. He had come from dead last until it was time for him to collect the paycheck, and in a matter of about ten laps, he ran me down and passed me. The finish was side by side, but he won with a slight lead.

A lot of people on that track were suspicious that Junior was pulling something. Rumor had it that Bill Elliott was so upset he didn't have whatever Spencer had, that by the time we went to Talladega, Elliott made sure he had it too. It was a curious rumor. At Talladega both of them were lifting in the corners, and I couldn't stay up with either one of them.

Was I frustrated? You better believe it. All things being equal, I believed those two wins should have been ours. We did not understand how their cars were passing inspection. In general, it was pretty annoying.

We next went to Loudon, New Hampshire, where we sat on our fifth pole of that year. We were very fast. By the thirtieth lap, I had lapped Dale Earnhardt. Again, I consider Dale a tough driver with a good car deal going, and I felt very pleased to pass him. It helped immeasurably that Larry and I were operating as a unit. Our chemistry was helping to make us formidable.

Larry had the uncanny ability to know what was going on out on the track even before I could tell him about it. As an example, during the Loudon race, I was leading when around lap 200 I started having problems. I had been running a really comfortable groove, when all of a sudden, it had gone away. Some drivers will stick to the old groove, run badly and moan and groan about the car. I prefer to slow down a little, do a little experimenting, and hopefully find myself a new, better line around the track.

After three or four laps Larry noticed that I was going about two-tenths of a second slower, and he radioed in something of a state of panic. "What's wrong, Ernie? Is everything okay?" I told him, "Larry, the groove I've been running has changed. It's gone." Larry said, "Search around and find a new one," which was what I was doing. After about fifteen laps, I started going faster again. Larry noticed that too. He said, "What's going on out there?" I said, "I've found me another groove." Larry was pleased. He was also in tune every step of the way with the incredible focus he's blessed with.

We were leading with forty laps to go, when I let the car get a little high up in turns one and two, and I found myself in what we call "the marbles," where the track was tearing up. I spun and hit the wall. Disappointed, I drove down pit road where the crew tried to make repairs. There was no help for it. I had hit so hard the battery had broken, and we couldn't even get the engine recranked. We had to park it. Meanwhile, the cagey Earnhardt, who was junk that day, nursed his car, rode around, and somehow found a way to finish second, causing us to lose a lot of points to him for the racing championship. As he pulled in, I recalled his advice to me early in my career: "Just stay in and finish the race." He consistently was true to his words.

We went to Pocono in late July. During the race the drivers with Hoosier tires seemed to be outrunning those with Goodyears. All day long I ran third or fourth behind Geoff Bodine, the two Burtons, and Joe Nemechek, who were on Hoosiers. Mark Martin, Rusty Wallace, and I were on Goodyears and we were half a lap behind them, and they plainly were driving away from us.

Larry would come on the radio and advise me, "Ernie, you're twenty seconds behind the leader." It takes about a minute to get around Pocono. I'd ruefully answer, "Larry, I don't know what to tell you. I don't know how we could get better performance. My car is good." It was the tires that made all the difference.

Nevertheless, no one ever said, "Let's change to

Hoosiers," because we knew that their advantage would only be a temporary one. We were a Goodyear-contracted team, and Robert felt in the long run we'd be better off fulfilling our obligations and staying on Goodyear tires. Robert suspected Hoosier would not be running tires long term. Additionally Larry was confident that if the crew worked hard they could overcome any tire disadvantage, just as we had at Sears Point. Once again, they were right. Hoosier came, and quickly went.

I would feel remiss if I did not add that I believe no race team could have worked harder than mine. We weren't a very large team. In the mid-'90s we were a relatively small, close-knit group of guys—Larry McReynolds; Raymond Fox, another close friend of mine who was Larry's right-hand man and who worked on the chassis; Joey Knuckles, who had been with Robert Yates forever, and who was the front tire changer on the pit crew; Doug Yates, Robert's son who worked day and night to try to make more and more horsepower; and Norman Koshimizu, who drove the truck and did a little bit of everything and who had been with Robert since his Di-Gard days in the 1970s. With everyone dedicated to a common goal, we all got along well. They had overcome the tragedy of Davey Allison's accidents and then worse, his death. I think it is admirable how they were able to stick together and become stronger as a result of all they had been through. They would not let themselves get knocked down. In fact, even if we won a race or sat on the pole, they never let up. They knew they had to work just as hard for the next race. There could be no better example of that than in how hard we prepared for the Brickyard 400 at Indianapolis in August.

A few months before the race, our team and the 4 Kodak team with Sterling Marlin tire tested for Goodyear at the Indy track. Our first test went well. We went back a second time, tested again, and were very fast. Again, this was still in the middle of the Goodyear-Hoosier tire war, and Goodyear was determined to improve its tire for the Brickyard 400. Goodyear paid the race teams to test. We were happy to do it because we were also learning and able to benefit from the experience. We put in a lot of effort getting ready for Indy, which in August 1994 became part of the regular NASCAR schedule for the first time. In that race I came very, very close to making the record books as the first NASCAR Indy winner.

When we went out and qualified for Indy, a Hoosier team in a car driven by Rick Mast sat on the pole. His primary competition looked most likely to be two Goodyear cars: one driven by Jeff Gordon and one by me. Unfortunately we got really loose during our qualifying run and had one of our worst efforts that year, finishing only fourteenth. We doubled our efforts to improve our race car the rest of the week. By the time they dropped the green flag to start the race, we were very competitive.

Initially Jeff Gordon and I had a spectacular duel. Gordon was fast, and so was I. For several laps we continually swapped spots.

Larry had been scanning the radio of the 24 car, and he heard Gordon tell his crew chief, Ray Evernham, "I get real loose when somebody's behind me." I could see that and so when Larry called to tell me, before he could say a word, I told him, "Larry, I know what you're going to say."

After a few laps went by, I drove right up on Gordon's

car. He got loose and had to let up on the gas to keep control, and I was able to pass him. If nothing went wrong, it looked like the race would be mine.

With five laps to go, I was sure we had it won. Then I suffered from rotten luck when we cut a right front tire. Shortly thereafter, the tire suddenly blew out as I was going down the straightaway. Fortunately, I managed somehow to avoid hitting the wall. I fought hard to keep the car on the track, but we had to pit under green. The incident tore the fender off, and though I was able to go back out and finish halfway back, the tire had cost me the race. It was a big disappointment.

At Watkins Glen, my Texaco/Havoline Thunderbird had another shot at winning. Mark Martin was a worthy opponent that day. We raced each other close all race long, both of us running well. Mark, however, managed to maintain a slight edge on me.

Track position is very important at Watkins Glen because restarts are single file, and with ten laps to go we pitted. Mark pitted right beside us. Larry and I decided the only way we could beat Mark's team was if we could outfox them somehow.

Late in the race I was on Mark's back bumper after a restart, but I just was not catching up to him. Both of us had enough fuel and tires to go to the end. Putting our ruse in action, the race team got on the pit wall. Larry held up four fingers, meaning he wanted me to come in and get four tires. We held the sign out, and all the guys on the pit crew got into position, telling the world that we intended to come in and pit.

The trap was set. On the track behind Mark, I was supposed to try to make Mark think I was coming in for four tires. If the Valvoline team thought we were pitting for tires, maybe they'd be afraid of how good we'd be with new tires, and they'd pit. Because I was running behind him, all I had to do after Mark drove down pit road was stay out on the track. The race would have been ours. It was worth a shot. Hell, it was the only shot we could think of on such short notice under those circumstances.

As I came around turn three I began to slow, trying to get Mark to bite at the trap. Their race team didn't know what to make of what we were doing. On the radio their crew chief, Steve Hmiel, was yelling to Mark, "They're going to pit. They're going to pit," which meant they were thinking about it. Despite our theatrical efforts (Larry and the crew continued to act like I was coming in) at the last moment Mark must have figured out it was all a hoax because he stayed out on the track and never went near pit road.

They stayed out, we stayed out, Mark won and we finished second and had a lot of fun doing it.

I'm glad I can remember that race. There was a time, after Michigan, when I couldn't remember much of anything, but particularly the events around the time of the accident. For a while it was a blessing not to remember that we had been a power to be reckoned with. It was left to the rest of the team to feel the agony of what had been left undone. While in my hospital bed in the ICU, I blissfully had no recollection that we were qualifying strongly every weekend and won more poles than most people could hope for.

Gratefully, my battered body did not know what had been instantly stolen from the team and from me—our second-place points standing. We were second only to

Earnhardt and even that small gap seemed to be closing every race.

Knowing all this would be pure hell. Today, I fully appreciate those facts. I'm grateful I'm alive to feel that frustration. But there's something else I know. I left a job unfinished. I don't intend to leave it that way.

15

I wish the only fallout from the wreck at Michigan would have been the damage to the car and to me. It didn't happen that way, though. Instead, it was like what happens when you throw a stone into a pond. There's a ripple effect. The wreck would have an effect on our race team that none of us could have foreseen. The beginnings of the discord on the team began, innocuously enough, while I was in the hospital.

Robert hired Dale Jarrett to sub for me in the 28 car, and when I came back in 1995, Robert made the decision to run two teams: in 1996 I would drive the 28 car, and D.J. would drive the new 88 car. With two race teams now, Robert had to hire a second crew chief for D.J.'s car. At the suggestion of Larry McReynolds, Robert chose Todd Parrott. This would be one suggestion that would haunt Larry for some time.

Larry had tried to lure Todd over to the Yates team for a couple of years, but Todd told Larry he wouldn't leave for any job except crew chief. It wasn't until my return that Larry was able to offer him that opportunity. Under the new arrangement Todd reported to Larry, who was supposed to oversee both race teams.

Robert started that second team for a number of reasons. One, the opportunity was there. Two, he was beginning to see that owners with more than one team had an advantage over one-car owners. One benefit is if you get $5 million to run one team, it doesn't take twice as much to run two teams, so more of the second $5 million is profit. Two teams, moreover, can share the same body hangar, the same painter, and the same chassis maker. Robert also was convinced he could make the parent team stronger by adding a second team because he would be able to spend more money on specialists and on research and development.

Another advantage to having two teams is that they can share information to make both cars run better. This often works very nicely, unless, of course, the two teams start bickering between themselves or unless one of the crew chiefs refuses to play ball (which happens more times than you would like to think).

As an incentive to make Larry more comfortable with a two-car concept, I think Robert gave him a percentage of the winnings of the new 88 car, in addition to his salary. It is my understanding that Robert felt that a two-car team might be a way to help Larry fulfill his dream to be a part owner in a race team. I don't believe Robert ever laid out specifics, but the way he set it out, Larry was going to oversee both cars, and if things worked out, sometime down the road his reward would be a piece of the team. Unfortunately for Larry, and for me, it didn't pan out that way.

There was a third unspoken reason why Robert went with two teams. Understandably, he was trying to hedge his bets in case I didn't come back 100 percent. What if I returned from my accident and no longer was competitive anymore? He still would have Dale. At first glance it looked like the smart thing to do.

When I returned in 1996 to run the full schedule for the first time since the accident, problems surfaced immediately between the two teams. From the start Robert and Larry had envisioned cooperation and a mutually beneficial relationship between the teams. Sometimes, on the outside, all that is visible is two drivers, running for the same owner, and they are called "teammates." However, as soon as one team feels the owner has given an unfair advantage to the other car, a rivalry develops that is fiercer than any rivalry with any other car. Initially, it may have looked as if the Yates cars were the same, but it was a little unnerving when D.J. and Todd were consistently running better than we were. I think it was hard for Larry when he would make an effort to work with Todd, and he didn't feel the effort was returned. It seemed Todd had ideas that were independent from an all-team approach.

As Larry explained it, it was like he had two extension cords and they weren't quite long enough to reach each other, but if he pulled them hard enough and held them, he could keep them plugged together. By the end of the year, Larry's hands gave out. He just couldn't hold the plugs together any longer. The whole situation was very disheartening.

It was a bright spot for us when I started the 1996 Daytona 500 on the outside pole. The car and the engine were everything I could have hoped for. In one of the two 125 qualifiers, which consists of half the field for the 500, there were four Chevrolets stacked up against my lone Ford. Of the Chevys, two of them were formidable Rick Hendrick cars. One serious concern I had was that they would double-team me if they got a chance. They didn't. Using my drafting skills, I beat them. It felt great being back on the track and flexing my muscles. They were skills I used to have and it was exceptionally satisfying to know I could still pull them out when necessary. Everyone in the stands, and certainly the crew, seemed to share in the sheer pleasure of my personal victory as well as my good qualification.

We had a good car for the Daytona 500, running fourth or fifth right behind Dale Earnhardt, when his ignition box went out on the front straightaway, shutting down the power. When he slowed suddenly, I ran into the back of him. The impact made Earnhardt a little bit loose, but he recovered and drove away while I spun out and hit the wall. I drove the car behind the pit wall and the crew worked on it, but try as we did, we were many, many laps back when D.J. and his 88 car won the race.

Things really seemed off at our next race in Rockingham. We missed on the setup by quite a bit, but were glad we didn't crash. That was something to build on. Still, we knew it wasn't what we were capable of doing. It only seemed distantly relevant that it was the first time I had run at Rockingham since they repaved it, which made it a little bit of a different track, something I had to get used to.

I think it was at Rockingham that I was beginning to notice that the two Yates teams, for whatever reason, were not pulling in the same direction. Robert didn't seem interested in mediating the situation or demanding cooperation.

At that point, I think it was up to him to make that crucial order, but it never came. Without Robert's overt support, Larry couldn't help but begin to feel a little resentful, not to mention frustrated.

When I didn't finish well at Daytona or Rockingham, I felt an incredible amount of pressure. Some of it came from within. Some came from reporters and fans who began comparing my performances to what I had done before the accident in 1994. Before I got hurt, I had driven more laps than any driver. I had done everything I could possibly do except win the championship. We had been a dominant team and felt the championship within our reach. Now I was coming back after being away two years, and there was no question I was still getting my sea legs back. I was trying to be patient with myself as the doctors had instructed, and under the circumstances thought things were going very well. Soon the question people seemed to be asking was, "Will Ernie Irvan ever be a good driver again?" My ambition was the same, that much I knew. I felt like it was an unfair question. Still it didn't keep me from putting more pressure on myself. I couldn't do much about things seeming a little off kilter between the two teams, though. It was a tough time.

When we went to Richmond, I crashed in practice. We were forced to use the backup car in the race, and right off, I banged into the back of someone and knocked off part of the nose. The cars are really aerodynamic, and if you knock off part of the chassis, you suffer the rest of the day. Incidents like that were getting us further and further behind.

We went to Darlington and for much of the race we were running along, gratefully doing well. A little bit behind on one of the pit stops, I was just in time for a wreck in turn four. Damn if I didn't go around and get in the middle of it. I came in and we had to fix the car. Larry had been grumbling about our performances, and after I came in Larry got on me. He said, "Ernie, we've got to quit tearing up the race cars. We're running out of cars, man," and I said something to him, and we yelled back and forth. It was clearly a symptom of our frustration and anxiety. Larry and I got over it in a hurry. I wish the rest of our circumstances could have improved as quickly.

After Darlington, Larry magnanimously agreed to use Todd's suspension rather than go with his own. Larry is a great team manager. He's decent with his people. He's good with the sponsors. He can do all that. He can also set a car up like nobody's business. As good as he is, it must have been tough for him to agree to use Todd's suspension. With Todd and D.J. doing so well, Larry did what he thought was best for the team, not what was best for his ego.

Using the new suspension, we finished fourth at Atlanta, in what was a really strong run. It was my best finish to date that year, and emotionally the boost I needed. I was a little more confident, but still had to worry about staying out of trouble. That seemed to be the hard part. We kept getting caught up in the random incidents that can knock you out of contention.

Even when we ran well, if I wasn't being compared to my past performances, my finishes were being compared to D.J.'s efforts. Though I had run fourth at Atlanta, D.J. and Todd had won it.

That they had run well all year long in the 88 car worsened the friction between Todd and Larry McReynolds.

Though Larry was supposed to be in charge of both cars, Todd was one of those crew chiefs who didn't want anyone—not even the other crew chief—to know what he was doing. Todd didn't seem interested in what we did on the 28 car. Conversely, Larry was still committed to being a team player. He would look at the 88 car and at what they were doing, but Todd would refuse to discuss anything with Larry. Understandably, Larry would grow frustrated with Todd's secretiveness. It was a bitter pill for Larry to swallow because Larry had pushed for Todd to get his job in the first place.

I would have thought that Robert Yates would have stepped in between the two by this time, but Robert tried to pretend that Larry and Todd didn't have a problem. When Larry continued to see that he would have to fight what would turn out to be a year-long battle with Todd without support from Robert, he was greatly upset. Larry could see the rest of the year would be long and hard.

Again, it didn't help any that I was still working on consistency myself. On Fridays I tended to struggle and not qualify well, but by Saturday I'd get my groove on the racetrack and be completely ready on Sunday when I got out racing. Not qualifying well was a distinct disadvantage. Starting at the back of the pack with the less competitive race teams would often lead to trouble. Mishaps or pileups happen frequently and early on. A lot of times you just don't want to get into that if you can avoid it.

When we went to Martinsville in mid-April, we qualified so poorly that we didn't make the field, and we needed to take a provisional to make the race. It may have been the first provisional the 28 car ever had to use under Robert Yates. Larry was determined to make the car better, and on Sunday morning before the race he literally rebuilt that car, changing everything from the A-arms to the trailing arms. I really admired that he did that and that he did it so well. That's support!

Despite Larry's herculean efforts, we qualified so poorly we had to pit on the back straightaway, another tremendous disadvantage. When the caution comes out and everyone goes to pit, the cars on the front stretch pit first while you are driving halfway around the track to your pit, and by the time you get there, those cars have gotten gas and their tires changed, and they leave and get to running hard to catch up with the pace car while you're being serviced. Pitting on the backstretch is such a disadvantage that even if you have a good car and you have a good pit stop, if you come into the pits fifth, you will go out twelfth or thirteenth, at best. It's the nature of having two pit roads.

I started the Martinsville race in the last row. Fortunately, most of the race was run under green. My car was performing so well I was able to finish second to Rusty Wallace. Had I not had to pit on the backstretch, I really believe I would have won the race.

At our next race in Talladega, I sat on the pole, which improved everyone's state of mind. During the race the car was running pretty loose, but we still managed to run in the top ten, until there was a terrible multicar wreck in turns one and two. It was really something. Ricky Craven almost sailed out of the racetrack. There was a picture in the paper of all the cars mangled together on top of each other. Somewhere in the middle of the pack you could almost see the 28 car underneath them all. So much for a top-ten spot.

The next week we went to Sears Point, where we did not qualify well. As usual, by race day we were back on track. We ended up tearing up a transmission and had to change it. As a result, the finish was not spectacular. Yet we all felt we were improving with each race. Encouraging each other, Larry and I would remind ourselves, "If we can get through the first half of the season and shake out the rust, by the time we hit the second half, we will be a team to be reckoned with."

Beginning at Charlotte at the end of May, things turned in our favor. We reeled off eight top-ten finishes in the next nine races and got as high as sixth in the battle for the racing championship. Although we weren't doing anything differently from what we had done in the earlier races when everything was going wrong, we were elated with the turn of events. Our restrictor plate program just kept getting better and better, and on July Fourth we finished fifth at Daytona. When we unloaded at Loudon, you could touch the car and almost feel its incredible potential.

Loudon is one of those racetracks where, whether I'm driving in a truck, a Busch race, or a Winston Cup car, I can get the job done. Though Loudon is a mile long, it is a flat short track. It is a relatively new track, built in the hills of New Hampshire, and it has been a great track for me.

We qualified sixth, but not far off the pole. In practice, we could see the car ran as well as anyone's. From the start I believed the car was untouchable as long as we didn't get caught in any pileups. We didn't.

We had long green-flag runs, and the car ran as if it could go on forever. There didn't seem to be any difficulties at all on the way to the checkered flag as I led the last hundred laps.

Larry didn't have much to say during those last fifty laps. He didn't have to. We both knew how much this win meant to the other person. It was an incredible bond I felt with Larry, borne out of the extraordinary times we had had together. Over the radio Larry kept me informed with guarded words. We still had a hundred laps to make.

He kept me posted on my lap times and just kept reminding me not to get overanxious, because we had a pretty good lead. We had an 11-second margin over D.J. in the second-place car. Larry just kept telling me to be smooth. Meanwhile, we continued to hold our breath, praying no caution would come out.

When victory came at last, it was sweet and we all shared in it. Psychologically, that was a very important win for me. It helped to silence some of the doubters whom I was trying diligently to keep from affecting me.

I followed that win with two fourth-place showings at Pocono and Talladega. At Indianapolis after leading most of the race I finished second to D.J. It was a great day for the Robert Yates race team. The finish trumpeted the message that, from now on, every weekend both the 28 car and the 88 car could be contenders. As for our car, we were glad we were hitting our setups. We sensed more good runs would follow.

If there were any skeptics left, I silenced them when I proved that the Loudon win wasn't any fluke by winning the second

Richmond race in mid-September. I beat Jeff Gordon to the flag in what was for me a very exciting finish. It was the first head-to-head battle I had with Gordon, who had been just starting to come into his own when I got hurt in '94.

The race was not without a few hitches. Just as I was humming along, I had a tense moment when the ignition started to go out. All of a sudden, my car died, and I lost track position. The crisis passed when I was able to flip switches and get it running again. By the end of the race, we were running faster than the rest of the cars out there. It was only a matter of time before I caught Jeff. He didn't give up the spot without a fight though. Working hard to hold on to the number-one spot I had just taken, I was grateful to take the checkered flag. It was a thoroughly enjoyable and satisfying win.

This win was critical at that time for a very important reason I didn't realize until the moment I won. It was then that I understood that I had to focus on exactly what our team needed to do—not what our team was doing and how it stacked up against the other Yates car. This was about *our* game, period. It was amazing what that shift in focus did for my frame of mind.

Just when I felt I was really using my own noggin, I suffered a concussion at Charlotte in October. We had arrived with the car in top-notch shape. It looked as if we were the fastest car out there based on the performances leading up to the race. With about ten minutes to go in Happy Hour, the final hour of practice, we wanted to test one more set of shocks. I went back out, and son of a gun if we didn't get a flat tire coming off one and two. Although I hit the inside wall, that incident was only the beginning of our trouble. That flat forced us to unload the backup car for the race.

We were only running fairly well in the race when I spun out in turn two. I was sitting sideways at the bottom of the racetrack when the 98 car drove wide open and smashed into the side of my car. I was very lucky he didn't hit the driver-side door. Fortunately it was the left front fender he hit. I was immediately airlifted to the hospital and spent the night for observation. I took a hard lick, and suffered a concussion, but since I ended up okay, I can't say my luck that day was all bad.

At the end of the 1996 season I finished tenth in the points, a terrific finish considering our shaky beginning. D.J. finished third in the standings, and I was happy for him. Clearly Larry and I showed we were a respectable top-five team. I was certain there would be a lot to build on for the next year.

To my great surprise, at the end of the 1996 season Larry McReynolds left Robert Yates and signed to become Dale Earnhardt's crew chief on the Richard Childress race team. As my friend, I would miss him. As my crew chief, I was very sorry to see him go. In the hospital after the Michigan wreck, Larry had promised me, "No matter what, I'm going to be there when you come back." Larry was true to his word. We ran a full season in '96, and he was there all the way for me.

I understood, though, how Larry felt about the way things were going between him, Todd Parrott, and Robert. In the end Larry couldn't hide his disappointment over the lack of coordination between the two race teams. All the trying had tired him out.

He felt that Todd had too much say-so over what was going on in the shop, and he decided to move on. Larry told me, "I'm supposed to be the overall crew chief, and I told Robert that for me to stay I needed things to be done accordingly."

The day Larry resigned, we went to dinner together. Larry wanted to explain why he was leaving. He didn't get into details. In general he said there were things he had asked Robert to do, and Robert did not seem to want to do them. The gentleman that he is, Larry never did say exactly what the deal was. Rumors abounded later. It didn't matter that he didn't supply the specific details. I had been there the whole season and watched him suffer while he worked his tail off trying to be a team player. Meanwhile, any goodwill he offered had been curtly rebuffed by the new, independent crew chief.

The next year it would be my turn to become so disillusioned.

16

TORTURE

My wife, Kim, and I traveled to New York in December 1996 for the annual NASCAR banquet where everyone was dressed up in tuxes and tails. The fact that the banquet calls for such formal attire indicates a few things. When NASCAR had the banquet in Daytona, it used to be that Junior Johnson and most of the other drivers would wear T-shirts, blue jeans, and work boots to the party. Times have changed. NASCAR's gotten bigger, with far wider media exposure and a greater number of corporate sponsors.

The banquet is televised nationally on ESPN, and part of the ceremony revolves around each of the top-ten drivers in the point standings getting up, thanking their sponsors, and making a brief speech.

I was the tenth-place finisher in '96, and I was first to get up and speak. This is no excuse, but I had had a serious head injury, and when I went to thank everyone, I thanked No Fear, who sponsors my truck, I thanked Raybestos, an associate sponsor, I thanked the guy who gave me a tractor for my farm, I thanked Robert, I thanked Larry, I thanked Kim, I thanked everyone under the sun, but I made what would be a monumental faux pas. I forgot to thank Texaco. It was immediately noted. Everyone seemed to notice. As I would later become painfully aware, Texaco seemed particularly sensitive to the oversight.

Dale Jarrett, who drove the other Robert Yates car, had finished third the year before and spoke after me. Texaco was just an associate sponsor on his car, but D.J. went out of his way to thank Texaco. I'm sure he was trying to smooth things over, but by then, I felt as if it only served to highlight my blunder.

I'm a race car driver. I have never pretended to be anything else. Furthermore, I have never professed to be a great speaker, nor have I felt comfortable talking in public. Simply put, I blew it. I was the first to admit it and quick to feel sorry for it. I still am. The Texaco sponsorship deal was made with five different divisions, and there were a lot of Texaco executives in attendance, and some of them were quite indignant about my omission.

It wasn't as if it had never happened before. Two years earlier Rusty Wallace got up and started talking, and he never thanked Miller beer, his primary sponsor. Afterward he said, "Damn, I forgot." It was an oversight, and everyone knew it was an oversight. Miller didn't care. Unfortunately for me, the men from Texaco didn't seem so congenial when it came time to overlook things.

After I left the podium, I walked over to the Texaco executives seated around a table to apologize. I said, "I can't believe I forgot to thank you. I'm really sorry." One of the executives could barely contain his anger. He told Robert Yates right then and there that he didn't want my contract renewed when it expired at the end of the '97 season—over a simple "thank you!"

Robert told him, "If you're not going to sign him when his contract comes up, there's no point starting the season with him. We need to make a change now. I don't want this hanging over our heads this season." Robert also told him, "However, I want to keep Ernie." The executive backed down. He told Robert that he would evaluate me at the end of the year to see if I had "changed my ways." Changed my ways how? There were grumblings about my not making enough appearances. But as best as I could recall, I had fulfilled my contractual obligations. I drove as hard as I could. I didn't goof off or refuse to do anything that was in my contract. I couldn't have been caught more off guard by this executive's reaction.

One aspect of my relationship with Texaco that really surprised me, though, was that they hadn't capitalized on my comeback as much as I thought they might have. In fact, it began to feel as if I was being shelved, and that stung because I knew I had always been loyal to them. I always wore my Texaco hat with the Texaco star. Hell, I even used Texaco gas. Talk about my actions speaking louder than words. When I returned from my accident and resumed racing, their ads featured Robert Yates and Larry McReynolds, or Mario and Michael Andretti. I'm sure there must have been some concern about whether or not I would ever be able to win races again. There was no reasonable guarantee that I could win. If you are betting conservatively, then you don't take a chance on promoting the comeback of somebody who might not come back. As a result, my comeback was pretty much wasted as a promotion vehicle. It was a shame, really.

Once in 1996 Kim and I flew to the Texaco headquarters in Houston, and I couldn't find a single picture of myself on their walls! When Kim saw the pictures of Michael and Mario Andretti and of Davey, but none of their current driver, she was disgusted. She felt that other sponsors were promoting drivers who hadn't done half of what I had accomplished. She was also upset that the Texaco officials seemed to be arriving at conclusions about me without bothering to talk with me or see things in terms of the big picture. Kim would tell a friend of ours who worked for Texaco, "They don't know Ernie. If he was doing drugs or beating me or cheating on me, that would be a reason to dislike him. But what has he done but work his tail off?" Over the three years I drove for the Robert Yates team I got to know several of the Texaco executives. But obviously not enough of them.

Texaco's coolness toward Kim and me also was reflected in the press we got. We felt the whole time we were with Texaco that we were always having to prove we were good people. The press was ready to slam me for anything I did. It was as though we were Texaco's stepchildren. It was really odd, and unfair. I suspect someone important at Texaco wasn't sold on me from the beginning. That's the only explanation we can come up with to understand why things evolved as they did.

It was very stressful, and I didn't even realize how much until I left. I think Kim felt the stress worse than I did, and there were times when she begged me not to re-sign with Texaco and Robert Yates at the end of the '97 season. She said, "Ernie, it isn't worth it. Life is too short. I can't live my life with this stress." She said, "We are not happy in these circumstances. You can't seem to please these people no matter how many races you win. I don't care if the 28 car has a rocket engine in it, it's not worth it."

Only now, looking back, can I see how right she was.

When Larry McReynolds left to go to the Richard Childress team at the end of the '96 season, Robert Yates had to find another crew chief. I called Robert and suggested my old friend Marc Reno. Marc and I knew what each other was all about, and that's a real plus to have with your crew chief. Marc and I had worked well together in the past, and I knew he was very capable of doing the job.

At the time Marc was working for James Finch running a Busch car for Jeff Purvis. He was content where he was. There was no politics, and Marc enjoyed working with Finch and Purvis very much. Just before Christmas '96, I called Marc and told him, "The Yates team has been mentioning your name to replace Larry up here. Are you interested?" A couple years earlier I had asked Marc to run my truck team with Joe Ruttman driving, and Marc had turned me down. Marc didn't feel comfortable with me being his boss, and I can understand that. Marc was happy where he was. This time, however, Robert would be his boss. When I mentioned the Yates deal, Marc was a little hesitant. I asked him, "If they call you up and offer you a deal, are you interested?" Marc was caught off guard but he said he would talk to Robert Yates about it.

Robert called Marc after Christmas, and the two met on New Year's Day. Marc was a close friend and neighbor of Larry's and there was no animosity between them that Marc was considering Larry's position. Larry was testing with

Dale Earnhardt that day, and Larry gave Marc his Carolina Panther football tickets. There was plenty of time before the game, and Marc drove his wife's Cadillac to Robert's shop. They talked for an hour and a half, and one of the questions Marc asked was, "Why do you have your shop in such a bad neighborhood?" Robert said, "A lot of people wonder why I stay here and don't move out. But it's primarily an industrial area, and we can run the dynos day and night without anybody complaining." Marc asked him, "What about break-ins?" "Don't you worry about that," Robert said. "Nah, we never get broken into. It's not that bad."

They shook hands after the interview, and when Marc returned to his car, he discovered that someone had broken into it and stolen personal items during his job interview! Marc never said a word to Robert. He just cleaned up the mess and drove home.

When Marc took the job with Robert, it was with a full understanding that I was going to re-sign with the Yates team at the end of the season. In their conversation Marc said he told Robert that there had been some talk that I wasn't coming back and he was concerned about that. Robert assured him, "We've cleared all the hurdles. Don't worry. Ernie will be back."

The 1997 season began, as every season does, with the Daytona 500. Both D.J. and I had good cars that day. D.J. and I were running together, around fourth and fifth, when in front of us Earnhardt and Gordon began running side by side. They came together, and Earnhardt spun. At one point, he became airborne right above me. As he descended, his rear spoiler caught my hood and ripped it right off the car and sent it flying high into the grandstand. It was a miracle no one was seriously hurt.

After the incident, I went into the infield care center to make sure the spectators who were hit by my hood were okay. I was thankful there were no serious injuries.

The next race was at Rockingham, and we didn't qualify very well. I haven't qualified well at Rockingham the last few years. As a result I had to pit along the backstretch, which is a serious disadvantage I'd rather not have to face. We had a top-five car, but unless there are a lot of green-flag stops, it's very difficult to run up front when you have to pit back there. Rockingham rarely has green-flag stops, and it didn't that day. We ended up finishing ninth.

The next race was at Richmond, where I was running fourth and having a great run. There were only four cars on the lead lap, and I was looking to go to the front when a caution came out. I pitted, along with everyone else, and came back out. We were all lined up on the outside, with the lapped cars lining up on the inside. Jeff Gordon was one of the lapped cars, and on his way up to the front, he started warming up his tires, weaving back and forth. I was annoyed as hell when he ran right into my fender and bent it a little. The incident cost me the race. We should have pitted but hoped for the best and didn't. The fender rubbed against a tire, which eventually blew out. I crashed into the fence and it killed our car. We took an easy top-ten run and turned it into a thirtieth. It seemed like a wasteful setback, and I was not happy about it.

Afterward reporters asked me about Gordon's recklessness, and I told the press I would "get him back." At that moment I meant it. It wasn't as if he did it on purpose, but my frustrations were cumulative. First it was Daytona where I was minding my business and Earnhardt spun and ripped my roof off, taking me out of competition, and now this fender bender with Gordon at Richmond had cost me. We're a very intense and competitive group, all of us. It's tough to just bite your tongue and say nothing over a period of time. Sometimes, when you have significant disappointments, the steam tends to rise.

My mood improved at Atlanta, where D.J. and I finished one-two. During the race NASCAR made me re-pit after the judges said I drove too fast down pit road. That cost me a little time, but it didn't make any difference. The only car faster than mine out there was D.J.'s, and his car was set up that small amount better than mine to give him an edge.

D.J. continued his winning ways at Darlington, and I finished twenty-first. In terms of the points, however, I was tenth, far better than how we had started out the year before. Overall, things seemed to be going relatively well, and there was no reason I shouldn't be optimistic looking ahead. I didn't realize that my trouble would come *off* the track.

On March 30, Kim's birthday, we decided to go out for a celebratory dinner with Marc and his wife, Raymond Fox and his wife, Tobey Butler and his wife, and Betty, a friend who works out with Kim and me, and her husband. Kim and I don't go out all that often, but that night we were having such a good time we didn't want the evening to end. We decided to go to a place called Twisters, not far from our home.

We were minding our own business, having a good time, listening to the music, when the disk jockey announced, "Ernie Irvan is here tonight. Would you please stand, Ernie?" I was not excited by his announcement. This was supposed to be Kim's night. Furthermore, I had hoped that we could discreetly have our birthday celebration. This DJ did not ask me in advance if I minded his announcing my attendance there. I felt it was inconsiderate on his part. After that, I thought it best to leave and told everyone so. Of our group of friends, everyone but Betty and her husband decided to leave.

Kim was having a good time. She knew I was upset, but it was her birthday, and she asked if we could stay for just a little longer. Reluctantly, I agreed. We were minding our own business when this woman came up to me and asked if I would dance with her. Kim, seeing that I was unsure about this, teased me. She said, "Go ahead, chicken." Our dance was quick and uneventful. When we were done, this woman went over to Kim, and I could see they were talking very animatedly.

She walked away, and about fifteen minutes later, when we were ready to leave, she came back and started pulling on the lobe of Kim's ear, accusing me of saying something crude to her. I hadn't been close enough to her for any length of time to tell her anything like that. Confused, Kim was ready to kill me. I told Kim, "I don't know what she's talking about!"

After this woman apparently felt she was finished physically and verbally assaulting Kim, she promptly left. Once Kim had a chance to gather in everything that had just happened to her, she decided that was not the way things ought to end. She intended to have the last word.

We went outside into the parking lot. The onerous couple was nowhere in sight. I said, "Kim, don't worry about it. She's gone. Let's go home."

We were about to get into our car to leave when a car pulled up with the woman, her boyfriend, and another couple inside. The woman yelled something at Kim, and Kim automatically called the woman something pretty nasty. It was like seeing Earnhardt's car flying over the top of my car. It all happened so quickly and the deterioration of the situation was so rapid, it was unbelievable. We were really taken aback when the woman jumped out of her car and, incredibly, started punching my wife! I went over to protect Kim, and when I got over there, the woman's boyfriend got out of the car, came over, and coldcocked me. It was a fiasco I really would have liked to avoid.

In the Charlotte papers the next day the account made it sound like my wife and I and a group of other people were having a drunken brawl in the parking lot of a redneck bar. The story was written in such a way that it seemed to beg the question: "What were you doing out late at night at a place like that?" Poor Kim felt worse about how the story made us look than she did about getting punched and bruised in the face.

I went to Robert Yates and told him exactly what had happened. I wanted to make sure he knew the details and the truth, no distortions. He advised me, "You need to make sure you don't put yourselves in that predicament again." No kidding. It was an unnecessary caution. In fact, I hoped it was a closed chapter. Unfortunately, it made for interesting press, especially when the truth was embellished and lopsided.

As for the Texaco people, I immediately told them what

had happened as well, and I was told, "Just make sure you stay away from that kind of negative publicity." That was an ironic piece of advice. Texaco had just been named as a defendant in several lawsuits for racial discrimination.

Kim wanted to go to the papers and tell our side of the story, but Texaco specifically ordered her not to do so. It didn't seem to matter that we felt our reputations were being tainted unjustly. Our orders were, "Don't discuss it." Additionally, we were asked not to press charges. I was in the hot seat at the time, knowing Texaco was deciding whether or not to renew my contract. The politically correct course of action was to follow orders, so Kim and I kept our mouths shut. Until now, I think the impression remained that Kim and I had participated in a drunken brawl outside a bar.

I didn't appreciate the press not getting the whole picture, and it really made me uncomfortable that Texaco did not stand up for me or encourage me to speak up for myself and my wife. Like a dark cloud hovering low to the ground as a slow-moving storm rolls its way in, it was an event that increased the tension in the air.

Right after that incident our next race was held at the new Texas Speedway. Robert had promised to tell me at Texas whether he intended to re-sign me or not. I knew from Marc Reno that Robert had assured him that everything would work out okay. Marc said Robert told him, "The Texaco people are thrilled to death with what Ernie's done this year. They still have concerns that once he signs, he won't be so accommodating. But I believe we're going to have this thing handled in Texas."

We had a really good car that day in Texas. Even when we discovered that one of our tires was terribly out of balance, we were able to recover from that. We had to come in and change it under the green, and we got a lap down. Still, after a caution came out, I raced the leader, Terry Labonte, and was able to get back to the line to get my lap back.

The caution had been brought out by a wreck, but my spotter, whose essential job it was to let me know what was going on ahead, missed seeing Greg Sacks spinning right in the middle of the track on the front straightaway. The spotter was inexperienced, and his failure to see and report that the track was blocked ahead would be a costly error.

I was on the inside, and Terry was on the outside, with both of us intently racing back to the line. I was keeping an eye on Terry's position and making sure I had enough room in the fourth turn. Hitting him would ruin everything.

As I changed my focus to look forward, I was shocked to see Sacks's car sprawled out in front of me right in the middle of the racetrack. The design for turn four in Texas is not adequate to accommodate speeds of more than 150 miles an hour. At 190 miles an hour, I had nowhere to go but straight into Greg Sacks. I know if my spotter had been watching well enough, things might have turned out differently. Even so, I'm still of the mind that the turn ought to be made safer.

With all those factors against me, I slammed into Greg Sacks, spun out of control, never having had a chance to make a correction. Jeff Gordon was racing back to the line like me, to get a lap back. Somehow in the press it became my fault that Gordon was involved in an accident. I knew it certainly wasn't going to help matters with Texaco. It didn't.

Robert Yates told me they would be letting me know at Charlotte where we stood on re-signing.

The burden for me was terrible. I really appreciated it then, when the team let me know they wanted me to stay; waiting to find out about that was hard on them, too. An ill wind, however, was definitely blowing as Robert contended with pressure from his wife, Carolyn and his son Doug, not to re-sign me.

When I first joined the Yates team, Robert had said he wanted to run the souvenir program. I had already been through a bad fight over souvenir revenues with Larry McClure. I didn't want to revisit that nightmare. Larry had hired an outside firm to run the souvenir business, and I didn't think that worked very well. When Robert said he wanted to run the souvenir business himself, I was open to a new approach that sounded more efficient. Robert saw how much money could be made from souvenirs, and as an entrepreneur, he wanted to have control of that aspect of his race team. I didn't mind because I figured Robert would pay me a fair share while I was driving for him. The whole time I was driving for him, we argued over the definition of "fair share."

The friction really started when Robert turned over the souvenir business to his wife, Carolyn.

It was about this time that Kim and I began to see how helpful it would be to have a business manager. I hired Brett Nelson, who then took over my battles with Carolyn so I could concentrate on driving. Hiring Brett turned out to be a wise decision on my part. Not only is he a shrewd businessman, but he is also a scrupulous record keeper. These traits would be invaluable when dealing with Carolyn, as well as others in the industry.

Brett worked very hard to make things work with

Carolyn. In discussions that he and I would have, we would both agree that Carolyn was trying to do a good job for the family business; however, there were times when we felt we were called upon to bend over backward.

I remember one time in particular when Carolyn called Brett at home, getting him out of bed at midnight because she was so overwrought. She accused us of cutting them out of things, being in cahoots with other people to make sure the Yates didn't get a cut. All sorts of things. As I said, Brett is meticulous in his record keeping, as well as very clear about what is and is not good business conduct. Thankfully, he had all the documentation necessary to help Carolyn see that her concerns were unfounded. She later graciously apologized. In her efforts to make sure business went the Yates's way, Carolyn could be a pretty colorful character, I'll say that.

I've heard since that she seems to be backing out of all that stuff these days. Back then when Brett, Kim, and I had to deal with Carolyn, we felt like we needed to be very careful. It felt like political suicide to be anything else.

I think Kim realized that the more time that lapsed, the harder things would be for us if Robert chose to listen to Carolyn. Under our contract Robert didn't have to tell me if he wanted to re-sign me until November. Kim strongly encouraged me to tell Robert that I wanted an answer by a sooner date than that. Her point was valid when she correctly reminded me that "If you wait until the end of the year, all the race teams will have filled their rides, and you'll be the odd man out."

Believe it or not, despite any discord between Texaco and me, or Carolyn and me, or Texaco and Carolyn, I liked what our race team was doing. I felt we had the potential to win more races. You can't ever predict when you're going to win, but I felt we were very capable of winning any week we went out there, and it was nice to know we were that strong.

We went to Charlotte, and both D.J. and I led the World 600. We had good performing race cars that weekend. We dominated the whole first half of the race, until things came to a halt for a long rain delay. When we went back out there the racetrack had changed dramatically. After the break, some people who had run well before the break now were running poorly. After they threw the green flag to restart, we were among them. Some people who had run badly before the break now were running great. Rusty Wallace had been a lap down, and before it rained, he couldn't have passed me in his best minute. But after the restart, Rusty climbed to the front and finished in second place when it was called at two in the morning with a hundred laps yet to run. We had been racing since five in the afternoon. Everyone was exhausted and not unhappy when they finally called it.

The Charlotte deadline that Robert talked about in Texas came and passed without a word from Robert or Texaco about my contract. I figured the further along we went, the better my chances they would re-sign me. In retrospect, I don't know why I wanted to re-sign so badly, considering how difficult things were. Part of it, I'm sure, was my pride. I also think that the Texaco Thunderbird was still a premier car capable of winning a lot of races, and that's what I love to do—drive good cars that can handle well and win.

At Dover I really thought winning was where we were headed without a dominant car. During the race we had one bad pit stop and I had to work my way back up to the front. I had the lead with ten laps to go when someone dumped a slick of oil onto the track, and I drove into turn one, slid, and hit the fence. It was very disappointing, particularly after all that hard driving after the bad pit stop.

I wrecked again at Pocono, and then during the week before the Michigan race Robert Yates called to see if he could come up to my shop to give me the details of all the things Texaco wanted me to do if I were to re-sign my contract. He had only been at my shop twice since I had known him. I was eager to get the contract signed, and I was glad to see him come up for that purpose.

He said, "Texaco wants you to make fifteen appearances." I told him that would be fine. He mentioned a couple of other conditions, and I agreed. I agreed to everything they wanted me to do.

Kim asked Robert, "What about all the rumors that you're not going to re-sign Ernie?" He said, "I'm re-signing Ernie. All we have to do is figure out the money." At that time I wasn't sure of the salary I wanted, and he wasn't sure what he wanted to pay me. I said, "So if we agree on salary, we can do it?"

Robert said, "Yes." Kim, still stinging from the way Texaco had treated me, wasn't as trustful that things could be tied up quite so easily. She told Robert bluntly, "If you don't want to re-sign him, just treat us decently and let us know, because we have a mortgage, we have a child, and we have to get ready for next year, just like you do." That's my Kim, never one to beat around the bush.

I was changing clothes before going to Detroit to sign a deal with Ford. I remember clearly Robert stood nearby and

I said, "We have a deal?" And he said, "Yeah." Robert and I shook hands, which to me meant that it was a done deal. I felt I had Robert's word that I would be back to drive for him in '98.

Kim said, "Robert, is it two years or three?" He began talking. Kim interrupted him. She said, "Robert, all you have to do is answer with one word. Is it a one-year, two-year, or three-year deal?"

He said, "Well, you don't want a one-year deal, so I'm having to work with the sponsor," and he started talking again. I asked again, "Robert, are we going to do this deal?" He said, "Yes." So I left, and he left.

About an hour after Robert left, the owner of one of the prestige race teams called to find out whether I was free to drive for his race team in '98. "Did you work out everything with Robert?" he asked, and I told him that everything had just been worked out. "I appreciate your calling and making me an offer," I told him. He said, "That's great. I'm glad you guys are doing that."

I've often wondered if the fact that I felt a certain amount of anxiety over the signing of my contract helped to divert my focus from returning to Michigan, where I had crashed. You might think I would have dreaded going back. In actuality, I didn't spend a lot of time thinking it over. It certainly would not have done any good. Those of us who race, in fact, have to train ourselves only to see the possibility of victory. This book is riddled with tragic stories, but concentrating on those things will not further our careers. My own personal tragedy at Michigan was not going to be any different.

When I went back, in fact, it was in a lighter frame of

mind. I had spent too much time worrying about my contract. The race itself was incredibly exciting, especially as I almost crashed there again during the second lap. I didn't, of course, and I really felt I had conquered something more than my competitors on the track. I had come as close to dancing with death as I possibly could without getting burned. Fate had shown the friendly side of its face that day, and I won.

I won!

To say it was an emotional victory is an understatement. The only shadow clouding the day was a comment Robert made in answer to a reporter's question about rumors he was not happy with me. His omimous reply: "One win doesn't solve everything."

Talk about raining on your parade.

17

A BITTER DIVORCE

When I got back to Charlotte, I confronted Robert at his office in the race shop. I said, "Do we have a deal or not?" He said, "I just need . . . a couple of more days." I said, "Didn't you just sit in my office last week and say we had a deal?" He said, "Yeah, but I'm having trouble . . ." and he explained that he didn't know whether he was even going to run the 28 car in 1998 or not. He said, "Ford is supposed to pay me what they need to on the 88 car. I'm not real sure." He said, "I need a couple of days. I'll let you know Wednesday at Daytona. Where are you going to be?" I said, "I'm going down Tuesday, and I'll be at the motel on Wednesday." He said, "I'll let you know by Wednesday."

He showed up on Wednesday, and when he saw me, he turned the other way, wouldn't come anywhere near me. At the track he avoided me. Kim said to me, "Ernie, call me a fool, but if someone's avoiding you, it's not good." I told Kim, "You're no fool. He's not going to re-sign me."

At Daytona, we didn't do too badly in the Firecracker 400, finishing ninth. Three days later, Robert called me on the phone to inform me that it looked like he and I weren't going to be able to agree on a new contract.

I said, "Now, Robert, didn't you just get done telling me you were going to re-sign me?" He said, "Ernie, we never did agree on the price." At first I didn't understand what he was saying, but then I caught his drift. I asked, "You're not re-signing me, are you?" Robert said, "I'm not going to be able to do it." He said, "This is the hardest thing I've ever had to do in my life."

I said, "Robert, there's nothing more to talk about." And I hung up.

Not being one who sits around and waits for opportunity to knock, I proceeded to make a few phone calls to see what arrangements I could make for the following year. When I called back the car owner who had called me the week before, he said that unfortunately he had just signed another driver. I made other calls. I knew I would land on my feet just fine, but I was very disappointed and hurt. I felt betrayed.

I had driven for the Robert Yates team for three and a half years. As far as Robert and I communicating back and forth, I still think it was one of the best relationships I ever had with an owner. What upset me most about the whole deal was that he had given me his word. Then, basically, he said it wasn't his word. From that point on, my trust in Robert was gone. You can't buy integrity, and one of the ways a person demonstrates that is by honoring his commitments, verbal or otherwise. It's true he always said to me, "If you don't want to be here, I don't want you to drive my race car." I walked away under the same policy. If he felt it was time to part company, then it was.

■ ■ ■

I did everything for Robert and for Texaco I ever said I was going to do. For the most part, he did for me pretty much everything he said he was going to do for me. When I signed with him he gave me his word he was going to do the best job he could to give me the best race cars every week, and he did that. Initially, we had a four-year deal the day we signed our contract. When I got hurt, they didn't have to continue paying my salary. Nonetheless, Texaco not only paid me through the rest of the year, but they also paid me for the next one. A cynic might call it good PR, but whatever the reasons, Kim and I will always be appreciative of the time it bought us while I recovered. Having everyone stand by me in my time of great tragedy made leaving Yates and Texaco all the more difficult. Regardless of our ups and downs, I appreciated them being there for me and my family when I was at my lowest point.

When Robert told me he wasn't renewing my contract, he also told the crew and press. Everyone knew I was driving the remainder of the 1997 season as a lame duck. It's hard to drive with the same enthusiasm when you know you're being released. I also was puzzled that I would be replaced by a rookie. I came to one possible conclusion: money from the souvenir business.

Before I got hurt, Robert had also promised me that if he ever sold the souvenir business, he would give me the opportunity to buy it. And why not? It was my likeness he was selling on all those T-shirts, clothing, mugs, and different products for sale. But around the time he let me go, he sold the souvenir business to a company called Action Performance for several million dollars. The deal angered

Texaco, who had sued Action Performance a few years earlier. Removed from the race team, I was in no position to talk to Robert about my share of the proceeds.

I never saw a penny from the sale of the souvenir business. By hiring a rookie, it was almost certain that Irwin wouldn't make demands for souvenir money either. The opportunity to drive the 28 car would most likely be enough.

Thus, in the end, it looks like the bottom line to our separation had to do with one thing primarily: money.

After the announcement that he was letting me go, Robert went to Marc Reno and Raymond Fox and told them he needed them to stay with him. He went on to tell them about the rookie deal with Irwin. Marc and Raymond were incredulous. They couldn't believe it. Robert said, "Yeah, Texaco is behind it, Ford is behind it, Raybestos is behind it. But I need you guys to commit to it. It's going to take a year or two for Kenny to get up to speed, and I want to keep the team intact." They got a pretty big signing bonus, making it very difficult for them to come with me, as Robert might easily have guessed.

I was determined to show everyone that I could win despite what had happened. In 1997 I won the Michigan race and sat on two poles, and we could have won as many as a half dozen races had I not wrecked or had engines not blown up. I should have won both races at Loudon. In the first one the motor blew up, and in the latter I came in second.

On qualifying day of that second Loudon race I woke up with the flu. When I went out, it seemed the car felt as lousy as I did. It wouldn't perform, and I had to start at the back. It was strange because any time I went out and practiced, the car was strong, we were the fastest car, but in qualifying the car just wouldn't go.

Once the race started, however, the car performed incredibly well. It gave me great pleasure and a lot of confidence in the race team to drive a car like that. Toward the end of the race Jeff Gordon beat us out of the pits and got ahead of us. I was on Gordon's back bumper, and Marc Reno, my crew chief, was begging me to pass him. But I knew the only way I could do that was to knock him out of the way, and I was reluctant to do that. I told Marc, "I can't rough him." Marc still wasn't convinced. He continued to prod me to do what I needed to do. I said, "No, Marc, I don't want to race him that way."

That second Loudon race was the last good one we ran. Each week we had a lot of problems during the latter part of the race. Everyone seemed to lose his focus, and our team deteriorated. I was bitter, and the guys were upset for me that I had to look for another ride.

Atlanta was the last race. I gave Robert Yates 100 percent that day, like I had done every day since I started with that team. I drove every lap like it was the most important lap, and I am proud to say I did that to the end.

18

After the word got out that I wasn't going to re-sign with the Robert Yates team, I received five or six offers from teams with solid race programs. Each one had attractive personnel to work with and each was a balm on my wounded pride. When I made my choice, I decided that the determining factor was going to be my relationship with the sponsor—how it would treat me, how it would promote me, how it would support me. For four years I had felt like Texaco's whipping boy. I vowed that during this next stage in my career I would sign with the team whose sponsor was genuinely interested in what I offered. I knew I had a lot to bring to the table. I chose the MB2 race team because of its sponsor, Mars/M&M, makers of such well-known brands of candy as Skittles, M&M's, Milky Way, Snickers, and Starburst. When their folks talked to me, they made it clear they wanted to promote Ernie Irvan, and they wanted me to promote their fine products.

When I joined MB2, the race team was only in its second year of operation. Derrike Cope drove the car the first year. I've known the team manager, Jay Frye, for a long time. Our crew chief, Ryan Pemberton, has never won a Winston Cup race, but he's gaining experience, and he has a good head on his shoulders. The three owners of the team, Tom Beard, Nelson Bowers, and Read Morton, have been great guys. They are behind the team all the way, and I know it won't be long before we are running competitively every week and contending for the Winston Cup point championship.

As I bring this chapter (of my book and my life) to a close, I am very optimistic about our race team. At the start of the 1998 season, my Skittles car was running in the middle of the pack, and some bad luck really hurt us in some of the races.

As our race team members became more comfortable with each other, I began seeing signs that soon we will be points contenders. At Indianapolis in late July, under cool temperatures and overcast skies, I was the first driver to go out to qualify. I drove my Pontiac onto the huge racetrack and broke the lap record (which I had set the year before) at a speed of 179.394. Then I had to wait in my motor home while forty-nine other drivers tried to beat me. None did. It was an exhilarating feeling to be back on top again. I expect the wins to follow soon.

We are starting to finish consistently at or close to the top ten, which is a significant accomplishment for a second-year team, particularly considering the strength of the well-established dynasties including that of Robert Yates.

I am confident we will reach the next plateau, running for the win. We have the faith, and we have the patience. I am not through winning Winston Cup races. My primary goal is to win the racing championship, and I feel that too is reachable.

Since my accident, I have proven I have what it takes to win. I'm as good as I always was, and I am just as fiercely determined to return to the top as ever. The only noticable difference in me after my accident is that I am more humble. After what happened, I realize how lucky I am just to be back doing what I love to do most. I think the adversities I have faced in my life have served to remind me that I am strong and persistent enough to overcome whatever may be thrown my way.

Those same struggles have served to make my victories all the sweeter. As I said, I'm not stopping here, though. There is always more to reach for. I look forward to it.

19

A NEW BEGINNING

Looking at the last chapter of the first edition of this book (which went to press last year in February), I realize how much the last two sentences still ring true. There *is* more to reach for. There is always more to reach for. It's just that now it's something different, something new to look forward to. Since those words were last printed, I have been involved in two unlucky accidents. One I suffered in Talladega. That was unsettling. Still, after a brief recovery period, I felt fine about getting back in the car. The other one—the last one—happened at the same racetrack exactly five years from the day that I almost died. Both accidents occurred during practice runs. Although my injuries were more extensive the first time in Michigan, both times I had to be cut out of the car and was unconscious when the medical crew got to me. When I crashed this last time at Michigan, the coincidences and the medical ramifications finally became too great to ignore.

The doctors told me I sustained a concussion and bruised my lungs from this last crash. During my recovery period, the doctors insisted that I take serious stock of the jeopardy my life was in. It goes without saying that when your job is to drive at competitive speeds close to 200 miles an hour around concrete surfaces that your risk for injury and death is pretty clear-cut. However, because I had had such severe injuries previously, the risk went up exponentially.

Until I had some significant time to heal, there was no way of telling how well my reflexes would return. I had to stop and consider that not only was I putting myself at higher risk, but the possibility existed that I would be putting my fellow drivers in more danger if I could not drive as expertly as I had in the past. These guys have not only been my competitors over the years, but also friends to me and my family.

It was difficult to really confront the notion that it was time to make a decision about whether I should continue on in a sport—a way of life for me, really—that I had been working at about as long as I had been walking and talking. As I mentioned before, my love affair with racing has not just been mine, it has also been my family's. My mom and dad have had their own racing careers and have vigorously supported mine. My wife and children have lovingly followed me wherever my job has taken me, generously adopting the nomadic lifestyle the sport demands. They made friends with my friends and their families, keenly felt my disappointments, celebrated my victories, and shared my dreams. It was hard to imagine that lifestyle would all change in one instant with one decision.

I certainly have been blessed to be recognized as one of NASCAR's fifty greatest drivers. But it wasn't just a career and reputation that I had built over the years; a business had also been created. If I permanently stepped out of my race car, the jobs of many people in that business might either become unnecessary or would change. Would I still need the same number of people to oversee my fan club, the licensing, and other aspects of the business? How on earth would I tell these people I intended to change all that? My wife would remind me that if I became incapacitated, or worse, died in my next car crash, what could I do for any of them then?

And what about the fans? I would truly miss seeing them at the racetrack. It was so inspirational and energizing. I will never tell you that I did not relish winning, but racing was about so much more than that. I knew the fans could feel the intensity of the competition that existed out on the track. That had to be one of the reasons they came—to share in that, to cheer on that competitive spirit.

Winning was so much sweeter in the races that I had to fight hard for—like one of my races at Charlotte where I battled it out with someone who is not only a friend, but is also one of my fiercest competitors, Rusty Wallace. Any race, though, win or lose, is a long, adrenaline-filled test of endurance and expertise. Win or lose, Dale Earnhardt's insistence that it was just about as essential to stay in the race as it was to win made me feel as if I had a piece of victory if I made it to the finish line intact. When I finished in the top ten, I felt as if I had claimed an even bigger piece of victory. It was clear to me that I would miss the fans; and I would sorely miss the challenges that came from my more-than-capable competitors.

I loved it. All of it. The doctors were clear, though—they absolutely could not, in all good conscience, advise me to race again. Looking at all the things I would be walking away from was one of the hardest things I have ever had to do. I fully appreciated how difficult it must have been for athletes such as John Elway, Wayne Gretsky, and Larry Bird to retire from their playing fields. However, after talking with the doctors, I knew my chances to cheat death were becoming slimmer. Walking away from the only way of life I had ever known was only eased by looking ahead to the future. No one has any guarantees, but if I left racing, I stood as much of a chance as the next guy to see my children graduate from college. I could look in my wife's eyes and know she would not have to face her and our children's future alone.

I am grateful that a little over five years ago I began to prepare financially for the day when I might have to make this decision—I hired an adept business manager. When Kim and my business manager, Brett, and I got together after this last accident, we were able to discuss the exciting options I had if I walked away from driving. I think it is unfortunate when athletes retire and, after an illustrious career, they have little to show for it. This, fortunately, would not be the case. There are many business opportunities for me to explore. Over the years, I have gained a lot of knowledge about the sport that I have lived and loved. Now I can use that knowledge as I change courses in my career.

As I was driving my daughter to school one morning after this last accident, a thought hit me just about as hard as the wall had up in Michigan. If I had prepared for this day, what was stopping me? Fear of change? Fear of the unknown? After the kind of career that I had lead, the risks I had taken, those fears suddenly seemed ludicrous when balanced by the potential my life still held. I realized if I stopped focusing on the changes that were taking me out of my comfort zone long enough to look ahead at the other possibilities that existed in my life, then those fears would pale in comparison to the excitement that the new opportunities and challenges could bring.

When we were considering the title of this last chapter, it was Kim who suggested the one that we finally decided on. When she proposed it, it seemed exactly right because it reflects just how we both were beginning to feel about our future. My role in racing had to change, no doubt about that. But when Kim and I put our heads together, it seemed increasingly clear that it was time I pursue some of the other options we had only talked about. Participating as an owner of a team was just one thing that I had peripherally given my attention to in the past. Now I can make that a reality.

I am not sure how long it will take to choose which road to travel, but whichever one that is, I will pursue it with the same dogged determination and attention that I have put into driving. I have come to realize that as many changes that came my way, some things would stay the same. My values, for instance, still require that I give 100 percent to whatever I am committed to. My family has always meant a great deal to me. My body may have taken a pretty good beating in this past year, but my competitive spirit is just as healthy as it ever was. The times when it looked like my career was over, I found out who my friends were. Now I know who I can count on and who I can't. I will take this knowledge and these same values with me to my next challenge. It's still show time—it's just a different show. No time to look back. There is still too much to look forward to.

Many heartfelt thanks, again, to all my fans.